# AMERICAN POLITICAL SCIENCE

## R L Cohen, PhD

# Humanities
## ACADEMIC PUBLISHERS

ISBN: 9781988557953 (Paperback)
ISBN: 9781988557960 (Hardcover)

Published Year: 2024

Published in the United States of America
Published by Humanities Academic Publishers

# CONTENTS

# CHAPTER 1

# KEY DEFINITIONS
# IN POLITICAL SCIENCE

The term government refers to the system through which a community arranges itself and distributes power to achieve common objectives and provide necessary benefits for the entire society. Governments worldwide strive to achieve objectives such as economic growth, ensuring national border security, and safeguarding the safety and well-being of their citizens. Governments also offer advantages and privileges to their citizenry. The benefits offered vary based on the country and its specific governmental system, but governments typically provide services like education, healthcare, and transportation infrastructure. Politics is the practice of obtaining and exerting authority within a government in order to establish and accomplish specific objectives, particularly those concerning the allocation of resources within a country. Governmental systems and economic systems are occasionally conflated. This is due to the strong correlation or coevolution between specific political ideologies or forms of governance and particular economic systems.

For instance, the economic system of capitalism emerged along with the concepts of democratic republics, self-governance, and natural rights in Western Europe and North America. During this period, the notion of liberty gained significant prominence. John Locke, a seventeenth-century

English political philosopher, posited that all individuals possess inherent rights to life, freedom, and property. This concept gave rise to the notion that individuals should have the liberty to willingly agree to be ruled. During the 18th century, both in Great Britain's North American colonies and later in France, the concept of self-governance through elected representatives emerged. This theory emphasized that only those representatives elected by the people should have the authority to enact laws that govern them, rather than a monarch.

Similarly, Adam Smith, a Scottish philosopher born nineteen years after Locke's demise, advocated for the unrestricted acquisition of property by all individuals. Smith advocated for individual autonomy and the retention of one's earnings, rather than being subject to government, company, and industry domination. Competition would guarantee that prices stayed at a low level and defective goods were eliminated from the market. By adopting this approach, businesses would attain financial gains, consumers would have their requirements fulfilled, and society as a whole would thrive. Smith expounded upon these concepts, which served as the foundation for modern capitalism, in his book The Wealth of Nations, released in 1776, coinciding with the authorship of the Declaration of Independence.

The United States witnessed the simultaneous development of representative government and capitalism, leading many Americans to associate democracy, a system where individuals control themselves, with capitalism. Conceptually, a democratic governance system upholds individualism and grants the liberty to exercise personal agency, rather than being subject to governmental control, regardless of its positive or negative implications. Capitalism is dependent on individuality. Simultaneously, prosperous capitalists like political regimes in which they may exert a certain degree of influence to protect their freedom.

Democracy and capitalism are not always interconnected. Undoubtedly, it can be contended that a capitalist economic system may have detrimental effects on democracy in certain aspects. Despite Smith's hypothesis that capitalism will result in universal prosperity, this outcome has not been definitively observed. In numerous capitalist nations, significant disparities in wealth can be observed between the proprietors of prominent enterprises, industries, and financial institutions, and individuals who engage in wage labor for others. Consequently, a minute fraction of the population may acquire significant control over the government due to their immense riches, surpassing the influence possessed by the rest of the population. This topic will be further explored in subsequent discussion.

Socialism is a viable alternative to the traditional economic system. In socialist countries, the government has and controls the means of wealth creation, including factories, vast farms, and banks, rather than private individuals. The government amasses wealth and subsequently allocates it to citizens, predominantly through social programs that offer services such as cost-free or affordable healthcare, education, and childcare. In socialist nations, the government typically possesses and regulates utilities, such as electricity, transportation systems (including airlines and trains), and telecommunications systems. In numerous communist nations, the government functions as an oligarchy, wherein only individuals belonging to a specific political party or governing elite are allowed to engage in governance. For instance, in China, the governance is carried out by individuals who are affiliated with the Chinese Communist Party.

## GOVERNMENTS AND REGIMES

The term 'politics' is derived from the Greek word *politiká* which refers to the affairs of the polis. Polis, on the other hand, corresponds to the Ancient Greek city-states, the majority of which possessed an autarkic/self-sufficient governmental system. Politics is therefore primarily the process by which individuals develop, defend, and alter the general principles by which they live. For this reason, politics, in its daily use, is identified with the art of government and state affairs.

Relating politics to the activities of the state makes it necessary to distinguish between the public sphere and the private sphere. These ideas highlight the distinction between private and public interests in the strictest meaning. Beyond personal interests, the public sphere includes issues that affect the well-being of the entire society. Adversely, the private sphere is about personal concerns unrelated to the wider population. In this regard, libertarians and classical liberals draw a clear line between public and private matters. For instance, family life and business relationships are deeply embedded in the private sphere, and it is deemed improper for politics to directly meddle with these relationships.

However, some philosophies argue that the public and private spheres cannot be clearly divided. For instance, 'personal is political' is one of the most significant catchphrases of feminists. This catchphrase challenges the idea of the distinction between the public and the private sphere, contending that gender inequality in the public sphere has its roots in culture and family. The private domain is also rejected by Marxists, who argue that economic relations alone determine all aspects of political relations and institutions.

One of the key proponents of deliberative democracy, Jurgen Habermas, defines the public sphere as a social setting where a variety of viewpoints are presented, issues pertaining to general issues are debated, and communicative solutions to collective problems are found. Although this term is largely recognized, political philosophy will continue to dispute whether certain topics are public or private.

Being a social science and concerning the governance of our communities, the definition of politics is unavoidably connected to both conflict – a competition against opposing forces – and cooperation – the act of achieving goals through collective action. That is, human beings are social animals, but they have different wants, needs, and opinions, so they differ in the decisions about the rules by which they live. These latter are thus essential for any social system, since rules help to determine who will win or lose future power struggles without having to resort to violence.[1]

---

[1] Roller, E. (2005), *The Performance of Democracies: Political Institutions and Public Policy*. Oxford University Press, Oxford.

In contrast to the notion that politics is a form of conflict resolution, some authors associate politics with the production and distribution of resources, values, and social statuses. This type of comprehension is also known as power politics. Power politics de-idealizes and redefines politics as a simple struggle for power. There is no such thing as legitimate politics in this regard, but there are winners and losers. Marx, for instance, does not view liberal democracy as a legitimate political system, but rather as an ideological deception manufactured by capitalists to defend their class interests. This is why, in a broader context, anarchists consider all governmental power to be illegitimate. This radical rejection of politics is not shared by the majority of political scientists. Moreover, the legitimacy of political authority is regarded as a fundamental theme in political science.

Therefore, politics is a process and not an outcome: due to the inescapable presence of diversity and scarcity, not all conflicts in society can be resolved, so the process of setting rules can create disputes among the population. These disputes are at the basis of two essential concepts to understand politics: authority and power. The latter can be defined as the ability to influence others, so it may not necessarily be political, while the former is a form of legitimate power, which means that authority is itself the right to exercise power. That is, individuals acknowledge that society requires a form of common agreement to ensure that rules are upheld, so politics is connected to exercise of authority, such that Easton defines it as the "authoritative allocation of values."[2] Yet, to reach this agreement, it is essential that human beings cooperate one with another up to the point that political power can also be defined as "acting in concert" as done by Hannah Arendt[3].

---

[2] Easton, D. (1976). "Theoretical approaches to political support.", Canadian Journal of Political Science, 9 (3), pp. 431-448.

[3] Phillips, J. (2013), "Between the Tyranny of Opinion and the Despotism of Rational Truth: Arendt on Facts and Acting in Concert.", New German Critique, 40 (2), 97-112.

Following a discussion of what politics is, it is necessary to quickly define political science. Experiments, observations, and inferences that can be repeated are the cornerstones of scientific inquiry, which seeks to provide robust explanations for observed and hypothesized phenomena. Thus, political science is defined as the social science that examines politics by means of the empirical method. In this view, the term 'political science' refers to an approach to the study of politics that is empirical in nature and is devoid of any value judgments. This method is the product of positivism. This highlights the clear divide that exists between the fields of political science and political philosophy, which is analogous to the gap that exists between empirical and normative analysis.

In this sense, science asks "what is it?" but philosophy asks, "what ought to be?" The disciplines of political science include, for example, what democracy is and the extent to which countries have democratic standards relative to one another. To argue why democratic regimes are superior to other types of regimes, however, is undoubtedly a question of political philosophy. Since it would be pointless for political scientists to analyze democracy apart from its normative claims, it is not always possible or desirable to maintain a clear distinction between political science and political philosophy. The importance of the collaboration between political science and philosophy becomes clearer when we revise the legitimacy problem of political authority.

The concept of legitimacy is essential to understand what the State – the current prevalent form of political organization of our societies -- is, since Max Weber defines it as a "human community that (successfully) claims the monopoly of the legitimate use of physical force within a given territory."[4] This means that other actors may use violence, but the state is the only actor legitimized to do so. To exercise its power, the State power must be organized, and in order to decide who is in charge of allocating

---

[4] Weber M. (2004 [1919]), The Vocation Lectures. "Science as a Vocation". "Politics as a Vocation", Ed by David Owen D. and Strong T.B., Hackett Publishing Company, Cambridge.

citizens' different values, societies need a form of government, namely a system or an organization for exercising authority over a body of people.

This argument describes the state as a legal monopoly of power; nevertheless, it does not elaborate on the source of the legitimacy of power. Weber recognized three sorts of political legitimacy, based on history and customs (traditional authority), charismatic authority, and a system of formal, legal rules (legal-rational authority). Modern societies, according to Weber, are increasingly defined by the exercise of legal-rational authority and a sort of legitimacy that derives from respect for formal and typically legal rules.

Contemporary democratic political authorities are examples of rational-legal authority. In democratic societies, the ability to shift political authority through elections is historically quite exceptional. During the Middle Ages, when it was believed that God granted dynasties the right to govern, it was not feasible for political power to be transferred by elections. The power to rule is personified by the assertion that the right to rule belongs to a dynasty or charismatic leader. Believing that the authority to rule is personal is predicated on the concept that ruling is not a scientific or rational practice, but rather an assertion of personal abilities and traits. This political assumption also explains the aristocratic and hierarchical organization of traditional societies. Modern democratic countries, on the other hand, adhere to the idea of political equality and do not assume that the peaceful transfer of power through elections will result in treason or political instability. On the contrary, it is claimed that democratic political decision-making systems will serve the common interests of society, hence denying individuals personal right to rule. Since governance is a rational practice, the transfer of political power via elections is regarded as a usual political procedure.

Politics produce different kinds of governments according to the level of control and authority exercised by the government over its population. At one end of the spectrum, the government makes all decisions about how individuals live their lives, and citizens are powerless to push back. On the other end, there is an anarchic system where individuals make the decisions for themselves, and the government does not exist. Hence, governments can exercise this authority in different ways, and the form of government, or the set of rules that regulate the operation of a government, are defined as the political regime. This latter defines only a form of government and must not be misunderstood with its negative connotation, namely regime as an authoritarian political system that restricts the people's liberties.[5]

The difference between 'government' and 'regime' is important. For example, the United States federal government is composed of the three main branches (legislative, executive and judiciary) and draws its powers from the Constitution, the President and federal courts. With the elections, citizens decide which party (Democratic Party or Republican Party) they want to direct these branches and who should be the President. Instead, regime defines the political institutional framework of the country. Examples of regimes can thus be "democracy," "authoritarian," or "totalitarian." The United States system of governance, namely its regime, is a democratic republic style, and this does not change with the elections. Elections are made to select – and to replace – governments while they cannot change regime type. Hence, regardless of whether Republicans or Democrats win the elections, the United States regime will remain a democratic republic. It is commonly acknowledged that republics are fundamentally classified into parliamentary and presidential systems. However, a parliamentary form of government can also exist inside a constitutional monarchy, as in the United Kingdom. The political regime of the United Kingdom is a constitutional monarchy with a parliamentary form of government.

Overall, we can find four main types of regimes: democracy, theocracy, autocracy, and totalitarianism. To identify the type of a political regime, we can take into account three fundamental factors: the political decision-making procedure, the source of sovereignty, and the extent

---

[5] Dietrich, S. and Bernhard M. (2009). "State or regime? The impact of institutions on welfare outcomes." *The European Journal of Development Research*, 28 (2), 252-269.

of the official ideology. Democracy's etymology comes from the Greek word *demos* ("the people") and *kratos* (power), and this implies that any democratic system must be based on a popular sovereignty, namely the principle for which the authority of the state and its government are created and sustained by the consent of its people, who are the source of political power.[6] This sovereignty can be exercised in two main forms.

First, in a democracy as self-government, citizens can be directly involved in politics and make the rules that govern themselves, as it was in the case in Ancient Athens, Greece. Today, direct democracy can be recreated in several ways, from deliberative assemblies to direct decisional means such as referendum, or the initiative process. The method by which citizens can become directly involved on a single issue by voting directly on an issue and proposing new laws or amendments to a state constitution is referred to as a referendum.

Second, modern democracy does not necessarily require a direct involvement in politics by the whole populace. Democracy can also assume the form of a republic, namely a form of government in which the people hold the power, but they rule indirectly by means of their representatives. This form of representative democracy, supported by Madison in his *Federalist Papers*,[7] is adopted in the United States and defines a regime where politicians rule society according to the constitutional law on behalf of the citizenry, but where the people still retain power due to democratic procedures such as elections, party system, and the division of powers. However, this form of government is not necessarily democratic, since there could be republics where citizens do not hold sufficient institutional means to control the elites ruling the country.

In this regard, liberal democracies and illiberal democracies can be distinguished. Liberal democracies are constitutional democracies. It is not sufficient that states have written or unwritten constitutions to

---

[6] Held, D. (2006), *Models of Democracy*, Stanford University Press, California.
[7] Madison J. (1982 [1788]), *The Federalist Paper by Alexander Hamilton*, James Madison and John Jay, Bantam Books, New York.

qualify as constitutional states. Constitutionalism seeks to protect the rights and liberties of individuals against the state by restricting political power through the separation of powers and checks and balances. Governments that do not successfully satisfy this political objective cannot be called constitutional government. For instance, Iraq under Saddam Hussein and contemporary Iran both have written constitutions. However, we do not classify these countries as constitutional government.

Additionally, we can categorize illiberal democracies within themselves. According to the annual Democracy Index produced by the Economist Intelligence Unit, for instance, the categories of regimes include full democracy, flawed democracy, hybrid regimes, and authoritarian regimes. Attempting to categorize regimes in an unorthodox manner reveals that it is extremely challenging to build democracy with all of its institutions. In general, democracies with strong democratic histories in Western Europe and North America are classified as full democracies, while countries with significant flaws in their democratic institutionalization are classified otherwise. Countries such as Brazil, Argentina, and India, in which democratic politics have not been fully established despite holding regular and fair elections, are examples of flawed democracies. Countries such as Paraguay, Mexico, and Ecuador, where elections are not fair and competitive, the media is controlled by the political authority, and civil liberties are not guaranteed, are referred to as hybrid regimes, even if they hold regular elections. These countries can be classified as illiberal democracies because they have moved away from the democratic ideal.

Authoritarian regimes are those without democratic political institutions, and political pluralism is either absent or heavily restricted. Many of the nations that fall into this category are dictatorship. There may be some formal democratic institutions, but in practice, democracy is more of a form than a substance. If elections take place at all, they are not held under democratic principles. There is a dismissive attitude toward violations of civil freedoms and abuses of those rights. In most countries, the media are either owned by the state or are under the authority of groups with ties to the government. Both criticisms of the government and general expressions of opinion are subject to widespread censorship. The judicial system is not free from outside influence.[8] This category may contain Russia, Venezuela, and Saudi Arabia.

In this regard, it is important to underline the difference between an authoritarian and a totalitarian regime. The former restricts only certain liberties of the population; it may also accept certain independent organizations and it does not necessarily rely on a strong ideology to influence the people's values. On the contrary, totalitarianism aims at controlling every aspect of citizens' life and does not accept any independent organization.[9] As mentioned by Benito Mussolini, father of Italian fascism, in a totalitarian state, there is "all within the state, none outside the state and none against the state."[10] Traditional societies cannot support totalitarian regimes. By utilizing all state structures and institutions, an incredibly powerful government can keep every structure and even every individual of the society under surveillance and control. Totalitarian regimes possess an ideology, such as Marxism-Leninism, Fascism, or National Socialism, which is required to produce a perfect society, as well as the ability to monitor and manage this ideology. It is very difficult for a totalitarian regime to form and consolidate in the absence of these two capabilities. While there are still several authoritarian regimes in the world, North Korea is the last totalitarian regime left.

Finally, a regime can also be a "theocracy," namely a political system where the government is controlled by religious officials who are regarded as divinely guided. Such government leaders are members of the clergy, and laws are not based on political constitutions but rather on religious law. This form of government was typical of early civilizations, and while the Enlightenment has rendered this regime obsolete in

---

[8]  Economist Intelligence (2021). Democracy index 2021: the China challenge, UK, p. 68.
[9]  Curtis, M. (1979), *Totalitarianism*, Transaction Publishers, New Jersey.
[10]  Ibid.

Western societies, some theocracies still exist in the Middle East, such as in Saudi Arabia and Iran.[11]

## Theories of power

A significant number of Americans harbor concerns regarding the existence of a privileged group of individuals who wield substantial control over the governance of the United States, while others perceive themselves as lacking any meaningful influence. The view in question is sometimes referred to as the elite theory of government. Contrary to that viewpoint, the pluralist theory of governance posits that political power is held by competing interest groups that collectively exert influence in the government. Pluralist thinkers claim that individuals engage in the political system due to the abundance of avenues through which they can approach the government. The U.S. system, characterized by its several levels and branches, offers numerous opportunities for individuals and organizations to interact with the government.

While 'government' and 'regime' are terms that define the way political power is organized within a certain state, different theories exist concerning the way scholars believe power should be framed, of which we can find four main paradigms. First, there is the pluralist theory, for which, if elected, representatives manage to represent equally the different interests present in our societies. Their rule could be both democratic and respecting the people's liberty. As an academic explanation pluralism developed after the end of the Second World War and reached its height during the 1950s and 1960s, periods of economic and political development for Western societies characterized by low social conflict.[12]

During this time, scholars stressed the beneficial consequences of social diversity for politics, advocating for constitutional ways of

---

[11] Cosgel M.M. & Miceli T.J, (2013), "Theocracy", *Working papers 2013-29*, University of Connecticut, Department of Economics.

[12] Dryzek J.S., Dunleavy P. (2009), *Theories of the Democratic State*, Palgrave Macmillan, Basingstoke.

accommodating this diversity on public policy issues. In this framework, group interest is the building block of politics, since this helps citizens develop their political skills and understand how democracy necessitates bargaining and compromise. For this framework to work properly, no group must be blocked from competing on equal terms with another one, and any category of people who share an interest must have the chance to form a group. Therefore, pluralists believed that electoral competition creates a *polyarchy*, namely a government of minorities where elections are competitive. In this system, diverse groups have the opportunity to make themselves heard effectively in the political system with politicians relying on the electorate's support for their re-election.

Considering politics as the result of the mediation between the requests of competing groups, pluralists hold that representative procedures ensure the representation of a large number of influential groups, thus avoiding the concentration of power in the hands of few individuals, which was the theoretical pillar of the second paradigm, namely the elitist scholars. This literature developed with Italian sociologists such as Gaetano Mosca[13], Roberto Michels[14] and Vilfredo Pareto[15], but later developed also in the United States thanks to scholars such as Charles Wright Mills.[16] This philosopher maintained that the common man cannot control politics, since power is centralized in the hands of a political elite that makes the fundamental decisions for everyone. Therefore, Mills defined elites as: "those political, economic and military circles which, arranged in a complex and stratified order, make decisions of at least national importance."[17]

[13]  Renzo S. (1952). "Note on Gaetano Mosca.", *The American Political Science Review,* 46.2 (1952), 603-605.
[14]  Michels R. (1915), *Political Parties: A Sociological Study of The Oligarchical Tendencies of Modern Democracy,* Hearst's International Library Company, New York.
[15]  Pareto V. (1935), *A Treatise on General Sociology,* General Publishing Company, Memphis.
[16]  Mills C.W. (1956), *The Power Elite,* Oxford University Press, Oxford.
[17]  Ibid.

Mills noticed that in the American society of his time, the greatest power existed in the economic, political, and military spheres.[18] These elites determined the direction of the state and reduced all minor institutions to below these top powers. Moreover, each sector extended and thickened its relations with the others, so there was a strong interdependence between them. The members of these elites could also be considered as a single whole since they behaved in a benevolent way among themselves and had common interests with similar social origins. Therefore, despite the theory that democracies should spread political power equally, these elites ruled centralized power in their hands.

The power of the elites is connected to the third paradigm, namely the bureaucratic theory. This view relies on Weber's famous theory for which bureaucratization was intertwined with the development of the territorial state and the capitalist economy.[19] That is, the development of mass citizenship increases both the quantitative demands on the state administration, and the qualitative demand for uniformity of treatment, which can only be met by a supra-local administrative system, operating on the basis of impartiality between persons. Hence, bureaucracy is a distinctive feature of the modern world because it constitutes an efficient structure of power and of administration over a large territory.

This process influences also the structure of democratic systems, since bureaucratization reduces the importance of the parliament in favor of the party, its leaders, and of specialized agencies. For example, the bureaucratic theory suggests that in the United States, those within agencies like the EPA, CIA, and the FBI, are the ones who have the real power within the nation. That is, 'democratization' did not lead to a great dispersal of power to the masses, even though this does not mean that parliament has become obsolete. Rather the opposite: certain democratic processes have become essential in politics, such as the selection of leaders by electoral

---

[18]   Ibid.

[19]   Lutzker, M. A. (1982), "Max Weber and the analysis of modern bureaucratic organization: Notes toward a theory of appraisal.", *The American Archivist*, 45 (2), 119-130.

competition, the provision through Parliament of a forum for public debate and review of policy, and a mechanism for removing leaders in the event of a serious loss of confidence.[20]

Finally, the last paradigm connected to political distribution of power is the social movement theory. This theory explains how social mobilization occurs, under which forms it manifests, and which political consequences it may have. This paradigm became particularly influential in the 1960s, when many in both the United States and Europe began to see civic protests as a means to improve politics. At first, these protests puzzled scholars because studies relied on a deprivation theory which taught that protests were a result of social sufferance, while social movements in the 1960s were the result of an increase in social welfare. Furthermore, answers to this puzzle created differences between American and European sociology.[21]

On the one side, American theories relied more on structural approaches that examined which social and political contexts enabled or restricted protests. Among the factors that increased political movements, scholars underlined features such as an increased access to political decision-making power, an instability in the ruling elites, and a lower ability of the state to repress these actions. Moreover, resource mobilization was of particular importance, since the more organized a community, and the more material, moral, cultural and human resources it possessed, the more likely a protest was to begin.

On the other side, the European strand focused more on social-constructivist approaches that focused less on social-class and material explanations, to argue instead that current protests are different from past labor movements based on social-class, since social movements are now based on post-material features as collective identity, gender, and

[20] Waters T, Waters D (2015), *Weber's Rationalism and Modern Society: New Translations on Politics, Bureaucracy, and Social Stratification*, Palgrave Macmillan, London.
[21] Morris, A. (2000), "Reflections on social movement theory: Criticisms and proposals.", *Contemporary Sociology* 29 (3), 445-454.

sexuality. On top of that, recent scholars such as Goodwin and Polletta argued that emotions, construction of meaning and agency, play a significant part as well in leading to the formation of social movements.[22]

As described by these paradigms, power is not organized in the same way in each country and this has significant consequences, not only for the people's political power, but also for one of the pillars of any political system, namely the people's liberty.

## Types of liberty

Overall, two main conceptions of liberty have dominated the political debate, namely Isaiah Berlin's division between a "negative liberty" and a "positive (or organic) liberty."[23] Negative liberty, which is the absence of external constraints on one's actions, includes civil and political rights such as freedom of speech, life, private property, freedom from violent crime, freedom of religion, habeas corpus, a fair trial, and freedom from slavery. Positive liberty requires the agent to take an active part in gaining control of themselves, since it claims, "I am free to the extent that I achieve self-mastery." Positive liberty mainly focuses on answering the question: "By whom am I ruled?" Therefore, the positive desire to govern myself is connected to the belief that it is essential to determine who is making the political decisions to assess if citizens are free or not. Hence, the main question on which this conception of liberty is framed is: "What does it mean to be free to govern myself?"

First, self-mastery entails that individuals must be a *subject* and not an *object*, namely a self-directed doer able to make decisions by herself and not something moved by external forces. Being a subject is important because only insofar as I am able to conceive policies and goals of my own (and I am afterwards able to realize them), can I consider myself

---

[22]   Buechler, S. M. (1995). "New Social Movement Theories", *The Sociological Quarterly*, 36(3): 441-464.

[23]   Berlin I. (1958), *Two Concepts of Liberty*, Oxford University Press, Oxford.

a self-mastered human being. Otherwise, I will just be an object, 'thing' directed by others according to their needs. In this framework, I am free to the degree that I can realize my own will, while I am enslaved to the extent that I cannot do so.[24]

On the contrary, negative liberty is the concept describing individuals having a personal sphere that must not be constrained by any external interference – a space within which they can act unobstructed by others. Conceiving freedom in terms of non-interference, it becomes essential to understand which hindrances damage personal liberty and which could instead be accepted. The negative liberty scholars' answer to this dilemma has a pivotal social component, since they maintain that citizens are unfree if others prevent them from doing what they could otherwise do. Individuals are then politically unfree when – and only when – they are prevented from attaining a goal by another human being: the wider the area where they are not hindered by other human beings in exercising their choices, the freer they are[25].

At first glance, it may seem simple to guarantee this liberty in a framework where all coercion is conceived as bad because it represses human desires. Total freedom lacking coercion. However, the fact that we live in social systems, where personal liberties are inevitably connected, creates disputes among scholars regarding how many "bads" we ought to impose to avoid larger evils. The problem is then how wide each individual's personal sphere should be, since if everyone was given unlimited freedom, we would live in a chaos where the will of the stronger would prevail over that of the weaker. In a negative liberty framework, the argument is thus: the line between the area of private life and that of public authority should be drawn to have the maximum degree of non-interference compatible with the minimum demands of social life.

Thus, the negative liberty solution differs from the one given by positive liberty. Whereas the latter aims to put authority directly in the hands

---

[24] Berlin I. (2002), *Liberty*, Oxford University Press, Oxford.
[25] Berlin 2002; 171-177.

of the citizenry, the former focuses on finding a minimum area of personal freedom that cannot be violated by anyone, and by this means, they aim to block authority. Hence, these two views focus on two different aspects of power: whereas positive liberty scholars focus on the *source* of the power in the hands of those ruling the social system, negative liberty scholars address the problem of the *intensity and amount* of power that rulers ought to have.

How should therefore negative freedom be restricted? Wouldn't that result in a chaotic order if everyone attempts to do whatever they please? For example, can press freedom involve publishing inaccurate information about another person? According to Mill, a person's freedom is justified if it does not violate the rights and liberties of others. The term for this is the harm principle. You can specialize in martial arts as you like, but you cannot beat anyone other than in self-defense. Individuals who are free to choose in a free society will have competing interests and objectives. This needs numerous legal norms for conflict settlement. In this regard, free societies are also characterized by the strict enforcement of the law. However, the rules of law here are intended to expand individuals' negative freedoms. In contrast, the purpose of the laws in a non-free society is to restrict negative liberties.

The primary criticism of positive freedom is that it is unclear what it means to be free from the influence of others and our own inner constraints. For instance, one of the primary justifications for compulsory public education is that ignorant persons are incapable of making wise decisions. In this regard, proponents of positive freedom claim that via education, individuals may make better decisions. Due to the impossibility of separating educational content from ideologies and conceptions of the good life, especially in the social sciences, there is a risk that public education may become a form of ideological indoctrination. The primary reason communist regimes such as the Soviet Union are regarded as totalitarian is their attempts to entirely eliminate individual preferences. Radical communist indoctrination might be viewed as a radical manifestation of the positive conception of freedom.

In light of this, libertarians take a firm stand against positive freedom arguments. However, modern social democracies are acutely conscious of the contradiction between negative and positive freedom. Consequently, social policies aiming at fostering the development of human capacities strive not to limit individual preferences with pre-conceptions of the good life.

Berlin's division has yet been criticized by the republican conception of liberty as non-domination, whose origins can be found in Rome and later in the commonwealthman tradition, with books such as *Cato's Letters* by Trenchard and Gordon[26] or Madison's essays in the *Federalist Papers*. This ideal centers around the threat of having to live at the mercy of another, since it maintains that liberty involves emancipation from any subordination under domination. That is, it is important to determine when a party 'A' is actually dominating party 'B.' According to Philipp Pettit, the answer is that 'A' is dominating 'B' if – and only if – the former practices interference at will and with impunity, thus posing an arbitrary imposition on the latter's life.[27]

Republican liberty as non-domination has two main features. First, liberty is the opposite of slavery, and even if the master were to be benign, 'living at the mercy of another' is considered a great evil to avoid. Second, if the interference is not arbitrary, but controlled by the interests and opinions of those affected, it is not a form of domination. This view cannot be represented by Berlin's dichotomy. On the one hand, the fact that I am free from the mastery of another individual has no direct connection with the achievement of my self-mastery. On the other hand, republicanism focuses on a different X from which we should be free than the one chosen by negative liberty scholars, since the latter think that X should be "interference," whereas the former maintain that it ought to be "mastery."[28]

---

[26] Trenchard J., Gordon T. (1971), *Cato's Letters*, Da Capo, New York.
[27] Pettit P. (1997), *Republicanism: A Theory of Freedom and Government*, Clarendon Press, Oxford.
[28] Pettit 1997; 52-61.

For this reason, there are two main differences between non-domination and non-interference. First, if one individual is subjected to a master, even though she does whatever she likes, thus enjoying non-interference, she is still a slave, since it is the opportunity to interfere at will that gives the dominating power to the master, despite whether or not the master will eventually use it. The problem of non-interference is even though the master may let the slave decide freely under some conditions, the slave will never be free. Conversely, non-domination grants greater security to personal freedom, since the master cannot interfere with the individual in any case.[29]

Second, interference may occur without people being rendered thereby unfree, since no domination exists if one interferes with my liberty but does so according to my will. Conversely, non-interference entails that every interference limits people's set of choices of some degree, and as such it constrains their freedom. Some interferences in people's lives are thus acceptable, especially if a third party interferes in a relationship where A dominates B to defend and free the latter. This aspect is central in relation to the rule of law, since it entails that a proper law is a non-mastering interferer if it does not compromise the people's liberty. On the contrary, in a non-interference framework, the fact that each law is an interference creates a difficult puzzle for the state, since its actions are seen as an inevitable constraint on an individual's set of choices.

---

[29]  Pettit P. (2012), *On the People's Terms: A Republican Theory and Model of Democracy*, Cambridge University Press, Cambridge.

## KEY TERMS

**Adam Smith:** A Scottish philosopher who advocated for individual autonomy and the retention of one's earnings, rather than being subject to government or corporate domination. He is known for his work "The Wealth of Nations," which laid the foundation for modern capitalism.

**Authority:** A form of legitimate power; the right to exercise power acknowledged by individuals in society.

**Autocracy**: A political regime where power is concentrated in the hands of a single ruler or a small group, with little to no political pluralism.

**Bureaucratic Theory**: A theory that emphasizes the role of bureaucratic structures and administrators in modern governance, often reducing the importance of elected representatives.

**Capitalism**: An economic system characterized by private ownership of the means of production, where individuals are free to acquire property and compete in the market.

**Charismatic Authority**: A type of political legitimacy based on the personal appeal and extraordinary leadership qualities of an individual leader.

**Communism**: An economic and political system where the government controls the means of production and wealth distribution, often governed by a single political party.

**Constitutional Monarchy**: A form of government where a monarch acts as the head of state within the parameters of a constitution, and political power is exercised by elected representatives.

**Democracy**: A political regime based on popular sovereignty, where power is exercised by the people either directly or through elected representatives.

**Elitist Theory**: A theory suggesting that a small group of elites holds substantial power and makes fundamental decisions in society.

**Government**: The system through which a community arranges itself and distributes power to achieve common objectives and provide necessary benefits for society.

**John Locke**: A seventeenth-century English political philosopher who posited that all individuals possess inherent rights to life, freedom, and property, advocating for self-governance.

**Legal-Rational Authority**: A type of political legitimacy based on a system of formal, legal rules and procedures.

**Negative Liberty**: The absence of external constraints on one's actions, emphasizing non-interference and personal freedom.

**Pluralist Theory**: A theory positing that political power is distributed among various competing interest groups that collectively influence the government.

**Positive Liberty**: The concept of achieving self-mastery and control over one's own life, often linked to active participation in governance.

**Power**: The ability to influence others, which may or may not be political.

**Public Sphere**: The realm of political activity and public interest, contrasted with the private sphere of personal life.

**Republican Liberty**: A concept of freedom defined as non-domination, where liberty involves being free from subordination to another's will.

**Self-Governance**: The concept that individuals should have the liberty to willingly agree to be ruled, often associated with democratic principles.

**Socialism**: An economic system where the government controls the means of wealth creation and distribution, often providing extensive social programs and public services.

**Totalitarianism**: A political regime that seeks to control every aspect of citizens' lives, often characterized by a strong ideology and the suppression of dissent.

**Traditional Authority**: A type of political legitimacy based on historical and cultural customs.

**Theocracy**: A political system where the government is controlled by religious officials, and laws are based on religious principles.

**Wealth of Nations**: A book by Adam Smith published in 1776 that laid the foundation for modern capitalism, advocating for individual autonomy and free markets.

# CHAPTER 2

# POLITICAL IDEOLOGIES

I deology is typically employed in a pejorative way in everyday language. To imply that a particular conduct or notion is ideological is to imply that it is the result of a biased, radical, or dogmatic attitude, rather than a result of careful examination. However, political ideologies are only partially coherent and comprehensive in terms of political ideas, theories, and actions. In political theory, concepts are not spontaneously created. Each problem or claim has a rich history and numerous sources from which it draws. In this regard, in order to evaluate and give significance to political theories and even actions, it is vital to comprehend the paradigm to which these concepts and behaviors are tied.

Thus, political ideologies are intellectual traditions that provide empirical and normative ideas and claims on human nature, historical evolution, and political-social systems that are only partially coherent. It is assumed that the intellectuals, who are presumed to be part of a ideological tradition, approach humanity, society, politics, and economics with at least some fundamentally shared assumptions and methods. In this regard, it is feasible to connect the concepts of philosophers to particular political beliefs.

This part will provide responses to the following questions: Who are the most influential thinkers within an ideological tradition? What are the essential principles and ideas of a particular ideology? What are the several schools of thought that arose from the same ideology at different points in history? What fundamental characteristics unite or distinguish these schools of thought? What influence have ideologies had on political systems in the past, and what are their projected future implications? What are the effects of ideological movements in multiple countries and what kind of diversity may be found in these ideas?

Through the transition from feudalism to capitalism in the modern age, three primary ideological traditions have emerged: liberalism, conservatism, and socialism. Nevertheless, we can also add minor ideologies such as anarchism, nationalism, fascism, feminism, and green ideology. Although the divide between major and minor ideologies is somewhat arbitrary, it gives a clear framework for analyzing the interrelationships and conflicts between various ideologies. Even if minor ideologies have their own conceptual vocabulary and political purposes, they are tied to large ideologies in a certain manner. Nationalism, for example, can be classified based on major ideologies, such as liberal nationalism, conservative nationalism, and anti-colonial nationalism. Nationalisms with diverse traits do not mean that nationalism is not an ideology on its own, but it would be impossible to make sense of these distinct varieties of nationalism without a strong reference to major ideologies. Due to space constraints, only the major ideologies will be discussed in this chapter.

## LIBERALISM

Liberalism is distinguished from other ideologies by its acceptance of individual freedom as a fundamental value and its argument that the government should be limited by the constitution to defend individual freedom. The primary tenet of this ideology is the concept of limited government. Philosophers like Jeremy Bentham, Immanuel Kant, Charles-Louis de Secondat Montesquieu, Alexis Tocqueville, Adam Smith, John Locke, and John Stuart Mill are a few people who made significant contributions to the growth of liberal thought beginning in the seventeenth century. Philosophers like Friedrich August von Hayek, Robert Nozick, and Ludwig von Misses were a few of the names that fueled liberal philosophy in the 20th century.

## TYPES OF LIBERALISM

There are three major liberal currents: classical liberalism, modern liberalism, and libertarianism. The fundamental policy distinctions between the various liberal currents relate to how the government governs relationships between the individual and society.

### *Classical Liberalism*

The primary framework of liberalism is classical liberalism, which is the first of these. The values of traditional liberalism, which came into existence in the seventeenth century, include fundamental human rights, limited government, the rule of law, and free markets. John Locke and Adam Smith are two influential founders of classical liberalism. Smith created the concept of economic liberalism while Locke created political liberalism. The primary concern of classical liberals in the 17th and 18th centuries was on defining the constitutional monarchy and the institutions of the market economy that were beginning to form in England and refining these developments.

The main issues that unite the classical liberals of this era are that political power should derive its legitimacy from the consent of the people, that the violation of the fundamental rights and freedoms of individuals by the state is immoral, and that free markets are an important guarantor of wealth and freedom. On the other hand, the classical liberals of the 19th century were focused on the social, political, and economic challenges generated by the economic inequities that were a natural consequence of representative democracy, fast social transformation, and widespread market economy. On the other side, liberals of the 20th century fought against the "threat" posed by communist regimes produced by socialist revolutions on constitutional democracy and the

market economy. During this time, when economic problems and economic systems dominated the discourse, liberal economists' influence in
liberal thought rose to the forefront.

On a methodological level, it is possible to divide classical liberalism
into two major categories: natural law theorists and utilitarians. Locke is
the most influential advocate of the natural law tradition. Locke, a social
contract theorist, argues that natural rights are inherent. This implies
that human rights existed prior to the establishment of both society and
the state. If individuals possess human rights before society and the state,
neither social practices nor state-established norms can violate these
rights. From this perspective, Locke maintained that the political sovereign cannot exist without the consent of the individuals who comprise
the political community and that once the government has emerged, the
political authority is once again accountable for preserving the rights of
these individuals. As is evident, Locke's political theory is predicated on
moral assumptions. One could claim that the United States Constitution
was drafted in accordance with Lockean ideals.

### Utilitarianism

In contrast, utilitarianism evaluates rules and behaviors based on their
outcomes. In this view, utilitarianism can be divided into two categories: classical utilitarianism and rule utilitarianism. Bentham created the
classical utilitarian theory. Bentham argues that empirically unprovable
normative assumptions, such as natural law theory, are superstitious and
that humans should be viewed as utilitarian animals that seek pleasure
and avoid pain. Bentham maintains that the policy with the greatest
good for the greatest number of people is always the correct one, regardless of the nature of the pleasure or pain involved. The utilitarianism of
Bentham contributed to political equality by promoting the principle of
one person, one vote. Bentham was unable to provide a clear solution for
preventing the tyranny of the majority, or the majority's seizure of the
rights of minorities. After Bentham, who did not distinguish between
pleasures and pains qualitatively, Mill asserted that there are qualitative

distinctions between 'utilities'. Mill highlighted these distinctions in the following aphorism:

> "It is better to be a human being dissatisfied than a pig satisfied; better to be Socrates dissatisfied than a fool satisfied. And if the fool, or the pig, is of a different opinion, it is only because they only know their own side of the question."

Rule utilitarianism, on the other hand, examines whether laws and institutions have produced positive results throughout history for the common good, as opposed to accumulating utilities. By reviewing the historical growth process of British political history, Hume argues that the laws and institutions that made England superior to other nations arose as a result of the maintenance of excellent institutions rather than the outcome of pure utility calculation. Hayek is the most influential advocate of rule utilitarianism in the 20th century.

Rule utilitarianism is also used to justify the unequal results of free markets. Production and consumption relations in the market based on private property and voluntary exchange create material inequality in terms of their results. Justice in the market economy and liberal political system, in general, is based on equality before law. Application of general, abstract and equal legal rules to individuals without discrimination constitutes the basis of the classical liberal idea of justice. The formal features of the law are to ensure that the rules do not serve a specific purpose or group.

However, the equal application of the rules does not mean that the results of social and economic transactions will be egalitarian. On the contrary, since equality before law opens a wide area of freedom to individuals, it causes individuals to gain unequal income and even social status. Thus, the market economy does not serve predetermined collective ends. Rather, individuals conduct market transactions for their own purposes, and each individual's pursuit of maximizing his own interests within the rules is considered justified. In this respect, it is uncertain in which direction the relations of production and consumption will develop in a market economy and cannot be directed towards collective goals in principle.

Governments usually intervene in the market economy with monetary and fiscal policies, and labor regulations. These interventions ultimately serve collective purposes. However, social justice policies that try to provide material equality will disrupt the structure and functioning of the market. Comprehensive interventions in the market economy will also deteriorate the wealth creation expected from the free markets and the level of individual freedom will decrease. The increase in economic planning means the decrease in individual planning, and the expansion of the public economy means the shrinkage of the private economy.

Classical liberals establish a causal relationship between individual freedom, the rule of law, and free market economy. Therefore, they argue that the rule of law and freedom cannot be institutionalized in countries where there is no robust market economy. For example, in communist planned economies, there are no general, abstract, egalitarian rules, and economic production and consumption are governed entirely by a chain of command. In this respect, communist countries do not have a rule of law in the Western sense. Therefore, classical liberals perceive comprehensive market interventions or destruction of the free markets primarily as a threat to individual freedom and argue that extensive direct interventions in the market economy will also destroy the rule of law. A classic example of such an argument can be studied in Hayek's Road to Serfdom.

## MODERN LIBERALISM

The notion of social liberalism/modern liberalism, which has existed since the middle of the nineteenth century, is the second movement to emerge within liberalism. In contrast to classical liberalism, this perspective places obligations on the state in some particular areas and promotes democratic participation, social and economic rights, and the notion of equality. Prominent philosophers in this school of thought include Thomas H. Green, John Stuart Mill, and John Rawls. Modern liberal philosophers, on the one hand, maintain the political values and civil rights championed by classical liberalism, while on the other, they argue that the unrestricted market economy treats disadvantaged individuals in society unfairly and hinders their potential personal growth. Modern liberals assign the state an active role in regulating economic and social connections to promote social justice and preserve social equality. Social policies such as unemployment benefits, union rights, price controls, and social health care aid are among the new responsibilities imposed on the state by modern liberals.

As mentioned above, classical liberals view the state as an umpire who enforces the rules uniformly to all members of society. In contrast, modern liberals view the state as the protector of its citizens. It is considered that disadvantaged individuals cannot change their social and economic conditions and do not always know what is best for them when left alone. For this reason, the state is granted broad authority over social and economic matters, and efforts are made to achieve the social goals set by politicians.

In addition to mistrust in the market economy and faith in the state, modern liberals view the unequal power relations established by private property as unfair. Consequently, material inequalities should be eliminated to some extent so that individuals can successfully exercise their civil and political rights and achieve self-fulfillment. Later papers by Mill are known to provide such defenses. However, A Theory of Justice by John Rawls, released in 1971, remains the primary source of liberal perspectives on social justice today.

According to Rawls, social and economic inequality can be justified if it benefits society's most disadvantaged members the most. Therefore, even while Rawls acknowledges that there are justified inequalities, he strictly conditions these inequalities and ascribes a social purpose to them. The demand for justice has collective ends that are independent of market processes, according to modern liberals who support social justice. For instance, market forces alone should not determine what happens to disadvantaged groups who lack marketable skills or who struggle in the markets. Governments must support these collective ends as a necessity of social justice by redistributing income, values, and status to ensure that societies have social goals that go beyond those that emerge from the markets. Insufficient service of private education, for instance, is one of the reasons why public education is compulsory. In this regard, people who did not have a good education because of unfavorable environmental circumstances cannot be held accountable for the negative social and economic circumstances they found themselves in. Therefore, modern liberals argue that others in society have a moral obligation to assist those who are disadvantaged in society owing to factors beyond their control.

## LIBERTARIANISM

The libertarianism that emerged in the 20th century is the third concept to emerge within liberalism. The state is regarded as a night watchman in this view, which was established by philosophers like Robert Nozick and Ayn Rand, and it calls for the government excludes from all spheres of social, economic, and political life. The libertarian concept holds that it is vital to leave the provision of all services, including those related to infrastructure, education, health, and social security, to the free markets at large, except for those related to security and justice.

Libertarianism is a political theory that originated in the United States, particularly during the second half of the 20th century. Libertarians, who think that individual liberty and the right to property are necessary conditions for a good society, require that all human relationships be based on consent. According to the principle of non-aggression, the only legitimate use of force is self-defense. Libertarianism is quite similar to Lockean classical liberalism; however, libertarians defend social and economic problems from the standpoint of property-based individual freedom in a more comprehensive manner than Locke did. Libertarianism is a political ideology created in opposition to the welfare state's nanny state conception, i.e., the conception of politics that claims guardianship over individuals.

In this context, individuals cannot be coerced to support social causes such as social justice or the greater good. Libertarians argue that the government's taxation of its citizens in the name of programs such as welfare expenditures, economic efficiency, or cultural development represents an unfair income transfer. For instance, libertarians contend that the government should not seek to advance the arts. They believe that art enthusiasts should cover their own expenses with their own funds. They think that no one can be obliged to accommodate another's artistic preferences. Similarly, it is ethical for individuals to voluntarily assist others. When the government or others compel individuals to provide social assistance, libertarians argue, individuals are compelled to sacrifice themselves for the benefit of others. For libertarians, this is equivalent to slavery or serfdom.

## CONSERVATISM

Although its origins can be traced back to antiquity, conservatism as a political ideology evolved throughout the modern era. It is possible to identify conservatism as an attitude or attitude among numerous philosophers and eras. In addition to ideologies such as liberalism and socialism, however, conservatism as a distinct political ideology was molded by criticisms of Enlightenment philosophy on the philosophical level and the French Revolution on the social and political level. In this framework, conservatism, which is a contemporary political philosophy, has had various thought traditions, significant political movements/parties, and a substantial social base till the present day.

Although the concept's intellectual roots were established in the 18th century, it was not used as a distinct political position or ideology until the first part of the 19th century. Notable conservative philosophers include Edmund Burke, Joseph Maistre, Adam Müller, Robert Nisbet, Hanry Sidwick, Michael Oakeshott, and Roger Verman Scruton. It should not be assumed, however, that the concept has the same meaning everywhere.

Temporally and geographically distinct articulations of conservatism have occurred. In contrast to the liberal content of Anglo-American conservatism, the authoritarian content of Continental European conservatism has increased. In the 20th century, conservatism was divided between paternalism, which favored reformist and interventionist programs, and liberalism, which somehow adopted free market principles. Discussions on the position of conservative political philosophy on the scale of authoritarianism-liberalism and totalitarianism-pluralism, as well as the various intellectual currents that evolved in this context, continue to exist today.

## TYPES OF CONSERVATISM

There is a significant difference between authoritarian European Conservatism and liberal Anglo-American Conservatism. Moreover, paternalist conservatism, which advocates and implements interventionist measures, contrasts with the pro-free market neo-conservatism that emerged in the 1980s.

## CONTINENTAL CONSERVATISM AND AUTHORITARIAN CONSERVATISM

Continental European conservatives reject both the Enlightenment and the French Revolution, along with all of their social and political ramifications, out of deep-seated hate for both. It is a counterrevolutionary and reactionary political ideology that advocates the rule of the traditional elite and yearns for the Middle Ages. In contrast to other conservative ideologies that value authority, hierarchy, and order, they promoted authoritarianism and autocratic governments. Defending authoritarianism is distinct from highlighting the importance of authority. This political tradition, often known as authoritarian conservatism in this regard, demonstrates little support for liberal democratic ideas. So much so that it justifies the obligation of loyalty even to a terrible ruler, despite individual liberty, rights, participation, and so on.

Authoritarian conservatives continued to promote hierarchical and autocratic systems throughout the 19th century, and conservative elites in Germany and Italy supported movements and organizations that opened the way for Mussolini and Hitler throughout the first half of the 20th century. Authoritarian conservatives, who rejected the limitation of political power through constitutions and parliamentary institutions, also supported power patterns such as Bonapartism and Peronism, which combined authoritarianism with a commitment to economic and social welfare to create a plebiscite dictatorship. These regimes combined populism with an authoritarian emphasis on obedience, discipline, and national unity to preach a sort of conservative nationalism. At this time, it is essential to consider the gap between authoritarian conservatism and fascism. Although they are distinct philosophies, when authoritarian conservatism is taken to its extreme, fascism is nourished. The existence of a conceptual framework is possible. In contrast to the Anglo-American tradition, thinkers, and arguments within the German conservative thought point to conservatism with a higher dose of authoritarianism.

## LIBERAL CONSERVATISM AND ANGLO-AMERICAN CONSERVATISM

Although it shares some conceptual underpinnings with authoritarian conservatism, Anglo-American conservatism has significant ties to liberal ideas. This tradition, which was inspired by anti-rationalist philosophers such as Adam Smith, David Hume, and Adam Ferguson, is empiricist, evolutionist, and liberal. Anti-rationalism is the belief that society cannot be ruled and understood by abstract rules based on pure reason. Individuals' behaviors are governed by their emotions, ambitions, and instincts; in the context of social connections, the reason is secondary to these passions. Edmund Burke, who is considered to be the creator of liberalism, was a Whig, and Adam Smith shared his ideas on ethics and economics to a great extent. This 'liberal' character will become apparent when this fact is explored. As a liberal conservative, Burke criticizes the Enlightenment's fundamental rationalism but accepts John Locke's empiricist epistemology. In contrast, abstract rationalism asserts that society may be recreated from scratch using just abstract rational principles. In this regard, liberal conservatism opposes the French Revolution fiercely, while supporting the British and American revolutions. It advocates 'moderate', 'balanced,' and parliamentary government.

There is no contradiction between traditional social order advocacy and market economy advocacy under the liberal conservative framework. As Burke views market laws as natural laws, he rejects all forms of economic intervention. Burke opposes authoritarian conservatism with his advocacy of limited government. But Burke attributes limited government to the political and social traditions of Britain. In this view, he does not consider the limited government to be an application of abstract liberal principles Liberal conservatives do not adopt particular liberal concepts and institutions as a unified whole and pragmatically incorporate them into their ideology.

## PATERNALIST CONSERVATISM AND NEO-CONSERVATISM

Paternalist conservatism, which advocates interventionist policies, can be observed in the policies of Benjamin Disraeli in England, the welfare statist policies of Lord Randolph Churchill, and the practices known as "moderate middle way" or "mixed system" after World War II. Interventionism refers to the active involvement of public institutions in addressing social problems caused by economic inequality. The term one-nation conservatism is also used to refer to this concept. Beginning in the period of Disraeli, conservatives projected that increasing industrialization, urbanization, and inequality would divide England into two distinct nations, the "rich" and the "poor" and promoted reformist/interventionist measures to combat this threat.

In this context, conservative governments expanded the voting rights of the lower classes, improved working and housing conditions, and enacted social reforms designed to shield individuals from the detrimental effects of the market economy. The objective of these paternalist interventionist policies is not to expand positive freedom, eliminate hierarchy, or establish social equality; rather, it is to prevent changes that could undermine hierarchy and organic social structure by means of state intervention. Paternalism refers to the governmental treatment of individuals in a manner comparable to a father's exercise of control inside the family. Just as a father makes judgments for his children based on his experience, knowledge, and authority, so too does the government know and apply what is beneficial for individuals. Conservative paternalism is primarily motivated by concern about the radicalization of the lower classes. During the post-World War II period, Christian democratic parties in a number of European countries embraced similar interventionist tactics. During this period, Christian democratic parties, which had begun to abandon their authoritarian views, advocated for political democracy, social reforms, and constitutional government, and sought to implement a social market economy and Keynesian welfare policies in opposition to the free market economy.

Neo-conservatism, which reconciles with the market-centered arguments of neo-liberalism and rejects the interventionist policies of paternalist conservatism, rose to popularity during the 1980s as part of the New Right program that formed in response to the crisis of the Western welfare state. During this time period, the neo-conservative notions of authority, tradition, national identity, and law and order, which were combined with the neo-liberal notions of market economy, economic efficiency, and individualism, advocated for market deregulation and political authority. Neoconservatism, which condemns welfare state policies by incorporating them with socialism, advocates for the restoration of law, order, and discipline that have been eroded by the revival of traditional values and moral principles. In this context, this entails strengthening the family, enhancing penalties, and reinforcing national identity. Within this context, it should be highlighted that especially American neo-conservatism supports the interventionist foreign policies and 'order of the world' of the United States.

## SOCIALISM

In chronological order, socialism is third among the major political ideologies. Socialism prioritizes collective action, shared property, and social equality. As a modern ideology, its primary objective is to expose the negative aspects of capitalism and propose alternatives to it. It views capitalism as exploitation and seeks the ways to abolish this exploitation or, if this is not possible, to at least mitigate its effects. It is precisely these formulations that give rise to various socialist concepts. At one extreme of the spectrum of socialists are radical revolutionary socialists who seek to demolish the market economy, eliminate private property, and replace the capitalist system with a communist regime. On the other hand, there are moderate socialists who, despite their critique of the market economy, do not demonstrate a revolutionary approach, accept liberal values occasionally, but suggest democratic formulas to establish equal opportunity for everyone to realize liberal objectives.

Socialism should be viewed as a spectrum that includes these two extremes. The welfare state policies in countries where moderate socialists were powerful show that this idea found a serious and practical application. However, instances where the most radical socialists gained power include the Soviet Union, China, Eastern Europe, Cuba, Vietnam, and North Korea. In the majority of the countries listed, socialism as an economic order has vanished or suffered a significant setback. Similarly, the social welfare policies shaped under the impact of socialism are the subject of severe criticism and heated debate. Despite these negative developments and the fading of socialism's power as an economic option, it remains the most significant topic of political and cultural criticism. For this reason, people/parties that uphold the socialist tradition and/or accept socialist ideas remain among the most formidable alternatives to power in a number of nations, particularly democratic nations.

## TYPES OF SOCIALISM

Despite the fact that Marxism has mostly dominated the socialist tradition, I will discuss the pre-Marxist socialists briefly here. In addition, I will provide a quick analysis of democratic socialism and social democracy outside of Marxism.

## UTOPIAN SOCIALISM

Since the commencement of the Industrial Revolution and the growth of the factory system, some philosophers have attacked the capitalist system for being inefficient, wasteful, irrational, or unfair. Beginning in the 1800s, these complaints became the distinguishing characteristics of a particular political attitude. In particular, people such as Comte Henri de Saint-Simon and Charles Fourier in France and Robert Owen in England became the forerunners of pre-Marxist socialist theory and the leaders of an anti-capitalist political movement with followers who committed to a particular program of action. Their works were widely read, their speeches attracted big audiences, and the concept of socialism spread to distant nations such as America. Within the context of the history of socialism, this process correlates with the first phase between the Napoleonic Wars and the 1848 upheavals. Not content with merely criticizing the current state of society, the people cited go on to advance their own ideas and plans for how society ought to be. In accordance with these ideas, each of the philosophers will provide a detailed vision of the perfect society of the future, revitalizing their own image.

This period in socialism's history is known as utopian socialism. This naming was attained by Karl Marx and the Marxist tradition in the years that followed. The justification for such naming is the Marxist tradition's evaluation of the ideas of the named individuals. Therefore, 'utopian socialists' hope for a general social transformation in which individualism, competition, and the dominance of private property are abolished, without recognizing the necessity of class struggle and without valuing the revolutionary role of the proletariat in the socialist transformation. In addition, the fact that earlier socialist movements were referred to as utopia and viewed as consisting of benevolence is tied to Marx and his followers' insistence that their socialism is 'scientific'. Because Marx's point is that he found the laws of social transformation, unlike the socialist tradition that came before him.

The abolition of capitalism is the most essential element shared by the utopias proposed by Simon, Fourier, and Owen. Each describes the capitalist system as wasteful, unjust, and unplanned. They seek a planned society that is efficient and egalitarian. As with capitalism, this society will eliminate the minority of non-workers who own the means of production and live in comfort and luxury. The ownership of the means of production was viewed as the method to achieving this objective, and it was believed that the majority of working people would live a happy life if they owned the means of production. From a methodological standpoint, St. Simon, Fourier, and Owen are attempting to build a brand-new science of human nature. Here, significant emphasis has been focused on the moral/ideological domain as the decisive foundation for all other elements of human behavior; an effort has been made to turn this discipline into a legitimate science that will answer the problem of societal cohesiveness. In accordance with these efforts, the existing moral, religious, and political ideology is regarded as the greatest barrier to the adoption of the newly revealed harmony rules.

Another defining characteristic of the anti-capitalist reaction exemplified by Simon, Fourier, and Owen is that it is an 'emotional' reaction to the poor working and living conditions brought about by the industrial revolution. This emotional aspect diminished the degree of realism and application of their proposed remedies. Utopian socialists know where they want to go, but their ideas on how to get there are unclear. Since these names lack a sufficient understanding of the historical dimension of social development, they believe that social disorders can be eliminated quickly by adopting and implementing their imagined ideal orders. When appealing to people's consciences and minds, they expect the ruling classes and administrators to accept new (socialist) social organizations. This led to the view that 'revolutionary' goals might be reached through 'evolutionary' means as a result of the belief that economic problems could be solved with economic remedies without a major change in the political structure. The evolutionist perspective observed here involves the notion that it will be sufficient to attract the powerful or wealthy by convincing them of the correctness and beauty of the new system, leaving the remainder to their common sense. However, the interests of the parties on the opposing side of this expectation necessitate the continuation of the current order, rendering the proposed ideas unrealistic.

## MARXISM

In the second half of the 19th century, Karl Marx's theories began to significantly influence socialist ideology and movements. While Marx's critical analysis of capitalist society laid the theoretical foundations for the political movement that bears his name, it has been influential in a wide range of fields, from justice to political economy, humanism to the relationship between the individual and society, and methodology to philosophy.

Marx's method might be referred to as historical materialism or dialectical materialism. The simplest definition of dialectics is the emergence of synthesis from the interaction between thesis and anti-thesis. The synthesis combines the best features of the thesis and the antithesis that formed it. Until a synthesis is reached, the reconciliation process between thesis and antithesis will be repeated numerous times throughout the vast expanse of history. Regarding this, materialism is the belief that all things are either composed only of matter or are ultimately dependent on matter for their existence and nature. It is possible for a materialistic philosophy to grant spirit a secondary position, yet the vast majority of materialism denies the existence of spirit or anything non-physical.

Marx believed that the mode of production is the only factor that determines everything about society. The material mode of production comprises of production forces and production relations, which Marx refers to as the base. The forces of production consist of means of production and labor power. Production relations define social formations and classes. Marx asserts that all social structures developed throughout history have been molded by class struggle. Class, on the other hand, refers to the economic position of a certain group in the mode of production. If you own the means of production, you are a member of the exploitative class, whereas if you are paid for your labor, you are a member of the exploited class. This explanation analysis, for instance, the class relationship between lords and serfs in feudal society and between bourgeois and proletariat in capitalist society.

However, history is not stationary and is inevitably in progress. This materialist historical progress is shaped by class conflict. The conflict between exploiting and exploited classes results in a social revolution that alters the social, political, and economic order. The exploiting class is the thesis, the exploited class is the antithesis, and the newly emerging social structure is the synthesis within this account. The emergence of the bourgeois class during feudalism and the conflict between aristocrats and the bourgeois gave rise to capitalism, a new social structure. Similarly, the conflict between capitalists and proletariat within the capitalist system will result in a revolution and pave the way for the formation of socialism. Additionally, the socialist system will be the end of history. Because, once the proletariat has eliminated the capitalists, a classless society will be built, and the conflict between thesis and antithesis will be resolved. Because workers would also control the means of production under socialism, exploitation, and class struggle, and ultimately historical progress will cease to exist.

The idea of the superstructure is one of the most massive implications of historical materialism.

According to the superstructure theory, the base determines all social institutions and traits, including the legal and political system, morality, religion, social practices, literature, art, and culture. The superstructure's role is to ensure the ongoing reproduction of this exploitative order because the main purpose of the base is to promote class exploitation. Therefore, Marx despises and opposes all bourgeois ideals, including democracy, human rights, and the rule of law. The same reasoning underlies Marxists' vilification of artistic and literary works that do not advance the cause of the working class. The liberal social, cultural, and political system known as the superstructure was created in the capitalist society to conceal the bourgeoisie's class interests from the working class. By creating the illusion that the capitalist order is just, the superstructure primarily aims to prevent the proletariat from developing class consciousness, which is synonymous with revolutionary awareness.

Marx and the Marxists did not contribute to the political ideas that developed under these systems because they saw the superstructure, or social and political system, as the bourgeoisie's ideological apparatus. Marx, for instance, lacks a personal philosophy of justice. The primary cause of this is that Marx saw politics to be a transient, historical process. Although he believes that exploited workers are not treated fairly in capitalist production relations, he did not provide a universal notion of justice. The universal cannot be historical, hence this cannot be the case. In this setting, rather than asserting theories on its own, Marxist political terminology primarily presents itself as a critique of capitalism. Marx's theory of the state is intimately tied to this intriguing Marxist perspective. The state, a superstructure apparatus, ensures the perpetuation of class exploitation as its primary function. However, when the extractive institutions vanish in the socialist society, the state will whittle away. Marxists have been willing to criticize modern theories, which they allege to be capitalist, rather than making original contributions to political theories, on the grounds that the state will eventually disappear.

A significant dispute has emerged over this shortcoming in Marxist theory, particularly in light of the totalitarian nature of the political structures erected by communist governments. Socialist writers employed the ideas of real socialism, or, to put it another way, actually existing socialism, to explain the distinctions between the Marxist ideal of socialism and communist regimes before the fall of the Soviet Union. The elimination of private property and the market economy prompted communist regimes to develop a comprehensive and extensive bureaucratic organizational system. This bureaucratic administration's failure to deliver the prosperity, equality, and freedom promised by Marx has given rise to a prolonged argument between communist and anti-communist writers.

The problem of alienation is another topic that weighs heavily on Marx's thoughts in relation to capitalist economic relations. Marx argues that all social classes in capitalist society experience political and social alienation that is founded on economic alienation. Labor is the source of alienation. People must work and produce in order to survive, and because this activity generates surplus value, the connection between man and nature is transformed into a dialectical one where the two parties interact and influence one another. In this instance, capitalism also creates a dichotomy between individuals and the outcomes of their effort. Because manufacturing activities are no longer a process of liberation through which people realize themselves, and people are no longer the masters of their products. People are subject to outside factors that prevent them from realizing their own freedom and creativity, and these forces also have control over their work. Thus, in terms of alienation, the outcome of capitalism for the proletariat is that it is alienated from the products it produces, the actual production process, all of its potentials as a human being, and other workers who are its own friends.

## DEMOCRATIC SOCIALISM AND SOCIAL DEMOCRACY

Democratic socialism or revisionist socialism is a nineteenth-century ideology that asserts socialist ideals may be accomplished through democratic politics without the need for revolutionary violence. Eduard Bernstein and Karl Kautsky are prominent democratic socialist theorists. These philosophers, who first sought to achieve socialism in a revolutionary manner similar to that of Karl Marx, came to believe that socialism could be achieved without revolution, particularly when the working class gained political rights through workers' parties. Democratic socialism has multiple origins. One of these sources is the nineteenth-century European social justice policies that sought to promote material equality through the transfer of wealth. The first instance of democratic socialism can be shown as German social welfare state. German welfare state intended to construct an order based on equality by distributing wealth to vast populations at the end of the 19th century. In England, Fabianism, another source of democratic socialism, evolved. Fabianism, an intellectual rather than political movement, sought to gradually replace the capitalist economy with a system of public production. Fabianism, which opposed the revolution, maintained that socialism could be established in England by democratic means, with the education of elites and the general public about socialism, on the grounds that socialism is a scientific fact.

Rapidly developing in the first half of the 20th century, workers' parties played a crucial role in the transition of democratic socialism into a powerful popular movement. After World War II, however, the workers' parties, following the example of the German Social Democratic Party, abandoned the goal of abolishing private property entirely. Instead, they adopted a welfare state model characterized by dominant public production and social democratic policies aimed at achieving material equality.

In this respect, democratic socialism and social democracy can be distinguished. The legal and political position of private property is not up for debate in contemporary Western social democracies, which are founded on competitive markets. Instead of supporting egalitarian principles through public production, welfare governments redistribute tax-funded budgets in accordance with social objectives. Social democracy cannot be founded on the anti-property and anti-market ideals of democratic socialism in contemporary democracies.

There are also claims that democratic socialism and democratic decision-making processes have significant flaws. It is not always possible for socialism to be compatible with its values, goals and democratic decision-making processes. In a democracy, political decisions are made by simple majority vote. In this regard, it is always feasible for the majority to deviate from socialist principles. In response to this argument, democratic socialists claim that the purpose of democracy is to ensure equality of power in society and that equality of power cannot be achieved without material equality. In this regard, they contend that only socialist principles can form a genuine democracy.

Regarding the ideology of social justice, democratic socialism and social democracy have another intricate link. Modern liberal philosophers significantly formulated the principles of social justice that provided the welfare state with political justification. Although contemporary liberal authors have advocated several extensive collectivist systems, they have framed their theoretical arguments and policy proposals inside a liberal political framework. Social democracy owes more to modern liberals than democratic socialists, at least in terms of the theory of social justice. In this context, the concept of the third way is an intriguing example of how workers' parties' conceptions of social democracy have evolved. This third way is shown as an alternative to "top-down" state intervention and free-market capitalism. It is widely associated with the government of Tony Blair and "new" Labor in the UK, but it was also influenced by the Administration of Bill Clinton in the USA.

During the early years following 1945, concepts and programs associated with social democracy had the greatest possible impact. They were promoted by socialist parties, as well as occasionally liberal and conservative ones, and the ultimate result was the expansion of economic and social intervention in the majority of Western governments. As a result of this, social democracy is frequently praised for having successfully tamed the unpredictability of capitalism while also bringing about more economic growth and greater social cohesion. However, the progress of social democracy took place concurrently with the "long boom" of the post-war period. When the "long boom" ended during the recessions that occurred in the 1970s and 1980s, the fundamental contradiction that exists within social democracy (between preserving the market economy and promoting equality) was brought to light. As a consequence, a significant number of people have moved away from the conventional social democratic stances in favor of ideals and policies that are more oriented toward the market economy. On the other hand, in the same way that the shortcomings of the social democratic pro-state position opened up opportunities for the New Right in the 1980s, developing reservations about the pro-market attitude of the New Right may open up new prospects for modernized or new social democracy.

The persistence of the concept of a third way reveals a profound disappointment with free market capitalism and state socialism. Politicians who advocate for third way make an effort, in essence, to develop a non-socialist critique of an unfettered free market economy. Concern about the arbitrary and frequently immoral consequences of market competition continues to be a primary criticism leveled against capitalism, even though the philosophical and ideological premises upon which this critique is based are constantly evolving. From this vantage point, the problem with capitalism is that it poses an ongoing danger to the cohesiveness of society as well as its overall stability.

Third, theorists are opposed to socialism for two reasons. First, they feel that collectivization and planning are unable to give a workable alternative to the free markets. Second, they believe that socialism is associated with a planned economy. Politics that take a "third way" are criticized heavily, mostly for two reasons. The first argument is that the concept of a third way is nothing more than a populist slogan that has no basis in either political or economic reality. The second argument is that third way ideas are fundamentally inconsistent due to the fact that they are unable to consider alternatives to the capitalist model of economic organization.

## KEY TERMS

**Adam Smith**: An 18th-century philosopher known for his work on economic liberalism and the development of classical liberal thought.

**Alienation**: A concept in Marxism referring to the estrangement of individuals from the products of their labor, the production process, their human potential, and their fellow workers in a capitalist society.

**Anglo-American Conservatism**: A branch of conservatism influenced by liberal ideas, emphasizing limited government, market economies, and empiricism.

**Authoritarian Conservatism**: A branch of conservatism that rejects Enlightenment ideas and promotes hierarchical, autocratic systems and loyalty to traditional elites.

**Bentham, Jeremy**: An English philosopher and founder of modern utilitarianism, emphasizing the greatest good for the greatest number.

**Bourgeoisie**: In Marxist theory, the class that owns the means of production and exploits the proletariat.

**Classical Liberalism**: A political ideology advocating for individual freedom, limited government, the rule of law, and free markets.

**Communism**: A political and economic ideology aiming for a classless society where the means of production are communally owned.

**Continental Conservatism**: A form of conservatism predominant in Europe, characterized by authoritarianism and rejection of Enlightenment principles.

**Democratic Socialism**: A political ideology that aims to achieve socialist goals through democratic means rather than revolutionary violence.

**Dialectical Materialism**: Marxist methodology that views historical progress as a result of the conflict between opposing social forces.

**Fabianism**: An intellectual movement advocating gradual and democratic transition to socialism, emphasizing education and reform over revolution.

**Historical Materialism**: A Marxist theory that economic structures determine societal and political structures, and class struggle drives historical change.

**Individual Freedom**: A core value in liberalism, emphasizing the rights and liberties of individuals over the authority of the state.

**John Locke**: A 17th-century philosopher who contributed to classical liberal thought, advocating for natural rights and government by consent.

**John Stuart Mill**: A philosopher who contributed to both utilitarianism and modern liberalism, advocating for individual liberty and social equality.

**Karl Marx**: A 19th-century philosopher and economist whose theories on capitalism, class struggle, and historical materialism laid the foundation for Marxism.

**Liberal Conservatism**: A form of conservatism that integrates liberal principles, advocating for limited government and market economies while preserving traditional social orders.

**Liberalism**: A political ideology emphasizing individual freedom, limited government, the rule of law, and free markets.

**Libertarianism**: A political philosophy advocating for minimal state intervention in personal and economic affairs, emphasizing individual liberty and property rights.

**Marxism**: A socialist ideology developed by Karl Marx, focusing on class struggle, the exploitation of the proletariat by the bourgeoisie, and the eventual establishment of a classless society.

**Modern Liberalism**: A form of liberalism that supports a more active role for the state in regulating the economy and promoting social justice to address inequalities.

**Natural Law**: A theory in classical liberalism, particularly advocated by John Locke, that certain rights are inherent and cannot be violated by the state.

**Neo-Conservatism**: A political movement combining traditional conservative values with free-market principles, emerging in the 1980s as part of the New Right.

**Paternalist Conservatism**: A form of conservatism advocating for state intervention to address social issues and protect the hierarchical social order.

**Proletariat**: In Marxist theory, the working class that is exploited by the bourgeoisie in capitalist societies.

**Rawls, John**: A modern liberal philosopher known for his work on social justice, particularly his theory that inequalities are justified if they benefit the least advantaged members of society.

**Social Democracy**: A political ideology that aims to achieve social justice within a capitalist framework, primarily through welfare state policies and wealth redistribution.

**Socialism**: A political and economic ideology advocating for collective ownership of the means of production, social equality, and the abolition or reform of capitalist systems.

**Superstructure**: In Marxist theory, the social, political, and ideological systems and institutions that arise from and serve to perpetuate the economic base of a society.

**Utopian Socialism**: An early form of socialism that envisions an ideal society based on cooperation and egalitarian principles, without recognizing the necessity of class struggle.

CHAPTER 3

# AMERICAN POLITICAL CULTURE

Political culture is a set of *shared* ideas, values, and beliefs that define the role and limitations of government and people's relationship to that government. Political beliefs and values are the primary elements that determine the political priorities and responses of citizens. Therefore, solely a rational cost-benefit analysis cannot be used to assess voter behavior and explain political phenomena. We can consider political beliefs and values that manifest political culture as the political personality of the average voter. These political values, which are commonly held by the average voter, are the primary determinants of a nation's political character. In fact, citizens evaluate political events based on these traits, and political reality can only be defined in relation to these values. In this regard, it may be difficult to demonstrate that political reality exists apart from political culture.

In addition to official norms, political culture consists mostly of unwritten practices and traditions. These practices and traditions are culturally transferred from generation to generation through socialization and are frequently referred to as "habits of the heart." Rather than studying and adopting them objectively, new generations frequently view reality in terms of these values. For instance, despite the fact that the American Constitution is a legal document that must be obeyed,

Americans also see it as quasi-sacred. Therefore, amending the American Constitution is not merely a matter of Congressional politics. Any change to the Constitution requires the genuine support of the American people.

President Roosevelt's attempt to increase the number of Supreme Court judges in 1937 is an intriguing example of a proposed constitutional amendment. At the height of his popularity, when the Supreme Court began to block some of Roosevelt's crucial New Deal legislation, he requested Congress for permission to increase the number of Supreme Court justices. The request of President Roosevelt provoked indignation across the nation. Opponents' primary concern was that this meddling in the legal system would compromise judicial independence. Roosevelt's request was denied with the support of the Democrats following a lengthy debate. Even the Democrats opposed the idea of President Roosevelt.

Even a prominent leader like President Roosevelt was not permitted to compromise judicial independence following the Great Depression of 1929. However, as time passed, Supreme Court justices realized they could no longer oppose social security legislation. Following Roosevelt's proposal, the New Deal laws were implemented without significant legal opposition.

The political culture that contributes to the stability of the political system should not be susceptible to significant change. However, profound economic crises and social upheavals can serve as catalysts for changes in political culture. In the instance of the Supreme Court, the American public's ambivalence between judicial independence and social security laws resulted in the formation of a new political mindset. With minor adaptations, the American political system has been able to stabilize itself in the face of significant social crises.

In many ways, the political culture of the United States diverges significantly from those of its Western relatives. American political culture is built upon values that limit the power of government. The emphasis on limited government originates from the United States being the first modern republic with a written constitution. The written constitution is an American invention in this regard. Before the United States, the establishment or even survival of a truly democratic republic across a broad geographical area was deemed unachievable by the majority of European political elites. Despite the fact that the United States engaged in a civil war over a century after its foundation, the country emerged from this conflict with enhanced political equality.

The direct foundation of a democratic system in the United States, without the establishment of a monarchical rule, separates it from other nations in which democracy is founded through revolutions or reforms. This distinction is typically referred to as the American exceptionalism. On the other hand, the Constitution of United States and American practices of self-government did not appear out of thin air. The Constitution of America is in part a redesign of political institutions founded on the rational principles of separation of powers and the rule of law, which matured in England following the Glorious Revolution, to fit the American federal system. For instance, the Constitution of America borrows heavily from the Instrument of Government issued by Oliver Cromwell, the leader of the Parliamentary army after the first English civil war, and the Bill of Rights issued in 1689 following the Glorious Revolution.

As will be shown in greater detail in the coming chapters, British political theory, especially John Locke's theories of natural law and social contract, are also essential components of American constitutional drafting. Furthermore, the first colonies founded in North America at the start of the 17th century created representative governments with approval from the British government. By the end of the eighteenth century, all colonies were autonomous through their representative governments. Such procedures cannot exist outside of British political philosophy and the British political tradition.

Certainly, the American political system and culture are markedly unlike from those of the British in certain areas. Despite its parliamentary components, the political system and social structure of England were aristocratic. The conservatism and traditionalism of British aristocracy clashed with the American people's rigorous egalitarianism and

dedication to liberal rational ideals. The originality of the American political system enabled the establishment of a state founded on rationalism
and principles of self-governance as opposed to a political creed founded
on myths and traditions. Before the American Revolution, despite all the
experience with limited government and liberal thought, the concept of
a limited government based on rational liberal principles was considered
a utopian vision. After the American Revolution, however, the majority
of intellectuals eagerly backed the French Revolution.

"Taxation without representation is slavery" was one of the slogans
that symbolized the drastic split with political and social equality between
the American colonies and Britain, and possibly the rest of the world.
Following Britain's imposition of direct taxes on Americans following the
Seven Years' War between Britain and the French-led union, this slogan
gained popularity. The introduction of direct taxes on top of those for-
merly imposed mostly through transactions was viewed by the American
colonists as a great injustice. American colonists, viewing themselves as
equal Britons, believed that direct taxes could only be enforced with their
consent. However, the British could not comprehend why the sovereign
state's right over its subjects was being questioned.

While it was widely acknowledged that taxation was a sovereign right,
the American colonists internalized the notion that a legitimate government could only be founded on consent more than any other society.
Americans did not anticipate that the concept of consensual government
would emerge gradually in an aristocratic culture. For them, consent-
based government was a moral imperative, and failure to implement this
idea meant the end of liberty and even servitude. Ordinary taxes for
another political community were a just and necessary reason for American colonists to rebel. Clearly, no other civilization would have interpreted taxation without representation as slavery during this time period.

As is evident, the distinct contrasts between the American and British political cultures prevented them from understanding one another.
In addition, the British Empire failed to appreciate the reason and commitment of those who resisted it. Thomas Jefferson charged the British

monarch with abusing his authority and stated that the king had failed to fulfill his responsibilities to his subjects. According to Jefferson, the king unfairly restricted the colonists' trade relations, taxed them without their consent, and deprived them of self-government. As meaningful and justifiable as Jefferson's resistance to the king was, the American rebellion was utterly pointless and unjustifiable in the eyes of the British ruler. In Democracy in America, Alex de Tocqueville observed that the American notion of democracy pointed to the emergence of a new type of society based on political and social equality. While this type of social structure appeared to come naturally from the American experience, it was revolutionary for the rest of the world.

However, the American political culture is woven together from political narratives that are vastly different across the nation. Every state has unique stories and a history defining the political narrative. We also see many instances when states do not get along or cooperate, and in these instances, cultures clash. Take, for example, the American Civil War, arguably the darkest and bloodiest hour in the country's history. That conflict represented an enormous fracturing in the political culture. The Union states maintained one set of beliefs on slavery, tariffs, suffrage, and government power, whereas the Confederates held diametrically opposite views. For years, the United States was divided on the most fundamental aspects of political culture, and it culminated in war. It was a loss of social cohesion that led to widespread suffering. This is one of the most critical reasons for studying the topic of American political culture and developing a better understanding of its dynamic input and output functions.

It is impossible to provide a tangible understanding of the American political culture. The political culture is unembodied and unspoken. Disparate views abound, especially with things based on personal experiences and exposure to other cultures. Those who have not traveled or met many people from other countries are more likely to think that the beliefs they share are objective reality, not just one set of many optional sets of narratives. In the political science subfield of comparative politics, scholars research other countries and discover widely different values on everything from group identification to suspicion of government, to tolerance of outside cultures. Examining these differences is one the primary methods researchers use to analyze societies objectively, avoid ethnocentrism, and disseminate information for learning purposes.

Political culture is easiest to recognize when one steps outside of it. Being inside of a political ideology or system can keep a person from seeing the 'big picture' of the political system. Political culture gives people a common set of assumptions about the world and a common political language within which they can agree. Let us now examine the essential values of American political culture and the historical events that gave rise to a new type of society in greater detail.

## FUNDAMENTALS OF AMERICAN POLITICAL CULTURE

Three fundamental political values have been dominant in the United States since the colonial period: freedom, equality, and self-government. Let's begin with the American conception of liberty. Individual liberty is the predominant conception of freedom in the American political system. Individual freedom, as described in the first section, refers to negative freedom or freedom of choice. Individual liberty is a fundamental principle of all modern democracies. According to Freedom House's 2021 Global Freedom Report, the United States got 83 out of a possible 100 points, placing it below a number of advanced liberal democracies. Considering that the study is based on the criteria of political rights and civil freedoms, it is important to remember that the emphasis on freedom in American politics does not always reflect the truth.

However, the American political emphasis on individual liberty is clearly based on Locke's idea of natural rights. Individuals do not need society's or the consent of the people to exercise their inalienable natural rights, according to Locke. Consequently, natural rights are rights asserted against the government and society. The public sphere includes matters that extend beyond the limits of natural rights, and the government's authority over the individual is restricted to this carefully defined public sphere.

Locke's theoretical claims have significant implications for the formation of American politics on a daily basis. For instance, two of the most prominent political debates in the United States are gun control and abortion rights. Conservatives are individuals who oppose gun regulation, whereas progressives are those who support abortion rights. However, both camps frame their arguments in terms of individual autonomy. In other words, it is simpler to garner public support if your political arguments are framed in terms of individual liberty.

This emphasis on individual liberty does not necessarily result in the development of legislative laws consistent with this theory, but it does result in the establishment of a robust political discourse among the people. It is rare to identify any nation where the concept of individual liberty is as deeply embedded as it is in the United States. For instance, the emphasis in Hollywood movies that the government supports public services via income taxes may lack political relevance in a great number of other nations. By paying taxes for public services, voters expect a check on the government.

This emphasis on taxation also reinforces the implication that the government's authority to govern is derived directly from the people. Even the anarchist American author Henry David Thoreau refused to pay taxes because he opposed the Mexican-American War, which began in 1846, on moral grounds. This political activism, referred to as civil disobedience, is fundamentally American. Individual liberty is an extreme reflection of the notion that moral standards can arise from the individual and that individuals can oppose government activities they do not morally approve of.

The second most important value of American political culture is equality. What is the origin for the concern for equality in modern political culture? In 19th century France, the motto of "liberte, egalite, and fraternite" (liberty, equality, and fraternity) became a chief concern after the violent French Revolution. Philosophers like Jean-Jacques Rousseau and

Maximilien Robespierre emphasized equality as an important ingredient in forming a social contract between members of society. Equality paves the way for the possibility of thriving democratic republics.

Equality can be divided into four main categories: equality before law, social equality, political equality and economic equality. Equality before law, defined, expresses that all citizens enjoy the same privileges, statuses, and rights in the eyes of the law. Social equality means that all individuals enjoy the same lawful status in society. Social equality is where the political/social hierarchy is free from institutional nobility. This would bar the existence of titled privileges such as those of barons or archdukes who inherit special benefits when they are born. Civil servants in the government are elected or appointed based on the law rather than heredity. Political equality is the means that every citizen has the same political rights and opportunities. This includes suffrage (voting) but it also includes the right to due process (trial by jury, right to an attorney). Although America has a dark history of universal suffrage being denied to anyone other than white landowning property owners, the United States has made great strides to create political and social equality for all people. Equality also is considered to be economic equality. Economic equality focuses on the differences in wealth. Social critics scrutinize wealth/income inequality out of concerns for justice and the loss of quality of life for those with less wealth. Others counter this by claiming that some inequality is unavoidable and that equality under the law is the only thing worth safeguarding. At any rate, the issue of equality, social, political or economic, retains an important point of divergence in today's political culture.

As described by Tocqueville in Democracy in America, Americans would rather be equal under slavery than unequal under freedom. This is why the rhetoric on equality has such a profound effect on Americans. A poorly justified claim of privilege, for instance, is perceived as an assertion of superiority, leading to severe criticism. The recent controversial affirmative action policy is an intriguing example of how Americans view equality. Opponents of affirmative action reject the positive privileges demanded by affirmative action for underprivileged communities on the grounds that they generate inequity between individuals. However, proponents of affirmative action claim that they demand it in order to alleviate the current impacts of systemic discrimination against particular communities. In other words, affirmative action is required to eliminate a social inequity produced by prior discrimination. In this regard, ideologically distinct parties explain their policies using the same collection of concepts.

Democracy is the third prominent political value in American political culture. Democracy is a decision-making process by which individuals register their preferences for their rulers (and the policies they promise). A democracy is a government which citizens rule directly and make government decisions themselves. In a democracy, the citizens have power over their government's decision making.

Is the United States considered a democracy? Yes, in some sense, but it is important to maintain precision of terms. With some exceptions (see the next section), the United States is not what you would call a "direct democracy," but rather a constitutional republic or representative democracy. Aristotle was one of the first to use the term "republic," which accounts for the United States and most countries in western civilization today. Under this model, citizens participate in politics by voting on representatives (members of Congress, the Senate, the President) who are expected to carry out the general will of those they govern. Elected officials, even your local mayor or councilmember, have a fiduciary responsibility to govern with the best interests of the people in mind. They are held accountable electorally. If they fail to satisfy their constituents, or are found guilty of a scandal, they run the risk of getting voted out of office.

In a democracy, the use of referendum can allow citizens to have direct access to creating a democratic state. A referendum is an election in which citizens vote directly on an issue. This is a way to employ "direct democracy." California passes laws and removes people from office with this method. An example of this, in 2020, was Proposition 17. This gave citizens the opportunity to vote on a referendum regarding voting rights for convicted felons released on parole. In that instance, it passed with 58% of Californians voting in favor.

In a democracy, we would assume a social, political, and economic equality amongst the people. Equal opportunity is the idea that every American has the same chance to influence politics and achieve economic success regardless of their race, gender, or class. It is the American dream that anyone can pull themselves up by their bootstraps, rich or poor, and have the same opportunities as anyone else. In the American political culture, the attitudes, beliefs, and assumptions that we create give order and meaning to public life. In a democracy, the American political culture gives Americans the ability to disagree but remain united ultimately.

Americans appear to have a natural inclination for democratic government, which can be viewed as an extension of the values of freedom and equality. However, in a democratic government, freedom is viewed as a result of equality. In other terms, freedom is the state of not being ruled by another individual. This is why democracies oppose the expert rule and place a higher value on political equality than technical expertise. Therefore, they feel that a government comprised of equals is superior to a hierarchical one ruled by the most knowledgeable individuals.

Political equality in the United States is founded on the adoption of the idea of one person, one vote. Nonetheless, equality and non-domination prevail in the representative democracy of the United States. In spite of the fact that decisions are taken more slowly in representative democracies than in authoritarian regimes, and that decisions can always be questioned, the fact that citizens can change and criticize their government is regarded as more significant than the shortcomings of democracy. The superiority of democracy over other kinds of government is almost indisputable in the eyes of Americans.

However, democratic government and limited government are not necessarily compatible. Ultimately, democratic decisions are determined by a majority vote among citizens of equal status. Democracy is a procedure for making decisions. Not always are democratic outcomes consistent with individual liberty or even equality. The violation of minority rights in democracies is a prime illustration of this issue. Therefore, the American democracy is a constitutional democracy based on the principle of limited government. So, constitutional government based on individual rights is essentially an American invention.

The right to "life, liberty, and the pursuit of happiness" is a strong embodiment of Locke's theory of limited government in the Constitution of the USA. In this regard, limited government is a result of the other three political ideals. American democracy should also be evaluated separately from democracies without a real constitution. American democracy is a liberal democracy in the conventional sense. The Constitution exists in order to avoid the self-destruction of democracy and to safeguard the natural rights of individuals. In this regard, the concern that democracy can become corrupted is firmly embedded in American political culture.

Thus, one can assume that American political culture is defined by the concept of limited government. Limited government is the political philosophy of a government limited in power. This is a key concept in the history of liberalism. Liberalism is a school of thought derived from the Enlightenment, found particularly in thinkers such as John Locke, Adam Smith, and David Hume. One might notice the similar sounding of the words "liberty" (from the Latin "*libertas*", meaning freedom from despotic control) and "liberal" (meaning free from restraint in speech or action). Each of these terms, in their most classical sense, refer to freedom and an aversion to external coercion. Locke and his adherents, like Thomas Jefferson, wrote in a time when many began to bring into question the legitimacy of the old, sometimes despotic, European monarchies.

The perception of individualism that dominates American political culture is one of the primary reasons why the system of limited government is so well-established in the United States. Individualism refers to moral individualism in this context. Moral individualism acknowledges that all humans are moral beings, i.e., they are capable of moral judgment. Again, we can defend this claim using Locke as support. While Locke argues that every individual is rational, he also implies that individuals can independently discover the natural law that maintains social order. In this situation, rational individuals can use their reason to determine the right action and limit their behavior in accordance with these moral principles. Obviously, these universal moral principles require codification and full implementation by positive law. Individuals are capable of respecting the rights of others, however, when rights are clearly defined and legally guaranteed.

Due to the government's well-defined and effective protection of individual rights, it is therefore possible for a social order to emerge through a contract between free individuals. Locke contends that natural law rules are negative claims. Therefore, the only legal obligation individuals have to one another is to respect each other's rights. In this regard, it is not surprising that positive claims are significantly less prevalent in American politics than in European democracies.

Negative rights claims ultimately support value pluralism. Value pluralism rejects a hierarchical ranking of individuals' political, religious, etc. values. Certainly, some values are favored over others, but the favored values are expected to be well-reasoned and few in number. This is where limited government and value pluralism intersect. The government uses coercion to implement its policies. This implies that every government policy must adhere to a particular hierarchy of values. If the government intervenes extensively in social and economic life, it will do so in accordance with a hierarchy of values.

In a communist regime, for instance, there are no individual values but only collective ones. The role of the state is to implement these hierarchical collective values in social and economic life. Nonetheless, because liberal democracies embrace value pluralism, they must reject state intervention in a number of areas. The United States emphasizes value pluralism more than its Western counterparts, at least in terms of discourse. The American opposition to the welfare state is the political arena in which value pluralism is most obviously reflected in American politics. Since the welfare state must pursue policies based on equality of outcomes, the imposition of certain value hierarchies becomes inevitable as welfare states expand. For instance, public education severely restricts the opening of private educational institutions and the ability of schools to design their own curricula. Public health care provides an analogous case study. In this context, we can evaluate the debates regarding the absence of public health care in the United States.

In American society, we hold the expectation that people will provide for their own forms of retirement and social welfare. Other countries, such as Great Britain, embrace community and communitarianism, insisting that people be protected by the government. For those people who prefer to have a social democracy, or community focused democracy, the public interest is best served when all of society uses the government as a mechanism to take care of its citizens through things such as universal healthcare and a social welfare system. In the United States, with individualism, it is not the government's responsibility to provide for full coverage of one's retirement, wellbeing, or employment.

## AMERICAN POLITICAL IDEOLOGIES

America has several different political ideologies. In modern times, it may feel like the competing political ideologies are polarized and in constant disagreement. Ideologies are the competing narratives we create to explain those disagreements. Typically, ideological division in the United States has been along economic terms, disputes between conservatives and liberals. Sometimes the disputes involve social dimensions as well though.

In the American political spectrum, conservatives on the right call for less regulation of the economy (lower taxes, freer trade, unrestricted competition). Conservatives are Americans who believe in reduced government spending, personal responsibility, traditional moral values, and a strong national defense. It is common to see conservatives known as "right wingers." However, conservatives or conservative presidents do not always follow the policies required by the conservative discourse.

For example, Ronald Regan and George W. Bush significantly increased public spending. Donald Trump, on the other hand, suspended the Transatlantic Trade and Investment Partnership, the planned free trade agreement between the European Union and the US. Trump's policy choice was widely supported by the conservative voters.

Liberals are the second political group in the American political spectrum. Liberals on the left call for more government regulation (like social welfare programs, universal health care, and free preschool programs). Liberals value cultural diversity, government programs for the needy, public intervention in the economy, and individual's right to a lifestyle based on their own social and moral positions. Modern liberals may differ from the Locke's classical emphasis on negative liberty, but they still emphasize positive liberty, couched within a need to safeguard society with economic safety nets. For example, a modern liberal would be socially-libertarian on something like drug possession, preferring not to criminalize it, but would seek state intervention on economic measures such as Social Security, a regulatory safety net.

Starting in the 1960s and 1970s, however, other non-economic issues started to motivate voters—issues like racial desegregation, civil rights, women's rights, including reproductive rights, prayer in school, and reducing crime. These issues split Americans along a political dimension much like a vertical line. When you combine the horizontal, economic ideological dimension with the vertical, social ideological dimension, you get four ideological categories that are important for understanding American politics today.

## A CLOSER LOOK AT AMERICAN IDEOLOGIES

American ideologies are distinct along economic lines. American economic conservatives are those that believe in the narrative that the government that governs best, governs least. Proponents of this ideology want to see the government provide less oversight on fiscal policy. An example of a political ideology that believes in less oversight is libertarianism.

Libertarians believe that respect for individual freedom is a central condition of justice. They believe that human relations should be based on mutual consent. Libertarians advocate a free society based on cooperation, tolerance, and mutual respect. Libertarianism states that each of us should be allowed to live our own lives as long as we do not violate the rights of others. They believe that individuals cannot be forced to take any action in the name of the collective good, such as economic stability, better cultural development, etc. Libertarians also believe that we should not use force except in self-defense. This principle is called non-aggression. Libertarians also uncompromisingly advocate a free-market economy and minimal government. They tend to favor policies like gun rights, reproductive rights, civil rights, assisted suicide, and legalized marijuana. Most want only as much regulation of the economy as it would take to keep competition fair and the market from tanking. Robert Nozick, author of *Anarchy, State, and Utopia*, gives the model of a "night-watchman" state, where the government exists only for the most basic functions. It would go no further than minimal governance such as police, courts of law, and a small military. This model omits most state intervention into economic and social matters. Some libertarians reject the legitimacy of the state altogether. This type of libertarianism is called anarcho-capitalism.

Although the US is not the most libertarian country in the world, some libertarian principles have become common sense for Americans. Things like the consensual nature of social cooperation and the need for the strict protection of the private sphere are commonplace social assumptions for Americans. However, libertarianism and conservatism are not the same things.

In terms of state intervention in social and economic life, American conservatives differ from libertarians. In practice, numerous conservatives demand various forms of government intervention. The most significant difference between libertarians and conservatives is in foreign policy. Conservatives frequently support US military foreign interventionism and typically do not oppose limiting individual rights in the name of combating terrorism or the war on drugs. In addition, the conservative belief that Judeo-Christian principles should have some influence in politics is diametrically opposed to the libertarian perspective on secular politics. For instance, homosexuality-related restrictions cannot be associated with libertarianism.

The progressives are those who are on the most extreme left end of political ideology. Progressives are those who are the farthest to the left on the political continuum. Social democrats, left-wings, and left-libertarians are those who believe in an even stronger role for the state in creating equality. Progressives represent various shades of leftist politics. Left-libertarians, for instance, share the same beliefs as libertarians regarding civil rights and pluralism. However, many post-Marxist groups do not embrace libertarian principles under any circumstances. Progressives share a commitment to social justice, universal healthcare, gender equality, labor rights, environmentalism, and opposition to big corporations. For instance, the Occupy Movement, which began in 2011, is a global progressive political movement against economic and social inequality.

Progressives made a substantial impact in America around the turn of the 20th century under the leadership of presidents like Theodore Roosevelt and Woodrow Wilson. This was during a time when the United States saw an expansion in population, industrialization, and urbanization. Progressive critics, like Upton Sinclair, believed that this coincided with an increase in corruption, business monopoly, and worker exploitation. The response to this was the creation of several new government bureaucracies such as the Food & Drug Administration (FDA), the United States Department of Agriculture (USDA), the Federal Trade Commission (FTC), and the passage of the 16th Amendment, which enabled the income tax. This would eventually go on to include the Prohibition of alcohol with the 18th Amendment. The biggest takeaway from this era was the bipartisan (Republicans and Democrats) embracing of a more hands-on and active approach to governance.

Social issues are a source of division between conservatives and liberals as well. Social conservatives put a priority on the government preserving a traditional social order. Social conservatives include several groups who believe that their vision of the social order (that is, how people should live their lives) is absolute and want to put it into law. Social conservatives receive some of the intellectual foundation for their views in the works of the Irish philosopher/statesman, Edmund Burke. Burke, as opposed to Rousseau, was more suspicious of the concept of social contract because he thought it would lead to the disintegration of tradition and customs. Social conservatives seek to enact protective laws for maintaining social norms but are wary of what they consider to be the "social engineering" of social liberals.

Social liberals have concrete ideas about what they think is right and don't mind stepping on civil liberties if necessary to realize them. The social liberal doesn't always gain many adherents because it pushes the limits of Americans' limited government, individualistic culture. There are some occasions, however, when social liberals can make an impact. Whenever a perceived crisis gains public visibility (i.e., the Vietnam War or the Civil Rights Era), social liberals may have a chance to persuade the public to vote to enact legislative changes that contradict the prevailing social milieu. Exceptional circumstances notwithstanding, since we tend towards limited government, Americans distrust the government and place limits on the authority the government can exercise over people.

Evidently, political culture manifests itself in numerous forms. You have probably encountered friends, family, and opponents who represent some or all of these viewpoints. It is not difficult to see how the competing sub-cultures might clash as they did during the American Revolution, the American Civil War, the Civil Rights Era, and perhaps today as federal, state, and local elections continue to be contentious. With this framework for comprehending political culture, we can learn about the current political context. What are the major points of contention between social conservatives and social liberals? How do they fuel the debate over the hot-button political issues (war, abortion, drug restrictions, education costs, etc.)? Can we reconcile these cultural differences without incurring violence and civil wars? How do individualists and communitarians get along under the umbrella of the same government? Understanding political culture is a useful way to make sense of the various political forces at play in American civic life.

## Key Terms

**American Exceptionalism**: The belief that the United States is inherently different from other nations, often based on its unique founding principles and history.

**Bill of Rights (1689)**: An English document that set out certain basic civil rights and clarified who would be next to inherit the Crown.

**British Political Philosophy**: The body of thought that originated in Britain and has significantly influenced American political institutions, particularly through the works of John Locke and the British constitutional framework.

**Civil Disobedience**: A form of political activism where individuals refuse to comply with certain laws as a form of protest, exemplified by Henry David Thoreau's opposition to paying taxes to protest the Mexican-American War.

**Constitution of the United States**: The foundational legal document of the United States that outlines the structure of government and the rights of the citizens, seen as quasi-sacred by Americans.

**Democracy**: A system of government where citizens have the power to elect their leaders and influence laws and policies, often characterized by equal participation.

**Direct Democracy**: A form of democracy where citizens vote directly on laws and policies rather than through elected representatives.

**Equality**: A fundamental value in American political culture that can be divided into equality before the law, social equality, political equality, and economic equality.

**Freedom**: One of the core values in American political culture, particularly individual liberty, which refers to negative freedom or freedom of choice.

**Glorious Revolution**: The 1688 revolution in England that led to the establishment of a constitutional monarchy and the principles of parliamentary sovereignty.

**Individualism**: A principle emphasizing the moral worth of the individual and their autonomy, deeply embedded in American political culture.

**John Locke**: An English philosopher whose theories of natural law and social contract significantly influenced American constitutional drafting.

**Judicial Independence**: The principle that the judiciary should be independent from other branches of government, highlighted by the controversy over President Roosevelt's attempt to increase the number of Supreme Court judges.

**Libertarianism**: An ideology advocating for minimal government intervention in personal and economic affairs, emphasizing individual liberty and mutual consent.

**Limited Government**: A political system where the powers of the government are restricted through laws and a constitution, ensuring that individual liberties are protected.

**Natural Rights**: Rights that individuals have simply by being human, which according to Locke, are inalienable and must be protected against government infringement.

**Political Culture**: A set of shared ideas, values, and beliefs that define the role and limitations of government and people's relationship to it.

**Representative Democracy**: A form of democracy where citizens elect representatives to make decisions on their behalf, as practiced in the United States.

**Separation of Powers**: A principle of governance in which the powers of government are divided among separate branches to prevent any one branch from gaining too much power.

**Social Contract**: A theory developed by philosophers like John Locke and Jean-Jacques Rousseau, suggesting that individuals consent to form a government that will protect their rights in exchange for certain freedoms.

**Supreme Court of the United States**: The highest judicial body in the United States, whose independence was defended during Roosevelt's attempt to add more justices.

**Value Pluralism**: The idea that there are many different values that may be equally correct and fundamental, and that individuals are free to choose their own values.

# CHAPTER 4

# CLASSICAL ORIGINS OF WESTERN POLITICAL IDEOLOGIES

Early Christian intellectuals regarded government as a means to promote and safeguard the Christian faith. Ultimately, numerous Christians concluded that the foundation and operation of government should primarily rely on the Bible rather than human reasoning. Tertullian, an early Christian philosopher from 155-220 CE, contended that divine revelations should precede human understanding and serve as the authentic basis for governmental organization. According to Tertullian, human reason should always be subordinate to the Christian perspective on life as revealed in scripture. Overall, Tertullian's theories significantly influenced Western political philosophy until the early 17th century. However, during this time, intellectuals like Thomas Hobbes emerged and advocated for a renewed emphasis on human reason.

## THOMAS HOBBES

The majority of the political systems that arose in Europe following the collapse of the western portion of the Roman Empire in the fifth century CE were kingdoms that actively supported and protected Christianity as a means to legitimize their authority. During the mid-1600s, Thomas

Hobbes (1588–1679) contended that the evaluation of politica
should not be based on their support for or promotion of a cei
gion but rather on their ability to maintain social harmony.

Hobbes posited that humans have the capacity to establish laws of
nature, which are principles derived from human rationality. If universally adhered to, these laws would result in the attainment of peace and
security. Nevertheless, a comprehensive terrestrial jurisdiction is necessary to ensure compliance with these rules. Without any governing body,
known as the state of nature according to Hobbes, adhering to the laws
of nature would expose an individual to potential assaults from those
who disregard them. Thus, it would be beneficial for each person to grant
authorization to a Leviathan, as described by Hobbes, which is a highly
influential governing body. This entity would enforce a balanced sense
of terror among all individuals, ensuring that they adhere to the rules of
nature. Hobbes contended that individuals should willingly enter into
a social compact, wherein they collectively pledge their allegiance to a
political sovereign who possesses absolute authority to enforce the laws
of nature.

## JOHN LOCKE

John Locke, an English philosopher and physician who lived from 1632
to 1704, adopted Hobbes's ideas about the state of nature and a social
compact among individuals. However, Locke's understanding of natural
laws differed significantly. Locke regarded natural laws as a collection of
ethical principles that can be deduced through rationality and are ultimately founded on the logically demonstrable existence of God. These
laws are universally applicable to all individuals. In contrast to Hobbes,
Locke believed that the natural laws and corresponding inherent rights
impose obligations on all individuals, regardless of whether a government enforces consistent punishments for violating them. The natural
law defines inherent rights and corresponding obligations towards others and oneself. According to Locke, individuals possess an inherent

entitlement to life, which consequently imposes a moral obligation on others to honor this entitlement. Individuals are morally obligated to refrain from committing suicide and to fully utilize their inherent abilities. Every person has an obligation to uphold the inherent entitlements of all other individuals.

John Locke, an Enlightenment philosopher, had a tremendous impact on the formation of early American governance. Locke employed the hypothetical scenario of the state of nature to ascertain the actions that rational persons, who are not under the authority of a government, would undertake. He envisioned a scenario in which, in the absence of societal structure, every individual would possess the authority to mete out punishment to those who infringed upon the inherent rights of others. Locke contended that humans in the state of nature would have the right to possess land only if they combined it with what they intrinsically possessed - their bodies and the labor of their bodies. Nevertheless, individuals were only permitted to obtain land if their acquisition did not impede the well-being and success of those who did not possess land.

Locke posited that in the hypothetical state of nature, a societal structure would arise where certain individuals would possess a greater amount of land compared to others, without causing any harm to the latter. He contended that individuals would only invest effort in acquiring substantial land holdings if they believed they could utilize that property to generate a profit through its development for the production of valuable goods. According to Locke, unequal land ownership would lead to a society where a large number of desirable items are created.

Within the context of a hypothetical scenario where individuals exist in a natural condition, it can be posited that they would eventually reach a consensus to establish a kind of currency to facilitate transactions. Subsequently, owners might hire persons to cultivate their land in exchange for monetary compensation, allowing them to prioritize the production of goods that people are willing to purchase with their pay. Even if proprietors were to obtain all land that was previously not owned, a commercial society would nonetheless arise, characterized by the unrestricted trading of goods and services. According to Locke, the ultimate outcome would be a much elevated quality of life for everyone, surpassing the initial conditions of the natural state. Based on this premise, Locke argued that the establishment of an economic system centered around private property would not cause harm to anyone, even if it led to significant inequality.

Locke posited that if persons in the state of nature adhered to the principles of natural law and recognized the advantages of private property, peace and prosperity would ensue. However, he contended that it is logical to anticipate the emergence of tensions. Envy may arise towards individuals who possess greater riches, and the capacity of each individual to enforce penalties for breaches of the natural law would ultimately result in disorder. Thus, individuals who possess reason and logic in their natural state would mutually consent to establish a social agreement that safeguards the entitlement to personal freedom and private possessions. This agreement would entail delegating the authority to enforce these inherent entitlements to a governing body whose primary objective is to protect and uphold these natural rights.

Within the state of nature, individuals possess the autonomy to select the precise structure that the government should adopt in order to carry out their responsibilities. One method to mitigate the potential for government misuse of the people's inherent rights would be to incorporate a restricted level of landowner representation inside the government. This policy would serve as a protection against unfair property taxation, which is a precursor to the notion, widely embraced in the American colonies, that taxation should not be imposed without some kind of representation by the people. Locke argued that if the government established by the people in the state of nature infringed upon their inherent rights and the principles of natural law, the right of revolution would empower the people to employ force in order to hold that government accountable and remove its leaders from power. Locke argued that individuals have the right to demand that governments protect their rights, including the protection of private property and the freedom to sell their labor for wages. Additionally, governments should be accountable to the people's right to revolt and should fulfill their obligations while minimizing the chances of violating the people's inherent rights.

## JEAN-JACQUES ROUSSEAU

A highly productive philosopher and writer Jean-Jacques Rousseau embraced Locke's concept of the state of nature, not merely as a hypothetical exercise, but rather as a genuine anthropological portrayal of human history. Rousseau contended that humans are inherently free but are constrained by societal restrictions in all places. The number is 20. Every individual possesses an inherent entitlement to liberty and an innate empathy towards other beings. Nevertheless, the human condition is dominated by an insatiable craving for material riches and societal standing, which has consequently given rise to the establishment of repressive political systems.

The Social Contract by Jean-Jacques Rousseau was written during a period characterized by shifting dynamics in the interactions between individuals and their governing authorities. Rousseau contends in The Social Contract that a group must cultivate an elevated collective identity as they tackle a shared problem in order to emancipate themselves. Charismatic leaders must foster a shared religious sensibility among the people, referred to by Rousseau as a civil religion, which establishes citizens as siblings and promotes the value of respecting religious diversity. Implementing this civil religion would enhance the feeling of shared identity among the populace.

Given the presence of this collective spirit within the group, it is necessary for the individuals themselves, rather than just their delegates, to convene and decide on the laws that will govern them. In order to prevent corruption, legislation should be enacted in a manner that is universally applicable, without granting any exceptions to specific individuals or groups. Furthermore, the process of creating laws should be free from the influence of political factions or elaborate rhetoric. It is important for individuals to convene regularly in order to reassess their legislation to guarantee that it continues to benefit the population in light of changing conditions.

Rousseau contends that the legislation enacted by such an assembly would ensure the collective desire, which represents the genuine benefit of every individual in society. These laws aim to decrease financial disparity and establish a system of civic education that would strengthen the civic religion and promote civic virtue, which is a deeply ingrained inclination to prioritize the well-being of the political community before personal gain.

Rousseau's views have exerted a profound influence. Thomas Jefferson (1743–1846) advocated for the regular convening of constitutional conventions in the United States, during which the entire constitutional system would be reevaluated. In recent times, Pete Buttigieg, a political leader and Secretary of Transportation, has contended that the power to modify the Constitution bestows a significant level of confidence in regular individuals to modify all laws according to their judgment. This is based on the well-established principle that there is no provision within the Constitution that renders a constitutional amendment unconstitutional. Essentially, any matter is eligible to be modified during the amending procedure.

The public nature of political activity also exhibits resemblances to Rousseau's ideas. During legal proceedings, jurors are required to publicly declare their verdict, in front of the community. Similar concerns to those expressed by Rousseau regarding how religious differences within a community can hinder the pursuit of the common good are present in other modern discussions, such as arguments surrounding public education. In countries like the United States, where the separation of church and state is legally protected, Rousseau's concept of a civil religion cannot be realized. In the United States, it is possible for the government to provide financial assistance to parents, which they can utilize to enroll their children in any private religious school of their choice. This scheme, known as educational vouchers, has been implemented by various states and allows parents to access schools that are often costly.

Critics of vouchers contend that public funding should remain impartial towards religious instruction and that the government should not financially support the availability of religious schooling. Some critics of vouchers argue that vouchers can lead to an increase in religious tension among the population, which aligns with Rousseau's belief in the importance of a civil religion.

## SOCRATES

Socrates, an Athenian philosopher in the fifth century BCE, argued that individuals ought to pursue the solutions to life's most fundamental inquiries through the use of logic. He advocated for embracing only those concepts that had withstood rigorous examination and can be expressed in a clear and explicit manner. The preservation of Socrates's legacy primarily relies on the works of his student, Plato (428–348 BCE). Plato's work, The Republic, presents a comprehensive and logical case for entrusting political authority to highly skilled persons who possess profound understanding of the underlying essence of the world and a sincere passion for wisdom. Plato had the belief that philosophers are the most suitable individuals to possess unrestrained political authority. These rulers would be immune to temptations of corruption and possess a deep understanding of what is most beneficial for the communities under their governance. Plato contended that such a government would provide genuine justice.

## ARISTOTLE

Aristotle, a pupil of Plato, concurred that an ideal political situation may be achieved by either a monarchy, where a supremely intelligent and virtuous king governs for the benefit of the people, or an aristocracy, where a collection of such virtuous rulers governs. Nevertheless, both Aristotle and Plato expressed concerns regarding the potential transformation of a government led by a single individual into a tyrannical regime, where the ruler acts solely in their own self-interest. Similarly, if power was concentrated in a small group, that group may transform into an oligarchy, which is characterized by governance by a few individuals who prioritize their own interests. Aristotle questioned whether it was safe to entrust political authority to the majority of individuals under a democratic system, considering the various potential outcomes. Aristotle hypothesized that this could potentially lead to a type of governance that would disregard the well-being of the entire society in favor of the desires of the majority.8 Presently, monarchs and authoritarian rulers frequently defend their authority by expressing doubt on the majority's capacity to achieve the collective interests of society.

Aristotle posited that the optimal scenario for the exercise of political power and the pursuit of the common good would be if the middle class, as it is presently known, constituted the majority of citizens. According to Aristotle, it would be ideal for political offices to accurately represent the differences in wealth among individuals. This means that both those who are wealthier and those who are less wealthy should have the opportunity to become political leaders. Additionally, the community should have a strong reverence for the rule of law. He referred to this type of governance as a Politeia.

In a *Politeia*, the government would prioritize the welfare of the public, enabling society to progress towards the realization of its citizens' genuine human capabilities. Aristotle contended that this would be the case due to the fact that individuals can fully realize their human potential only by engaging in logical discourse, deliberation, and evaluation of things pertaining to the welfare of a society. In order to fully realize one's potential as a human being, it is necessary to engage in political participation, which encompasses activities that revolve around the exercise of political power. This exercise is characterized by debate and deliberation focused on the collective welfare of society.

## JOHN STUART MILL AND THE ADVANCEMENT OF INDIVIDUAL FREEDOM

John Stuart Mill, an English writer, advocates for the complete integration of women into the rising rights of communities rooted in classical liberalism in his book *The Subjection of Women* (1869). Mill's publication in 1859, titled *On Liberty*, presented the idea that contemporary civilizations should enhance their dedication to the principle of individual freedom. Mill contends that society benefits from promoting open discourse and deliberation on all perspectives, regardless of their unpopularity, as even esteemed leaders with widespread support are prone to grave errors. The individual contends that liberty should be expanded not only in relation to speech and the media, but also to ensure that legal constraints do not impede the freedom of adults, even if their actions result in personal harm, as long as their actions do not harm others. Mill's level of dedication to personal freedom is such that he supports ideas that classical liberals like Locke would disapprove of. Locke argues that the primary function of government is to uphold the natural law, which includes the protection of individuals' lives and inherent abilities. According to Mill, personal liberty should be safeguarded by both legal means and cultural norms that promote freedom, even if the exercise of that freedom carries a potential danger for the individual, as long as it does not cause harm to others. Mill bases this approach, known as the harm principle, on two underlying beliefs: that freedom fosters a culture of exploration and open discussion that enables individuals to reject harmful concepts, and that the immense importance of personal freedom necessitates nothing less.

## FRANKLIN D. ROOSEVELT (FDR) AND HIS ADMINISTRATION'S ECONOMIC POLICIES KNOWN AS THE NEW DEAL

The Great Depression, which occurred from 1929 to 1941, had a profound influence on the classical liberal tradition. During the depths of the Great Depression, almost 25 percent of the American workforce was jobless, and a significant decline in economic activity caused many businesses to go bankrupt. From 1933 to 1939, President Franklin Delano Roosevelt (FDR) implemented the New Deal, a comprehensive series of economic regulations and social welfare programs aimed at safeguarding consumers, stimulating economic growth, enhancing labor conditions, and alleviating financial burdens on retirees. The programs encompassed the Federal Deposit Insurance Corporation (FDIC), the Federal Housing Administration (FHA), and the Social Security Board (now known as the Social Security Administration).

FDR challenged the classical liberal notion that government growth should be limited, instead calling for trust in the government's ability to stabilize the economy and establish safety net programs. FDR contended that by doing this, it would guarantee the enduring resilience of classical liberalism's dedication to individual rights and protection against government misconduct. It would prevent the necessity of increased government control over private property and stricter limitations on individual freedom, which are two more serious dangers to classical liberalism's focus on individual rights and limited government.

## FRIEDRICH AUGUST VON HAYEK

Many intellectuals, such as economist F. A. Hayek (1899–1992), expressed doubts about the extent of government growth during the New Deal. Hayek acknowledged the necessity of increasing the state's involvement in overseeing economic activity. However, he argued that only a substantial and intrusive government, equipped with significant enforcement authority, would be capable of effectively managing the economy of a large nation. Hayek's central argument in The Road to Serfdom is that widespread state planning of the economy grants the government excessive authority, resulting in a curtailment of individual freedom and the potential for government control over all aspects of people's lives. Hayek argues that an enlarged government leads to the establishment of entrenched bureaucrats who evade democratic responsibility. According to his argument, once state rules and large-scale programs are implemented, it becomes extremely challenging to reverse them. Furthermore, the expansion of economic restrictions ultimately results in decreased wealth for everyone. According to Hayek, the ultimate outcome would be the emergence of a new type of serfdom, characterized by restricted freedom, entrenched social hierarchies, and widespread poverty.

Hayek contended that the enactment of significant regulations would likely lead to the establishment of a command economy by the government, wherein the pricing of products and services would be determined by the state. Hayek argues that this would have a negative impact on economic prosperity. He believes that prosperity relies on the effective and logical distribution of resources by producers and consumers. This can only occur in a free market, where prices are determined by supply and demand, and government regulation is minimal. The free market conveys information to producers and customers through product pricing, indicating the availability and desire for different things. Prices increase when there is an unmet demand, prompting manufacturers to redirect their production towards the things that buyers desire. When a product is over produced, prices decrease and production transitions to manufacturing different products. Hayek argued that depending on the government to determine prices would result in excessive production of certain items, insufficient production of others, and a decrease in the overall quality of life.

## KEY TERMS

**Aristocracy**: A form of government in which power is held by the nobility or a privileged class.

**Aristotle**: An ancient Greek philosopher and student of Plato, who theorized about political systems and the concept of Politeia.

**Civil Religion**: A term used by Rousseau to describe a shared religious sensibility among citizens that promotes civic virtues and respects religious diversity.

**Classical Liberalism**: A political ideology advocating for individual freedoms, limited government, and free-market economics.

**Divine Revelations**: The belief that insights or truths are directly revealed by a divine source, often considered superior to human reasoning.

**Enlightenment**: An intellectual movement in the 17th and 18th centuries emphasizing reason, individualism, and skepticism of traditional doctrines.

**F. A. Hayek**: An economist who argued against extensive government intervention in the economy, warning it could lead to a loss of individual freedoms.

**Franklin D. Roosevelt (FDR)**: The 32nd President of the United States who implemented the New Deal to address the Great Depression.

**John Locke**: An English philosopher who theorized about natural laws and rights, significantly influencing early American political thought.

**John Stuart Mill**: An English philosopher advocating for individual liberty and the expansion of freedoms in society.

**Leviathan**: A term used by Thomas Hobbes to describe a powerful governing body necessary to enforce laws and maintain social order.

**Natural Law**: Ethical principles believed to be inherent in human nature and discernible through reason.

**New Deal**: A series of programs and regulations implemented by FDR to recover from the Great Depression.

**Oligarchy**: A form of government in which power is held by a small group of people.

**Plato**: An ancient Greek philosopher, student of Socrates, who wrote "The Republic," advocating for philosopher-kings.

**Politeia**: Aristotle's term for a mixed form of government representing both wealthy and less wealthy citizens, focused on the common good.

**Rousseau**: A philosopher who emphasized the importance of collective identity and civil religion for a functioning society.

**Social Contract**: A theory posited by Rousseau and Locke about individuals consenting to form a government to protect their natural rights.

**Socrates**: An ancient Greek philosopher known for his method of questioning and emphasis on logical reasoning.

**State of Nature**: A hypothetical condition used by philosophers like Hobbes, Locke, and Rousseau to discuss the origin of societies and governments.

**Thomas Hobbes**: An English philosopher who argued that a powerful government (Leviathan) is necessary to maintain social order.

**Tertullian**: An early Christian philosopher who argued that government should be based on divine revelation rather than human reason.

# CHAPTER 5

# POLITICS AND ECONOMIC MODELS

## Why would the discussion of economic models and politics occur intertwined?

The first answer to why these two fields are connected is that human beings are a social species. That is, each individual defines her own needs and desires in cooperation with others, so we must find a way to socially organize these relations. If we lived in a world where resources are infinite, this would not be necessary, since all citizens could just fulfill any of their desires as they please. However, in our empirical world scarcity plays an essential role. This refers to the fact that human and non-human resources are finite and society is thus only capable of producing a limited amount of goods.[30] In short, there are not sufficient resources to produce all the wares that people desire or want to consume. For this reason, societies have to find a way to redistribute the limited amount of goods and wares at their disposal. This is the role of economics, which is defined as the process for deciding who gets the material resources

---

[30] Hahnel R. (2003), *ABCs of Political Economy. Modern Primer*, Pluto Press, London.

and how they get them. Hence, economic goods are those wares that are relatively scarce and need to be allocated according to a certain criterion.

In democratic systems, the reelection of governments is directly related to economic performance. Although there is no absolute rule, any administration will wish to hold elections during a period of economic expansion and rising income levels. This is because economic growth and stability is one of the most influential elements in shaping voter preferences for political parties. Voters hold governments accountable for economic performance as a result of their direct or indirect influence over the economy. The performance of national economies is frequently determined by political decisions including monetary and fiscal policy and economic regulations. In this regard, political decisions influence economic decisions and economic output.

An economy is the sum of all exchanges, or all ongoing buying and selling, in an area. While all economies today are built around goods, services, and money, they differ radically from one another. Each country's economy can have structural differences according to how wealthy its citizens are, how wealth is distributed among the population, and the technology by which wealth is produced. Structural differences in economies can profoundly change countries' political decision-making processes, voter behavior and expectations, and even political regimes.

In addition, some economic indicators can provide data on the functioning and success of the political system. For example, GDP and per capita income are the most commonly used data to categorize the socio-economic status of countries. The gross domestic product (GDP) is an estimate of the total value of completed products and services produced within the borders of a country over a specific time period, often one year. Popularly, GDP is used to measure the size of an economy. For example, as of 2021, the GDP of the US is $25.2 trillion, that of the UK is $3.2 trillion and that of India is $3.4 trillion. While these ratios are often seen as a by-product of the level of industrialization of countries, they only yield more meaningful political results in terms of GDP per capita. In this respect, the annual per capita income in the US is 69 thousand dollars, in the UK it is 47 thousand dollars and in India it is around 2,400 dollars. Therefore, when measuring the level of development of countries, it is more accurate to examine national income per capita rather than GDP.

Per capita income in developed economies is much higher than in developing countries. For example, while the GDPs of the UK and India are close to each other, the population of India is 1.14 billion people, while the population of the UK is 68 million people. These figures show that economic productivity in India is extremely low compared to the UK. According to the Fraser Institute's annual Economic Freedom of the World report, countries with high per capita income are those with a developed market economy and a robust liberal democracy. So how rich a country's citizens become is clearly directly related to its politics.

In addition to the per capita national income, the GINI coefficient is an important economic indicator that is used when measuring the degree of development of countries. The GINI ratio is an extremely valuable indicator of the prevalence of income inequality in a population. Predictably, countries with more comprehensive social welfare systems have GINI coefficients that are lower than those of other nations. For instance, economic disparity in Northern European nations is significantly smaller than in the United States.

Moreover, there is a direct relationship between the institutional framework in which political decisions are made and the institutional framework in which economic decisions are made. In this respect, we cannot analyze political values in isolation from economic models. For example, individual freedom can only exist in a political regime based on a sound market economy. As the famous monetarist economist Milton Friedman pointed out, individuals who do not have any use rights over economic resources cannot have control over their lives in line with their priorities and goals. This is why classical liberals and libertarians always emphasize the direct relationship between private property and individual liberty. For example, should the market of readers or government bureaucrats decide which books should be published or not? The more discretion governments have over economic resources, the less discretion individuals have over their own lives and plans.

Certainly, it is possible to argue that individual liberty is an exaggerated political goal and that equality should be politically favored. However, it would be a contradiction to place a high value on individual liberty and at the same time advocate the abolition of private property. Similarly, the rule of law is in many ways related to free markets. The decentralized decision-making processes required by the market economy necessitate abstract, general, equal rules of law. Therefore, the rules of law on which a market economy is based grant immunity to individuals and limit the discretionary power of the government. In contrast, a centrally planned economy would be largely governed by orders and directives in line with the social goals set by politicians and bureaucrats, and the immunity rights of citizens would be largely eliminated.

As political values evolve, so do economic models. It is logical, for instance, that the concept of economic and social human rights has come into conflict with free market economies, particularly following World War II. The majority of economic and social rights relate to goods and services that cannot be provided on the market or cannot be produced in adequate quantities. When these commodities and services, which can be defined in a variety of ways and to varying degrees, are deemed justifiable, direct state interference in free markets and private wealth is required. A progressive tax policy, for instance, may only be justified in light of social objectives. In this regard, the scope, breadth, and institutions of the welfare state will dictate directly the structure of the market economy.

The link between political values and economic models can be extended to definitions of political regimes. For example, before the collapse of the Soviet Union, what constituted a "real" democracy was a heated debate among political scientists. During this period, constitutional or liberal democracies were heavily criticized. Socialist writers argued that true democracy could only be established in communist societies, claiming that material inequality, especially in capitalist countries, made democratic rule impossible.

This discussion on democracy is very informative as it clearly demonstrates the relationship between political ideals and economic models. It is now widely accepted that a democratic government requires regular and competitive elections and at least two political parties. In the Soviet Union, however, it was not possible to have a second political party and it was illegitimate to have alternative politics outside the communist party. The elections that were held were not expected to conform to universal standards in any way. However, it could be argued that only in a classless society would government serve collective purposes and true political equality be possible. By calling Western democracies formal democracies, the formal conditions of liberal democracy were devalued by socialist writers. For this reason, the idea that the Soviet Union, a one-party dictatorship, had built a true democracy could be debated in academic circles for years.

As demonstrated by the preceding illustration, there is a close relationship between our evaluations of economic models and our political ideals. This is a complex process in which the political and economic meanings we give to concepts are linked, as opposed to a one-sided relationship in which one determines the other in an absolute manner. Analyzing this topic is a field of study for both political science and political economy. The link between economic models and political systems contains both descriptive and normative features in this regard.

Before proceeding to analyze the main economic models and related political debates, it is important to define the political economy. The study of the political meanings of economic models often requires the use of political economy methods. The term "political economy" has been around for a long time, and throughout that period it has taken on a wide variety of meanings. Political economy, according to Adam Smith, is the study of how to best direct a country's resources to maximize its ability to create and distribute wealth. Marx was interested in the impact that controls over the means of production had on the course of history.

The term "political economy" has been used with competing definitions during the majority of the 20th century. The relationship between economics and politics has been seen as both a field of study and a research strategy at different times. Even the approach to methodology was split in two: the economic approach (also known as public choice) focused on the rationality of individuals, and the sociological approach focused on the larger institutions that shaped that individuals' behavior.

Political economy, in its broadest definition, is the economic study of government and politics. Therefore, rather of being a singular method, it is a set of related methods. This method integrates many of the concerns of political sociologists because institutions are no longer neglected and are often the target of the inquiry. Politics becomes the study of political economics since political behavior and institutions are themselves academic fields. Methodologies previously used only in the field of economics are now integral to political science. In most cases, the individual serves as the unit of analysis.

## POLITICAL ECONOMIC APPROACHES IN HISTORICAL PERSPECTIVE

Economic policy was not an essential political problem in the closed autarchic economies of the Middle Ages, which were founded on economic self-sufficiency. Nonetheless, since the move from autocratic economies to modern economies open to international commerce, the means by which nations enhance their national wealth have become a significant economic concern. In contrast to the medieval age, when continual economic expansion was not expected, economic growth is now one of the primary objectives of political powers in the modern era.

### Mercantilism

In this regard, mercantilism was the first kind of political economy to arise. During the 15th and 17th centuries, mercantilism effectively connected national wealth to export surpluses. The more a country exports goods and services, the better, but importing goods and services is as undesirable. This economic policy grants governments the authority to directly and broadly intervene in the production and consumption processes. In order to sustain economic growth, governments have devised vast regulations governing what individuals produce, how they produce, and what they consume.

Mercantilism led to economic protectionism. Since goods and services coming from abroad were considered harmful to the national economy, the goods to be imported were strictly listed. Except for these lists and the persons and firms appointed by the government, imports were prohibited. In the national economy, the government granted monopoly powers to various individuals and firms in order to give these producers an advantage in the international market. For example, sectors that had not yet developed in the national economy were called infant economies and these sectors were completely protected from foreign trade. International trade is considered a zero-sum game. This means that international trade is not based on mutual interests, but on a winner-take-all game/zero-sum game. For this reason, mercantilism is also known as economic nationalism. Because the goal of international trade was determined as national interests.

This perspective has significant flaws. In a world where all nations embrace mercantilist policies, international trade and economic cooperation between nations are severely constrained. When countries perceive each other as economic adversaries, antagonism and sometimes conflict are inevitable. According to the famed French economist Frederic Bastiat, "when goods don't cross boarders, soldiers will." Therefore, mercantilism ultimately led to economic expansionism via wars and invasions. Specifically, mercantilists, who deprived themselves of the opportunity to influence natural resources and international markets through trade, attempted to achieve their economic objectives through colonialist practices.

Especially when the economic history of modern Europe is analyzed, it is clear that the economic warfare created by mercantilism resulted in global catastrophes. Among the economic reasons of World Wars I and II, it is simple to recognize economic nationalism's role in interstate conflicts. After World War II, the common market was the most crucial measure to avoid another war in Europe. Europe's adoption of a free trade strategy to prevent economic nationalism from generating conflicts between large industrialized economies was no accident. In this regard, the European Union is built on a policy of international free trade that was intended to combat the issues posed by economic nationalism.

## Adam Smith and Invention of Free Markets and Minimal Government

The publication of Adam Smith's *An Inquiry into the Nature and Causes of the Wealth of Nations* in 1776 was the most significant intellectual cause for the change from mercantilist policies to free trade in Europe. Smith argued that the increase in the division of labor and specialization was the primary cause of the wealth of nations. This claim, which initially appears to be a technical matter, conceals broader economic and political arguments. But first, let's explore what type of efficiency is indicated by the division of labor.

Smith elaborated on the advantages of dividing production processes and assigning them to different people in order to maximize output and efficiency. The notion behind the "division of labor" concept was that if a worker specialized in performing a single activity, he would inevitably increase his speed and precision in carrying it out. Once the thought process was eliminated and the numerous manufacturing actions became second nature, it was possible to increase output. He, for instance, claimed that ten workers could manufacture 48,000 pins each day if each of the 18 specialized duties was assigned to a specific worker. The average production per worker each day is 4,800 pins. But without labor division, a worker would be fortunate to produce even one pin per day.

The productivity gains from the specialized division of labor that Smith observed in just one pin factory are enormous. When we apply this division of labor to an industry, to a national economy and even to international markets, we increase the scale of the division of labor enormously. One could argue that the productivity gains that would result from an increased division of labor at the national and international level are beyond the imagination of 18th century readers. In this respect, contrary to mercantilism, international trade cannot be a zero-sum game. On the contrary, it is argued that a global economy in which production processes are supported by international division of labor and specialization can generate previously unimaginable productivity gains.

To achieve the efficiency envisaged from the international division of labor, governments must abandon their interventionist and regulatory policies on national economies. Who will thereafter oversee the production and consumption processes? Smith contends that the price mechanism will drive production and consumption processes far more effectively than the government. At the junction of the supply of goods and services that producers are able and willing to produce and the demand for goods and services that consumers are able and willing to consume, prices are established. If producers and consumers are allowed to freely exchange on national and international markets, then production and consumption levels are naturally established. Smith used the metaphor of the "invisible hand" to describe the price mechanism in order to demonstrate that the price-setting process does not require government involvement.

Consequently, although Smith appears to be discussing the division of labor, which is a strictly technical production process, this is in fact a profoundly political subject. If the magnitude of the division of labor is the primary predictor of productivity and if price levels can be established without direct government interference, then it is likewise incorrect for political forces to claim political authority through economic nationalism. This is because politicians and bureaucrats are unaware of which commodities and services serve the national interest. Given the dynamic structure of international trade and the fluctuating supply and demand relationships of the global economy, the knowledge on which commodities and services should be produced and which should be imported is in constant flux.

If it is not a meaningful claim that the processes of production and consumption should be directed by governments in the national interest, then by whom and for what purposes should economic processes be directed? Smith simply but forcefully states that the processes of production and consumption should be driven by individuals seeking to maximize their own self-interest. Human beings are by nature utilitarian in economic matters. But in a well-functioning market, economic utilitarianism is not harmful to society as a whole, but rather beneficial. In the market, individuals have to satisfy the needs of others in order to satisfy their own needs. In markets where we depend on each other for the mutual satisfaction of our needs, everyone pursues his or her own self-interest while actually serving the interest of the general public. Smith supports this claim with the following example[31]:

> "It is not from the benevolence of the butcher, the brewer, or the baker, that we expect our dinner, but from their regard to their own interest. We address ourselves, not to their humanity but to their self-love, and never talk to them of our own necessities but of their advantages."

If individuals following their economic interests in free markets are the most essential elements in the process of wealth creation, what role do governments play in the economy? Smith suggested that the government should enforce contracts and grant patents and copyrights to encourage inventions and new ideas. In addition, he believed the government should provide public works, such as roads and bridges, that individuals could not provide. Surprisingly, he desired that users of these public works pay proportionately for their use. Smith also maintained

---

[31] Adam Smith, Wealth of Nations, Book 1, Chapter 2.

that tax rates should not be excessively high and that wages could only be increased through capital accumulation and labor productivity growth. These responsibilities assigned to the government by Smith are today known as minimal government.

Smith also opposed British imperialism by stating that Britain's expenditures and wars to hold on to the American colonies were much higher than the revenues it obtained from the colonies. Similarly, he opposed the monopoly powers of the East India Company, which managed Britain's eastern trade, and argued for the institutionalization of free trade and voluntary exchange between countries. He argued that importing what countries produce expensively and exporting what they produce cheaply would promote mutual interests and strengthen peaceful relations of dependence between countries. Imperialism, on the other hand, would fuel war and conflict.

Smith's ideas on international trade inspired the British economist David Ricardo to develop the law of comparative advantages a century later. Although individuals, firms or countries have the potential to produce different goods, in order to benefit from the efficiency of the division of labor, individuals, firms or countries should produce the goods and services that they are most advantageous in producing. Therefore, they should give up the production of other goods and services. Ricardo's theory is essential for comprehending globalization because it gives a solid theoretical foundation for the notion that free trade across nations is advantageous for all parties.

With the industrial revolution in England in the 1830s, the international division of labor and the theory of comparative advantages found wide application for the first time in history and opened the doors to a global economy. The Industrial Revolution was a period of scientific and technological advancement in the 18th century that changed predominantly rural, agrarian cultures into industrialized, urban ones, particularly in Europe and North America. Due to the development of new technologies and techniques in textiles, iron production, and other sectors, goods that were once carefully fashioned by hand began to be mass-produced in factories by machines.

Today, the global economy based on the law of comparative advantages has developed beyond the predictions of these philosophers. Supranational corporations, supranational trade organizations, and international trade law have played important roles in the functioning of the global economy beyond the dreams of Enlightenment philosophers.

## Marxism as a Classical Economic Theory

Smith's explanation reveals that the basic axioms assumed to drive human behavior have far-reaching political implications. Marx, as a critic of capitalism, based his fundamental assumption about individuals on the assertion that human nature is not fixed. Since the economic infrastructure determines the actions of individuals, axiomatic claims centered on individuals are incorrect from the start. Instead, he stresses the systemic elements that influence individual behavior. In this regard, Marx's citation of technology as a structural component is particularly intriguing. Marx asserts that every economic age has its own technology. The industrial revolution would not have been feasible without the steam engine, but capitalism enabled not the singular use of machines, but their systematic application in the factory system. Marx believed that the use of machines by capitalists lowered worker pay, created a new proletariat, and oppressed the existing proletariat.

Marx, on the other hand, admired the wealth generated by the Industrial Revolution and believed that this technological knowledge could be effectively utilized for the benefit of the working class in a socialist economy. Marx holds that there is no correlation between technological productivity and market-based institutions such as private property and contract law. In contrast, whereas under capitalism technology is a weapon of worker exploitation and alienation, it would serve the working class in a socialist society.

Therefore, there is no need for practical knowledge disclosed by market processes other than technological expertise. Since technological knowledge can only be converted into an efficient method of production within the division of labor and specialization that occurs on the market, the use of technology cannot rely just on technical knowledge, according to Smith. It is only relevant in the institutional context in which the technology will be utilized. Marx, however, believed that technological knowledge could be easily transferred from the capitalist system to the communist system in order to assist the working class.

According to Marx, the idea that human needs are subjective is also wrong. For it is not possible to argue that needs are determined through market processes or that the products demanded in the market are necessarily human needs. The goods and services on the market are commodities produced for profit and the link between them and objective human needs has been broken. Add to this the claim that it is the labor of workers that gives the value of goods and services, and the basic presuppositions of a socialist economic system are revealed. Since labor is the main criterion of value, capitalists or market processes and rules have no contribution to the production of value. Therefore, there is no need for capitalists or market processes to produce value.

Marx is, therefore, not concerned with questions of what, where, when, and how to produce. Such problems are only a problem of chaotic market processes, and under socialism, there will be no problem of how to allocate scarce resources among diversified needs. Once capitalism is abolished, production processes based on technical knowledge to meet objective human needs will be established by the collective management of the working class.

As can be shown, the vast contrasts between Smith and Marx have simple origins in human action. During the 19th century, economists abandoned the objective labor theory of Smith and Marx in favor of the subjective theory of value. I shall explore the controversy that the subjective theory of value produced for socialist economic planning in the section on planned economies.

## Neoclassical Economics

The classical school of economics assumed that the market value of goods and services was determined by the labor used in their production. This was called the labor theory of value. Marx even accused capitalists of exploitation of workers, since workers produced goods and services with their labor while capitalists had surplus value without using any labor. But if the prices of goods and services in the market have nothing to do with the labor spent on them, does Marx's claim of capitalist exploitation still hold?

Before drawing political conclusions from economic theory, let us start by explaining the theory of diminishing marginal value. An early assumption of neoclassical economics was that consumer utility, not production cost, is the most significant factor in establishing the value of a good or service. Based on the works of William Stanley Jevons, Carl Menger, and Léon Walras, this method was established in the late 19th century. The law of diminishing marginal utility states that the more an item is used or consumed, the less satisfaction is derived from each additional unit utilized or consumed.

Therefore, market prices are determined by the preferences of individuals and businesses and have no direct relationship with labor. Individuals and businesses engaged in market transactions are called rational agents, and their preferences are reasonable under specific conditions. Agents who are rational maximize their utility based on their priorities and market conditions. Traders participate in a competitive bidding process with other traders in order to create transactions that involve the purchase and sale of items. These transaction prices serve as signals to other producers and consumers, encouraging them to realign their resources and activities along lines that will yield greater profits. It is claimed that these market transactions involving rational agents will enable the markets to reach equilibrium.

Neoclassical economics attempted to mathematically explain Smith's economic theory with certain axiomatic presuppositions based on rationality. The set of concepts presented by neoclassical economics, especially after the 1950s, has been used not only to explain economic behavior but also to explain all kinds of social phenomena. For example, in addition to sociological, psychological or cultural explanations of family life, the economic explanation of family life can also be explained with neoclassical economic terminology. It is possible to come across studies that explain the evolutionary development of family structure with economic theory.

However, besides economics, politics is the field where neoclassical economics has been utilized the most. In this framework, the evolution of public choice theory and new institutional economics is crucial to political theory. By eliminating moral justifications from political research, public choice theory attempts to transform politics into a purely positive science. The objectives of politicians and bureaucrats, for instance, are not to serve the public interest and devote themselves to public service but rather to maximize their personal priorities. In this scenario, the sole objective of politicians is re-election, whilst bureaucrats seek to maximize their budgets. James Buchanan, one of the founding fathers of public choice theory, describes this strategy as "politics without romance." Buchanan has made significant contributions to the field of political science, particularly in exposing the arbitrariness/randomness of democratic decision-making processes.

New institutional economics is mostly concerned with politics. New institutionalism, made famous by Douglass North's work, explores the formation of political institutions by adapting rational choice theory to the concept of institutional equilibrium. Rather than the propagation and adoption of liberal values, North describes the evolution of liberal democracies in Europe as a process of power struggle among political elites finding an equilibrium.

Axiomatic presuppositions about how individuals act directly affect political analysis. The fact that neoclassical economics expresses its theories in a mathematical language has increased its prestige among social sciences and political debates have been increasingly influenced by economic theory. In this context, objections to neoclassical theory have also been directly related to the perspective on politics.

## Keynesian Economics and Government Intervention

The most important criticism of neoclassical economics comes from John Maynard Keynes. Keynesianism was the main source of criticism of free markets, especially after the Depression of 1929. According to Keynes, the claim that individuals are rational and that markets always move towards equilibrium is largely false. In reality, individuals act on wild instincts, not rational calculations, and may make many economically harmful decisions in the face of economic uncertainty as a reflex of self-preservation. For example, in a time of economic uncertainty, if consumers save more than the market needs instead of consuming, panic may start in production processes, leading to unnecessary closures of businesses. In this case, a deflationary pressure arising from the abundance of products could disrupt the structure of markets and the economy would inevitably shrink.

Keynes argued unequivocally that markets do not always reach equilibrium on their own and that the products and services generated in markets do not automatically clear. Consequently, what should governments do when irrational panic spreads throughout the markets? Budget equilibrium and free markets are the foundation of conventional fiscal theory. However, when the economy begins to shrink due to uncertainty in the absence of a fundamental cause, it will not be possible for the market to self-correct and reach maximum capacity utilization and full employment. For this reason, Keynes encourages governments to provide money to the public, particularly in times of crisis, through the use of fiscal policy, i.e., by substantially boosting public expenditures. Thus, individuals will contribute to the expansion of production processes by investing cheaply acquired money in the market. In accordance with Keynesianism, monetary growth through fiscal policy will have a multiplier effect on the economy. Monetary growth will boost aggregate demand, and the money flowing in the economy will increase national revenue by a greater amount than the amount spent.

During the COVID-19 pandemic, it is not surprising that governments around the world have prioritized Keynesian fiscal policy. Governments, who covered the income demands of those who were unable to work during the pandemic by printing unbacked money, are now attempting to contain inflation by implementing restrictive monetary policies. If governments are so competent at stabilizing the market, the Smithian concept of minimal government will have little relevance.

Historically, the most important reason for the popularity of Keynesian policies was the Great Depression and the World War II that followed. These two major social crises created a state of great uncertainty and led to a period in which not only governments but also citizens demanded more government intervention in the economy. With the rapid development of welfare states in Europe after World War II, a consensus for social democracy emerged. That is, right and left-wing parties and the majority of the population strongly supported government redistribution of income through social policies.

The concept of market failure explains one of the most significant points of the social democratic consensus. Failure of the market has two distinct meanings. The first is associated with the idea that market agents have no social purpose and maximize their individual utility. Aside from the goals pursued in the market, society may have several necessities that should be supplied not by the invisible hand of the market, but by the visible hand of the government, i.e. by central planning. For example, providing everyone with a sufficient income to live humanely or providing appropriate health care for all. It is argued that such social objectives are too crucial to be left to the uncertain production and consumption processes of the market.

The second is based on a critique of Keynesian arguments for the economic efficiency expected from free markets. Managed/regulated markets are demanded instead of free markets, and big government is proposed instead of minimal government. This is defined by the belief that state intervention, especially in the form of social welfare, can expand freedom by protecting individuals from the social ills that threaten individual existence. The famous Beveridge Report, released in the UK in 1942, called for state intervention against the following five ills that plague society: want, ignorance, idleness, squalor and disease.

## *Monetarism*

The great economic expansion of the 1950s and 1960s is considered a great success of Keynesian policies. However, the stagflation of the 1970s greatly shook the intellectual hegemony of Keynesianism. Stagflation is a situation of high inflation accompanied by economic stagnation. In stagflation, the general level of prices continues to rise as the economy continues to shrink despite monetary expansion. Unemployment, loss of real income and fear of the future lead citizens to question the ability of governments to manage markets. The most prominent thinker to criticize Keynes during this period was the American economist Milton Friedman.

In addition to the phenomenon of stagflation, the 1970s also saw the side effects of the comprehensive welfare state, such as bureaucratic inefficiency, social inertia and corporatism preventing governments from making policy. The main problem with Keynesian fiscal policy was the realization that governments did not have as much control over the effects of monetary policy as they thought they did. The economic growth generated by monetary expansion in the short run misdirected the consumption and savings behavior of consumers and the investment behavior of producers in the long run. In particular, the trade-off between short-term needs and long-term investments became inefficient as price signals were distorted by inflationary pressures.

Moreover, people' investments in private markets have declined as a greater proportion of their income has been eroded by rising taxes and inflation. The drop in private investment caused by an increase in public expenditures is known as the crowding-out effect. As opposed to Keynes' multiplier effect, the crowding-out effect inhibits the expansion of markets. In addition, as Friedman demonstrated, the fact that government interventions have little effect on the velocity of money circulation enables monetary expansion to generate inflation rather than economic development over the long term.

Likewise, Austrian economist Friedrich von Hayek, a prominent critic of Keynes and socialism, opposed state intervention, believing that market processes were too complex for governments to regulate. Hayek argues that extensive government intervention distorts the price mechanism and the price signals that assist market agents in making production and consumption decisions. Due to the complexity of labor division and specialization in contemporary markets, there is no technological and fixed data to guide trade processes. This information must be determined by market players during exchange processes. In contrast, government interventions misdirect these exchange mechanisms, resulting in unintended negative outcomes.

In addition to Keynesian critiques, public choice theorists' attacks on the welfare state have contributed significantly to the changing intellectual climate. Public choice supported market-based economic policies by refuting market failure arguments with the government failure argument. The argument for government failure challenges the capacity of governments to attain specified social goals. Therefore, market failure for a product or service does not inherently warrant government intervention. Instead, the proper investigation should establish whether market-based or bureaucratic solutions should be implemented. Theorists of public choice frequently prefer market-based approaches to bureaucratic ones.

The economic crises of the 1970s, combined with the intellectual triumph of libertarian economists such as Friedman and Hayek, paved the way for the birth of the political program known as the New Right in the UK and the US. Margaret Thatcher in the UK and Ronald Regan in the US launched a new wave of liberalization and free trade around the world with a strong return to traditional free market economic policies. The emphasis on reform of the welfare state, low inflation, private sector efficiency, and balanced budgets led to a revival of classical liberal policies. By critics, these economic policies are also known as neoliberalism.

## Key Terms

**Adam Smith**: An 18th-century philosopher and economist known for his book "An Inquiry into the Nature and Causes of the Wealth of Nations," which laid the foundations for classical free market economic theory.

**Beveridge Report**: A report published in the UK in 1942 that called for state intervention to combat five social ills: want, ignorance, idleness, squalor, and disease, leading to the development of the welfare state.

**Classical Economics**: An economic theory that emphasizes the importance of free markets, the division of labor, and minimal government intervention, primarily associated with Adam Smith.

**Comparative Advantage**: A theory developed by David Ricardo suggesting that individuals, firms, or countries should produce goods and services in which they have a relative efficiency advantage, promoting global trade benefits.

**Crowding-Out Effect**: An economic concept where increased public sector spending leads to a reduction in private sector investment, as the government borrows more from the financial markets.

**Division of Labor**: A concept introduced by Adam Smith, where the production process is divided into different stages, each performed by different workers, leading to increased efficiency and productivity.

**Economic Freedom of the World Report**: An annual report published by the Fraser Institute that measures the degree of economic freedom in various countries based on criteria such as government size, legal system, and property rights.

**GINI Coefficient**: A measure of income inequality within a population, where 0 represents perfect equality and 1 indicates maximal inequality.

**Great Depression**: A severe worldwide economic downturn that occurred during the 1930s, leading to widespread unemployment, poverty, and significant changes in economic policies.

**Gross Domestic Product (GDP)**: The total value of all finished goods and services produced within a country's borders in a specific time period, commonly used to measure the size and health of an economy.

**Industrial Revolution**: A period of major industrialization and technological advancement during the 18th and 19th centuries that transformed predominantly agrarian societies into industrialized and urban ones.

**Invisible Hand**: A metaphor used by Adam Smith to describe the self-regulating nature of the market, where individuals' pursuit of self-interest unintentionally benefits society as a whole.

**Keynesian Economics**: An economic theory developed by John Maynard Keynes, advocating for government intervention and fiscal policy to manage economic cycles and mitigate the adverse effects of economic recessions.

**Labor Theory of Value**: An economic theory proposed by classical economists like Adam Smith and Karl Marx, suggesting that the value of a good or service is determined by the amount of labor required to produce it.

**Marginal Utility**: A concept in neoclassical economics that describes the additional satisfaction or utility gained from consuming one more unit of a good or service, which typically decreases with each additional unit consumed.

**Marxism**: A socio-economic theory developed by Karl Marx, focusing on the struggles between classes, the exploitation of labor by capitalists, and the advocacy for a classless society through socialism and communism.

**Mercantilism:** An economic theory and practice prevalent in Europe from the 15th to 18th centuries, emphasizing national wealth accumulation through export surpluses and government intervention in the economy.

**Monetarism:** An economic theory primarily associated with Milton Friedman, emphasizing the role of government in controlling the money supply to manage inflation and economic stability.

**Neoclassical Economics:** An economic theory that focuses on how the perception of utility and consumer preferences determine the value of goods and services, often employing mathematical models to explain market behavior.

**New Right:** A political movement in the late 20th century, particularly in the UK and the US, advocating for free market policies, reduced government intervention, and a return to classical liberal economic principles.

**Public Choice Theory:** An economic theory that applies the principles of neoclassical economics to political science, suggesting that politicians and bureaucrats act in their own self-interest rather than the public good.

**Social Democracy:** A political ideology that supports economic and social interventions to promote social justice within the framework of a capitalist economy, often involving the welfare state and progressive taxation.

**Stagflation:** An economic condition characterized by stagnant economic growth, high unemployment, and high inflation, challenging traditional economic theories that linked inflation to economic growth.

**Welfare State:** A government system that provides social insurance and assistance to its citizens, including health care, unemployment benefits, and pensions, aimed at reducing poverty and inequality.

# CHAPTER 6

## ABSTRACT MODELS OF ECONOMIC SYSTEMS

The analysis of the relationship between economic systems and political institutions is basically based on the definitions of two competing economic systems, capitalism and socialism. However, an important problem with this analysis is that while the abstract principles of capitalism and socialism can be more or less agreed upon, it is not possible to find a pure application of these two forms. Moreover, authors may choose to define these economic systems according to their ideological positions. Hence the debate on different types of capitalism and socialism. They are much more useful analytical tools when these concepts are assumed to be ideal types.

### CAPITALISM

Capitalism is usually defined as an economic regime where enterprises and/or private citizens own the means of production and where employers pay a wage to their employees to manufacture goods with the purpose of afterwards selling them to produce profits. Even though these general traits are usually largely accepted in the literature, there is not a specific definition of capitalism that is unanimously accepted, so it is difficult to trace back its origins. If one argues that capitalism is simply the most natural way to allocate resources within an economic community, then it has always existed and it is an intrinsic feature of human beings. That is, human beings' nature is made of the will to enrich oneself or her community, so capitalism has always existed and will always exist. Yet, others argue that capitalism is not related to human beings' nature, but it rather developed as a result of specific economic phenomenon, such as the development of agriculture, or slavery in ancient societies. Hence, capitalism is a precise historical feature that has not always existed and it will not necessarily last forever[32].

That said, there is a widespread agreement concerning the fact that capitalism is an economic system where production is not planned by a central government but it is dictated by laws of demand and supply – defined as the economic relationship between the amount of a commodity that producers want to sell at a certain prince and the quantity consumers wish to buy - in the market economy. The term market is thus central to capitalism, and it refers to the decision-making of multiple individuals about what to buy or sell, which creates different levels of demand and supply.

This is also how price is determined since prices represent the equilibrium point at which the quantity of goods supplied by producers equals the amount required by consumers. More in detail, prices represent the compensation – usually measured in a certain currency - given by consumers to producers in return for one unit of goods or services. Prices are thus influenced by different factors that do not remain constant over time, such as production costs, demand of the product and availability.

While this standard definition of capitalism is correct, it does not explain why we need a definition of capitalism other than that of a free market economy. For example, according to Ludwig von Mises, a prominent free market advocate "The market economy is the social system

[32] Weingast B., Wittman D.A. (2006), *The Oxford Handbook of Political Science*, Oxford University Press, New York.

of the division of labor under private ownership of the means of production". Mises's description of the market economy and the preceding explanation of capitalism are approximately identical. In this regard, it is important to keep in mind that the discussion on capitalism is a value-laden ideological debate. This is because socialists have a negative connotation to capitalism and assert that it is an exploitative economic system. Marx's decision to place capitalism rather than liberal democracy at the core of his critique arises from his belief that liberal democratic institutions are the product of the economic system.

The advocates of the market economy, on the other hand, adopt and use the word capitalism, but use it more as a slogan in the ideological debate against socialism. There are also thinkers who define capitalism as a separate process within the market economy. For example, according to Craig Parsons,[33] "Capitalism is when people who own money (known as "capital") make more money without directly doing the labor to produce goods or services. They make their money by owning businesses that make a profit, investing their money in someone else's business and getting a return on that investment, or charging interest on loans to others. Capitalists make profits on their capital."

It is also possible to follow the debates on the definition of capitalism in the varieties of capitalism. If the production and consumption of goods and services are realized entirely through market prices, it is possible to call it free-market/laissez faire/enterprise capitalism. Although it is not possible to see an ideal free-market capitalism, the first example that comes to mind is the USA. However, it is possible to identify which countries are more free-market based on international indexes of economic freedom. According to the Heritage Foundation's 2022 Index of Economic Freedom, the top 10 countries with the freest markets in the world are as follows: Singapore, Switzerland, Ireland, Luxembourg, New Zealand, Taiwan, Estonia, Netherland, Finland and Denmark. The US ranked 25th in the mostly free category. Interestingly, Netherland,

---

[33] Craig Parsons, 307, Introduction to Political Science

Finland and Denmark, which are considered to be important social states, are in the top 10.

For free-market capitalists, capitalism is not just a model of wealth production. Capitalism is the foundation of modern civilization and liberal values such as individual liberty and the rule of law can only exist in a capitalist system. Moreover, even if capitalism creates economic inequality, the mass production on which capitalism is based increases the material wealth of the masses in a way that no other economic system can match. According to Mises, the consumer is sovereign in capitalism. Consumer sovereignty is based on the fact that the goods and services to be produced are ultimately formed by consumer preferences and that most of the production consists of the daily needs of the ordinary consumer rather than luxury goods. Moreover, the perception of luxury consumption is constantly changing due to the efficiency created by capitalism. For example, the use of cars, computers, or cell phones are no longer luxuries but basic necessities in capitalist societies.

However, it is also possible to come across definitions such as social capitalism and state capitalism. The first country that comes to mind in the context of social capitalism is Germany with its "social market economy" established after World War II. In addition to Germany, Austria and most Scandinavian countries can also be included in this category. This economic model is based on the concept of a social market, which is an attempt to reconcile market competition with the need for social cohesion and solidarity. In a social market economy there is no need for excessive state interventionism. An analysis of the economic freedom index reveals that most social democracies have competitive markets. However, trade unions are often represented by works councils and participate in annual rounds of industry-wide wage negotiations. This connection is supported by comprehensive and well-funded welfare programs that provide social guarantees to workers and other disadvantaged populations.

The concept of state capitalism is sometimes used in the literature to describe the economic model of some countries. In these countries, especially investment activities are directed by various bureaucratic organizations and investors' access to capital can be determined as a result of various political processes. In countries lagging behind in industrialization, it is observed that governments identify various strategic sectors for economic development and rapid industrialization and make planned investments in these areas. The political regimes of these countries are not always liberal democracies. The fact that there are examples of countries where capitalism does not intersect with liberal democracy is a prominent feature of state capitalism from time to time.

Japan, South Korea, Taiwan, Singapore, and Hong Kong are among the East Asian nations that are defined by state capitalism. The defining feature of these nations is their export-oriented economic policies. Their primary purpose is to dominate select international markets, not to strengthen domestic startups. Samsung or the chemical sector in South Korea and Taiwan's high-tech manufacturing are instances of successful state capitalism. Important practices in Japan include the lifelong employment strategy and comprehensive employee benefits.

From this short review, it is evident that capitalism is not a monolith, but rather manifests itself in political science with multiple facets and manifestations. As aforementioned, all scholars agree that capitalism is the economic regime where capital goods belong to private citizens, but since the way it is organized has differed significantly over time, there have been different visions related to what capitalism actually is. Due to this difficulty in defining what capitalism precisely is, there has never been an academic agreement on its 'political economy', but rather many different perspectives on some specific questions related to its ethics, equality and morality. More pertinent to the economy, there has always been a debate on how much we ought to regulate markets.

On the one hand, there are those sustaining a Laissez-faire/free-market capitalism, for whom capitalist markets should be completely free from any economic interventionism such as subsidies and regulations. This view is based on two pillars. First, on an integral conception of freedom as non-interference for which individual economic liberty must not be curtailed by the state's intervention. Second, that markets are capable of self-regulating and that best results are thus achieved when the market is left to its spontaneous order.[34] Hence, there is no space for government intervention in the economic sector. Laissez-faire developed in the 18th century, but this view is still influential, since neoliberalism - one of current the dominant economic paradigms - has drawn from it most of its structural features.[35]

On the other hand, most scholars acknowledge that we should have forms of regulated capitalism to control markets in a certain way, even though decision-makers should mainly be individuals rather than public agents as the government. In this system, individuals may decide they want the government to step in to regulate behaviors that are not in the public interest and to fix externalities created by economic liberty. As for previous features, the spectrum of "how much" government ought to intervene is wide and can be differently connected to capitalism. Yet, another important economic theory, socialism, maintains that it is not a matter of regulating capitalism, since we can reduce capitalism's problems only insofar as governments keep total control of the economy.

## SOCIALISM

Socialism is defined as an economic system where there is a social ownership of economic means of production, together with a planned market economy. According to Marx, forms of planned and public economy can be traced back up to primitive human-gatherer societies, but it is only with the modern era that this theory proposed itself as the alternative response to capitalism.[36] This latter commodifies land, means of production and work to create profit, but this can be seen as opposite to the

---

[34] Hill, L. E. (1964), "On Laissez-Faire Capitalism and Liberalism'.", *The American Journal of Economics and Sociology*, 23 (4), 393-396.

[35] Ganti, T. (2014), "Neoliberalism.", *Annual Review of Anthropology*, 43, 89-104.

[36] Saitta, D. J. "Marxism, prehistory, and primitive communism.", *Rethinking Marxism*, 1 (4), 145-168.

fabric of society. Some scholars thus started pointing out that the problem of capitalism was private property, since they maintained that even if we control and 'tame' private property with social justice, the fact that some individuals own the means of production unavoidably leads to the exploitation of those who do not own them.[37]

Capitalism was thus seen as contrary to "objective" human needs such as creative work, diversity, solidarity and satisfaction of needs. As a response, socialism aimed at structuring an economic system more compatible with these objective economic needs. At first, socialism was more a utopian ideal. Analyzing workers' poor conditions, some scholars – such as Shaker's Christian socialism or the Hutteriti in the United States - maintained that the source of workers' problems was that they were working in large factories exploited by their employers. On the contrary, the solution was to be found in small communities that would have resolved material scarcity by structuring societies on a commune spirit. Hence, this first period lacked a proper economic theory and was mainly based on utopian ideas.[38]

The first glimpses of an economic theory that promoted equality as a way to achieve a meritocratic society arose with the anarchist Pierre-Jospeh Proudhon, or with anti-capitalist scholars such as Robert Owen and Charles Fourier.[39] Yet, it was Henri de Saint-Simon who first coined the term "socialism" as the alternative system to capitalism who could have granted equal opportunities to the people.[40] Finally, socialism became a proper economic theory thanks to the famous work of Karl

[37] Brenkert, G. G. (1979), "Freedom and private property in Marx.", *Philosophy & Public Affairs*, 122-147.

[38] Bestor A. (2018), *Backwoods Utopias: The Sectarian Origins and the Owenite Phase of Communitarian Socialism in America, 1663-1829*, University of Pennsylvania Press, Pennsylvania.

[39] Prichard, A. (2013), *Justice, order and anarchy: The international political theory of Pierre-Joseph Proudhon*, Routledge, London.

[40] Simon, W. M. (1956), "History for utopia: Saint-Simon and the idea of progress.", *Journal of the History of Ideas* 17 (3), 311-331.

Marx and Friedrich Engels "Das Kapital" (Capital),[41] where it is possible to find the basis of the main socialist economic concepts. Since Marxist economic theory has been explained under the previous headings, Marx's views on the crisis of capitalism will be briefly mentioned here. For Marx, capitalism is not only based on exploitation, but is also inherently unstable.

The accumulation of capital is crucial to the instability of capitalist economic growth. Capitalism is inherently led to continuously accumulate wealth by gaining from investments' returns and by profiting from workers' surplus value. For this reason, capitalism must continuously find new markets and opportunities to expand itself worldwide and to repeat the accumulation process. Capital accumulation cyclically finds social and economic barriers that lead to periods of crisis which often result in further centralization of the means of production in the hands of fewer capitalists. The constant concentration of capital in the hands of a smaller capitalist will make class conflict and exploitation much more intolerable and obvious. For this reason, it is argued that the beginning of the socialist revolution will arise from this internal contradiction that capitalism cannot overcome.

In this framework, class conflict is an inherent characteristic of the economic system that according to Marx could be fixed only with a revolutionary movement aimed at the abolishment of private property so as to favor public property as the means of production. After Marx, other scholars not necessarily connected to socialism – such as J.S.Mill and J.M.Keynes – acknowledged that capitalism was unstable and that if the economic system was to 'tame' social conflict and to produce better results both in the different economic fields and in the market, it required some form of public intervention.[42] This debate on the

---

[41]  Marx K. (2019 [1867]), *Das Kapital (Capital) A Critique of Political Economy*, Benediction Classics, Oxford.

[42]  Taylor Q. (2016), "John Stuart Mill, Political Economist: A Reassessment", *The Independent Review*, 21 (1), 73-94.

connection between public intervention and market liberty has been a central feature of political economic debate over the last century, even though there currently are almost no countries framed on an integral socialist model.

Nowadays, we identify a socialist economy as a system where commodities are produced directly to be used, rather than to be sold to create profit. A central feature of the socialist economy is that it is 'planned' which means that economic inputs are assigned directly by using resources to produce value according to the needs. This is opposite to what happens in a market economy where value is assigned indirectly by letting the market and economic cycles decide the inputs. A planned economy requires the public ownership of the means of production, even though this varies from a complete ownership by the state (statism) to mixed forms of ownership by workers' cooperatives and a common property by all society.

Socialist industries do not encompass hierarchical relationships, but should be based on workers' self-government where each worker has the same decisional power over collective decisions as others.' Yet, most historical examples of socialist countries, such as the Soviet Union or Yugoslavia, framed the management of their factories on a rigid bureaucracy that implemented the will of the state, thus leading to the debate related to whether or not such states were actually economically socialist or "collectivist bureaucrats."[43]

Aim of socialism is thus to 'neutralize' the capital by tying investments and capital to a social planning aimed at eliminating the economic cycle and the overproduction crisis typical of economies that rely on private property. In this way, socialist theorists maintain that workers could obtain more equality, freedom to access the resources they need to live and they would not be exploited of the value produced by their work. Over the last century, there have been several attempts to implement

---

[43] Verdery, K. (1996), *What was socialism, and what comes next?* Princeton University Press, Princeton.

socialist economy in practice, even though most of them encompass certain capitalist features such as salaries given to employees and forms of partial free market.

Most of the social historical examples were structured on an economy planned by a central government who decided the kind and number of commodities that had to be produced, as it was the case in the Soviet Union, in the Vietnamese socialist republic or in Cuba. This economic regime reached its peak in the 80s, when almost 1/3 of the total world population lived underneath such economic regimes, even though all these economies together generated only 15% of world's GDP. However, with the dissolution of the Soviet Union in 1991, countries steadily changed their economies to more liberal forms, such that nowadays only a few countries – Cuba, North Korea, China – adopt this economic regime and aside from North Korea, this socialism is more liberal than the centrally planned version of the Soviet Union.[44]

An interesting example of the socialist economic model in theory and practice is market socialism. As Mises argued, an important source of the inefficiency of the socialist economic model is the absence of any mechanism to provide information about the relative scarcity of goods and services. In market economies, prices indicate how relatively scarce goods and services are in the market. For example, if the price of a good rises rapidly, other things being equal, it is understood that this good has become scarce in the market and entrepreneurs start producing it to make a profit. Similarly, if the price of a good is falling, this price movement informs entrepreneurs that no more of that good should be produced. Since economic resources can be used to produce many different goods and services, how these economic resources are allocated among different goods and services is governed by the spontaneous ordering of the price mechanism in the market.

---

[44] Sabry, M. I. (2017), *The Development of Socialism, Social Democracy and Communism: Historical, Political and Socioeconomic Perspectives*, Emerald Group Publishing, Bingley.

When socialists abolish private property and free exchange, they also abolish the price mechanism. In real life, however, socialists have faced the reality that limited resources cannot be allocated smoothly among supposedly objective needs. Ignorance of the relative scarcity of goods has led to the creation of many shortages in socialist economies, often leading to the production of many goods and services that cannot be demanded. Problems of interregional transportation of goods have been characterized by a similar problem of ignorance.

Some socialist economists who recognized this problem, notably the Polish socialist economist Oskar Lange, developed the theory of market socialism. The basic idea was to create a market for the exchange of raw materials and to obtain price information on these economic resources. Part of this model was also applied in Czechoslovakia. There are some important problems with market socialism. First, if the market is more efficient than central planning, why is the production of other goods and services managed by bureaucratic mechanisms? Second, in the face of constantly changing economic conditions and demands, it is recognized that the socialist economy cannot adapt its production processes to new conditions and needs. There does not seem to be a sound justification given by market socialists for why a comprehensive welfare state based on a market economy should not be preferred over this system.

For these reasons, Mises argued that economic planning is impossible in socialist economies. Although socialists found the production processes in a market economy irrational and chaotic, they could not provide a satisfactory answer to the fundamental economic problem of how to allocate resources between goods and services in a centrally planned economy. Marx argued that this problem was only a problem of capitalism and assumed that socialism would not have the problem of inability to produce. But in theory and in practice the problem of scarce resources clearly exists.

## KEY TERMS

**accumulation of capital**: The process by which capitalism continuously accumulates wealth by gaining from investments' returns and profiting from workers' surplus value.

**capital goods**: Goods owned by private citizens in a capitalist economy, used to produce other goods or services for profit.

**capitalism**: An economic regime where enterprises and/or private citizens own the means of production, and employers pay wages to employees to manufacture goods for profit.

**central planning**: An economic system where production decisions are made by a central government rather than by the laws of demand and supply.

**class conflict**: The inherent struggle between different classes within an economic system, particularly between capitalists and workers in a capitalist economy.

**consumer sovereignty**: The concept in capitalism that goods and services produced are ultimately determined by consumer preferences.

**demand and supply**: The economic relationship between the quantity of a commodity producers want to sell at a certain price and the quantity consumers wish to buy.

**economic freedom**: The degree to which a country's economy is characterized by free-market principles, often measured by indexes like the Heritage Foundation's Index of Economic Freedom.

**exploitation**: The perceived unfair use of workers' labor to generate profit for capitalists.

**free-market capitalism**: A form of capitalism where markets are completely free from government intervention, such as subsidies and regulations.

**market economy**: An economic system where production and prices are determined by unrestricted competition between privately owned businesses.

**market socialism**: An economic system that combines elements of socialism and capitalism, where markets are used to exchange raw materials and obtain price information, but production is managed by central planning.

**planned economy**: An economic system where economic inputs are assigned directly by using resources to produce value according to needs, as opposed to a market economy.

**price mechanism**: The process by which prices are determined by the interaction of demand and supply in a market economy, signaling the relative scarcity of goods and services.

**private property**: The ownership of goods and means of production by private individuals or corporations.

**production costs**: The expenses incurred in manufacturing goods, influencing the prices of goods and services in a market economy.

**public property**: The ownership of goods and means of production by the state or the community as a whole, characteristic of a socialist economy.

**scarcity**: The limited availability of resources, a fundamental economic problem in both capitalist and socialist economies.

**socialism**: An economic system characterized by social ownership of the means of production and a planned market economy.

**social market economy**: An economic model that reconciles market competition with social cohesion and solidarity, seen in countries like Germany and most Scandinavian nations.

**state capitalism**: An economic system where the state directs investment activities and certain sectors of the economy, seen in countries like Japan, South Korea, and Taiwan.

**surplus value**: The difference between the value produced by labor and the wages paid to workers, which capitalists profit from in a capitalist economy.

**utopian socialism**: Early forms of socialism based on idealistic visions of small, cooperative communities, lacking a formal economic theory.

# CHAPTER 7

# FEDERALISM

What is federalism? Federalism is the division of governmental power among the various public jurisdictions. In antiquity, government was much more unitary or "top-down" in its execution and delivery. Before power-sharing arrangements became common, political systems had been either unitary systems or confederal systems. Power was usually exercised in a *one-way direction*. A unitary government is a national polity governed as a single unit. The idea is to have the central government exercising all or most political authority. Most of the world's governments (nearly 90 percent) are unitary. A strong central government lends power to subnational governments, who cannot make and execute policy on their own. Unitary governments can create or abolish subnational units of governments. Federal governments typically cannot. The U.S. national government, for example, can't decide that Wyoming would be much better as a part of Montana, or that two Dakotas is just one too many. A confederation is a group of independent states or nations that yield some of their powers to a national government. A confederation, in which a group of states are equal partners in a government, aims to prevent a strong central government from dictating to its members, it also means nobody's in charge. A Confederation differs from a unitary government by the way the subsidiary states much more sovereign authority. During the period of American history when the country was governed under the Articles of Confederation (1781 to 1789), the individual states had more autonomy but also less cohesion with neighbouring states. Critics of that regime claimed that the absence of a weak central government left the young republic vulnerable to crises without mediation or judicial arbitration. Shay's Rebellion, a tax revolt that took place in Massachusetts, was considered the crisis that ended the United States' attempt at confederate governance.

America turned away from a unitary government style and tried a Confederation style of government for 10 years. The United States has used the federal form of governance since 1789 and the ratification of the United States Constitution. American federalism is not just the division of powers between the federal government and the states but is further nuanced by local governments. In U.S. federalism, for example, states have the ability to regulate trade within their borders, but only the federal government can regulate commerce that crosses state borders. National governments usually retain the sole ability to provide for national defence and the conduct of foreign relations, whereas both the states and the national government can create traffic and environmental laws. Both levels have the ability to raise revenues and spend money, while only national governments can address topics relating to international trade. Larger nations sometimes turn to federalism to manage widespread territories, such as the United States, Canada and Australia.

In American Federalism, some of the powers that the federal government possesses it also shares with the states. These are called concurrent powers. Federalism is a system of implementing public policy across multiple layers of government. The process of testing and spreading ideas across multiple levels of government from federal, state, and local levels is known as diffusion. Diffusion is the spreading of policy ideas from one city or state to others. An example of diffusion comes whenever local governments borrow policies. If New York City were to construct an ordinance that fined litterers $100 per offense, and San Francisco copied and administered the same policy, then it was a diffusion of New York City's original concept.

## THE FEDERALIST PAPERS AND FEDERALISM

The Federalist Papers are a collection of 85 newspaper editorials written in support of the Constitution under the pseudonym of Publius, whose real identity was three Federalists: Alexander Hamilton, James Madison, and John Jay. The word 'federalism' does not appear in the Constitution of the United States. It has been adopted and became manifest within the governmental structures as inspired by The Federalist Papers. James Madison, writing as Publius, addressed the concept of Federalism in The Federalist Papers.

There are many different topics in The Federalist Papers. In Federalist No. 39, Madison defines "republic" and establishes three rules which must apply:

1. What is the foundation of its establishment? Only the possess *ultimate* sovereignty over the government.
2. What are the sources of its power? The elected officials chosen by the people should not break the rules or abuse their power.
3. Who has the authority to make future changes? When someone is chosen to rule the country, he or she should only be in that position for a certain amount of time and must be held accountable (through impeachment if necessary) if found to have committed high crimes or treason.

The republic defined by Madison consists of the different elements of the government leadership. A Madisonian republic is a system of government as defined by these three stipulations where the citizens elect representatives to make decisions for them. This constitutes most civic officials within the three branches of government: the executive, the judicial, and the legislative. There are still some offices that are *not* directly accountable to the people. This includes justices on the Supreme Court of the United States as well as United States senators prior to the passage of the 17$^{th}$ Amendment. Federalists like Madison believed that there needed to be a balance of direct election (popular vote) versus internal appointment by informed elites.

Madison, along with the other framers, was aware of two methods of arranging the government: confederate or federal. The Articles of Confederation was the country's original attempt at confederacy, which was a loosely assembled body of state governments prior to the ratification of the Constitution. The second version of government is called federal, national, or consolidation. It is also known as a unitary system.

Madison's essays proposed a five-component model for the American federal system. The first component was the method of ratification. The establishment of the Constitution was not a mere proclamation or decree by central authorities. Rather it was voted upon by the various member states before becoming the supreme law of the land. The second component was the sources of power for national officers. Here Madison emphasized how the bodies of Congress (House & Senate) as well as the presidency should arise. The presidency, for example, would be subject to direct election by the people, but administered as a function of the states through the Electoral College. The third component considers the apportionment of representatives based on the census. This determines how many representatives there are per state. This third component was the establishment of the representative as a national officer. The people thus gained a national representation. The fourth component referred to a fixed number of senators; two per state. People are not represented in the Senate, the states are. The Senate reinforces the federal nature of the Constitution. Madison's fifth component was the power of the presidency. The president's power is derived from elections and governed through the Electoral College system. As was mentioned before, the popular vote of the citizens is involved with determining the president, but it is the Electoral College (based on the size of the state and its apportionment of senators and representatives) that ultimately elects the president.

# FEDERALIST PAPER 10 AND FACTIONS

Federalist No. 10 was published on November 23, 1787, under the pseudonym "Publius." It addresses the question of how to reconcile citizens with interests contrary to the rights of others or the interests of the greater community. During the late 18th century, the concept of factions bothered the founding fathers. Madison saw factions within society as inevitable due to the nature of man. As long as humans hold differing opinions, have differing amounts of wealth, and own differing amounts of property, they will continue to form alliances with people who are most like them. The result is that they may work against the public interest and infringe upon the rights of others. Madison warns against these dangers.

Federalist No. 10 continues a theme begun in Federalist No. 9, "The Utility of the Union as a Safeguard Against Domestic Faction and Insurrection." Scholars and jurists contend that Federalist 9 and Federalist 10 are an authoritative interpretation and explication of the Constitution. The question of faction undergirds the development of modern interest groups and the role in which minority groups are protected from majority opinions.

In addition to the problem with factions, Federalist No. 10 continues the discussion of the question broached in Hamilton's Federalist No. 9. Hamilton there addressed the destructive role of a faction in breaking apart the republic. The role in which people form groups and allegiances dictate how effective a republic will be. The question Madison answers, then, is how to eliminate the negative effects of factions. Can a faction exist without the consequences to the republic? Madison defines a faction as many citizens, whether amounting to a minority or majority of the whole, who are united and actuated by some common impulse of passion, or of interest, adverse to the rights of other citizens, or to the permanent and aggregate interests of the community. In Madison's definition, he identifies the most serious source of faction to be the diversity of opinion in political life which leads to dispute over fundamental issues such as what regime or religion should be preferred.

Distribution of property was at the core of the debate during Madison's time. At the heart of Madison's fears about factions was the unequal distribution of property in society. The reality of property ownership was that some people owned property and others owned nothing, and Madison felt that people would form different factions that pursued different interests based on such a gap in ownership.

Recognizing that the country's wealthiest property owners formed a minority and that the country's unpropertied classes formed a majority, Madison feared that the unpropertied classes would come together to form a majority faction that gained control of the government. This fear of the minority rising became part of the framing of the American Constitution. Specifically, Madison feared that the unpropertied classes would use their majority power to implement a variety of measures that redistributed wealth in a disordered fashion. In short, Madison feared that a majority faction of the unpropertied classes might emerge to redistribute wealth and property for populist purposes and to the dismay of the ruling class, which would inevitably result in conflict.

## MADISON'S ARGUMENTS FOR FACTION LIMITATION

Madison first assessed two ways to limit the damage caused by factions: remove the causes or control the effects. He then described the two methods of removing the causes of factions: first, destroying liberty, which would work because liberty is to faction what air is to fire. The second option would be to create a society of homogeneous opinions and interests, which is difficult but not impossible. Madison particularly emphasized that economic stratification prevents everyone from sharing the same opinion. He concluded that the damage caused by factions can be limited only by controlling the effects.

Madison further contended that a person may offer two ways to check majority factions: (1) prevent the existence of the same passion or interest in a majority at the same time or, (2) render a majority faction unable to act. Madison concluded that a small democracy cannot avoid the dangers of a majority faction because small size means that undesirable passions can very quickly spread to a majority of the people, which can then enact its will through the democratic government without difficulty. A republic is different from a democracy because its government is placed in the hands of delegates, and, as a result, can be extended over a larger area. The idea is that, in a large republic, there will be more fit characters to choose from for each delegate.

## FEDERALIST 51 AND CHECKS AND BALANCES

The notion of checks and balances became fundamental in the formation of government. Federalist No. 51 is titled: "The Structure of the Government Must Furnish the Proper Checks and Balances Between the Different Departments." It was another essay by James Madison. This document was published on February 8, 1788, under the pseudonym Publius. Federalist No. 51 addresses a means by which appropriate checks and balances can be created in government and advocates a separation of powers within the national government One of its most important ideas, an explanation of check and balances, is the often-quoted phrase, "Ambition must be made to counteract ambition." In government, it is well known that people will seek to be self-promoting. Madison's idea was that the politicians and the individuals in public service in the United States would all have proclamations and ideas that they would work hard to enact-- this is true for Madison's time as well as now. The solution to ensure that laws and strong ideas were not enacted by a small group of partisan individuals was to use a federalist system where each level of government had different branches, each branch having the authority to impact the operation of the other branches. One of the primary ways that Federalist Paper 51 was able to encourage checks and balances was to tie it to the concept of liberty and an aversion to centralized tyranny. The concentration of power into one branch or level of government is antithetical to liberty. Whenever one branch or institution (of any sort) gets too much power, they become corrupted and tyrannical. As Lord

Acton reminds us: "power corrupts; absolute power corrupts absolutely." Checks and balances can be a remedy to the corruption of power.

The system of checks and balances, as espoused by Madison and philosophers like John Locke and Jean-Jacques Rousseau, was designed to allow an independent function of the various branches of government within certain constraints. For example, the legislative branch would draft laws that would have to be signed (or vetoed) by the president. The Supreme Court could strike down the laws if deemed unconstitutional. The president appointed members of the court, but only by an approval vote of the Senate. It was a way to avoid allowing any one branch to gain too much influence and power.

## CHANGES IN FEDERALISM OVER TIME

The balance of power between states and the national government changes over time. Because the balance of power between state and national government was clearly left open to some interpretation by the founders, it left a lot of power to the Supreme Court for interpretation. Looking at federal/state power relations over time, we can see two trends:

1. Changes like industrialization, urbanization, and advances in science and technology have led citizens to look to the government at all levels for assistance, protection, and security.

2. There is an undeniable shift of power over time from the states to the national government, particularly since the culmination of the Civil War, but some of it as early as the ratification of the Constitution.

There have been some key moments where power has shifted from the states to the federal government. John Marshall's tenure as Chief Justice of the Supreme Court (1801–1835) marked a drastic shift of power from the states to the federal government. Marshall was the third Chief Justice of the Supreme Court. He believed in the Federalist vision of a strong national government. One of the ground-breaking cases heard under his tenure was *Marbury v. Madison*. *Marbury v. Madison* (1803) gave the Supreme Court the power of judicial review to determine if congressional laws, state laws, or executive actions are constitutional. This ground-breaking change in the role of the judiciary extended the role of checks and balances to the judicial branch with stronger enforcement.

A second key moment that shifted the power from the states to the federal government was the extension of the "Necessary and Proper Clause" in *McCulloch v. Maryland* (1819). The result of this case allowed that clause to be interpreted broadly to include many powers that were not in the Constitution.

The third key moment that shifted the power from the states to the federal governments was *Gibbons v. Ogden*. The extension of the Interstate Commerce Clause and the right to regulate commerce emanating from *Gibbons v. Ogden* (1824) opened the door to federal regulation of commerce, broadly understood to mean most forms of business. The landmark decision in which the Supreme Court of the United States held that the power to regulate interstate commerce, granted to Congress by the Commerce Clause of the United States Constitution, encompassed the power to regulate sea navigation.

## FEDERALISM: THEN AND NOW

Nowadays, advocates of national power tend to be Democrats whose ideology leads them to believe, like the Federalists, that national power is not a threat to individual liberties. Republicans tend to be more like the Anti-Federalists in their distrust of national power and their preference for keeping important decisions at the state level. Republicans have long advocated *devolution*, or the returning of power to the states. Their enthusiasm for that position changes somewhat when they are in control of the federal government. When Republicans control Congress and the executive, many of them are less wary of the reach of the national government because it is doing their bidding. Similarly, when Democrats are out of power, they look to the states to enact their agendas. Today the battle over federalism seems to have less to do with its old framework of limited government versus big government and more to do with the battle for power between two highly polarized parties.

During the first 150 years of the United States, the country practiced something called Dual Federalism. Dual Federalism (1789-1933) is when you have a clear division of governing authority between national governments and state governments. One example of this is layer cake federalism, which is when you have a clear division between the authority of the state government.

During the 1930s, President Franklin D. Roosevelt's New Deal programs involved a strengthening and combination of federal/state functions. This included new regulatory agencies such as the Tennessee Valley Authority (TVA). This concept became known as Cooperative Federalism. Cooperative Federalism (1933-1981) is the mingling of governing authority between different levels of government. Cooperative federalism featured a much larger role for the federal government, with more money flowing to the states, along with marching orders to go with the cash. States became conduits for federal policy, with federal matching funds there to entice the states to administer programs such as welfare.

President Ronald Reagan (1981-1989) changed how American federalism operated. It was coined New Federalism. New Federalism was a version of Cooperative Federalism but with less oversight by the federal government. It left more control to the state and local levels. New Federalism was characterized by the administering of Block Grants from the federal government to local governments. This was a way of transferring federal funds to local jurisdictions.

During the Obama administration, President Barrack Obama became known for Progressive Federalism in 2009. Progressive Federalism known as modern federalism is when the national government has broad goals but relies on local and state innovation to make sure they are met. Sometimes the federal government has pushed programs onto the states (pay for it yourself). At other times, the federal government has attempted to dictate to the states (the Defense of Marriage Act, No Child Left Behind, the continued criminalization of marijuana and hemp). The Feds have given states money via block grants with few restrictions, categorical grants with lots of restrictions, and revenue sharing with no restrictions. Typical federal funding still often involves matching funds for a specific purpose.

### 4.7 Tools Used in Modern Federalism

The modern tools used in federalism today are tied to the types of funding and programs that the federal government grants the state governments. One type of tool used by the federal government to fund state programs is a block grant. A Block grant gives funds that come with flexibility for the states to spend the money as they wish within broad parameters. Block grants were first introduced in 1966 as a channel for the federal government to give money to specific areas they wanted to improve. These examples in the 1960s included transportation and education. A second tool used by the federal government to fund the state governments is a categorical grant. A categorical grant is a grant of money with specific instructions on how it is to be spent. Finally, a third type of funding tool used by the federal government is an unfunded mandate from the federal government to the states. An unfunded mandate is when Congress will tell the states to do something but provide no funds for administering the policy. Unfunded mandates include local, state, and federal requirements not in synergy. For the unfunded mandate, there are federal laws or regulations that the local or state government must pay in order to enact a new law.

As one can tell, federalism has taken many shapes and forms in our country's history. There has been a general decline in the influence of the states, but the institutions of government remain similar to what was conceived by the founders of the Constitution. The United States has evolved considerably since the Articles of Confederation and the old debates over the various Federalist Papers. Things are different and they will undoubtedly change more with the passing of time. What will be the future for federalism and power sharing in America?

## AMERICAN FEDERALISM- WHO REALLY IS IN CHARGE?

American federalism reflects a strong distrust of centralized government. This fundamental distrust of centralized power, along with the perhaps grudging admission that some of it was necessary, led to both the division of federal power into three branches, and the division of power between the states and the national government. So who has the power? The U.S. Constitution does seem to provide some space for a strong national government in a number of places:

1. The "necessary and proper" clause (sometimes called "the elastic clause" because of its ability to stretch to cover a lot of ground) of the Constitution (Article I, Section 8, clause 18): This says Congress shall have the necessary and proper authority to do what needs to be done.

2. The supremacy clause (Article VI, clause 2): The Constitution is established as the supreme law of the land.

3. The commerce clause (Article I, Section 8, clause 3): Only Congress has the ability to regulate interstate commerce.

4. The spending clause (Article I, Section 8, clause 1): Congress is expressly granted the ability to raise taxes and spend money.

Couple these features with the power of the presidency and the national government's greater ability to raise money, and you have a recipe for a strong national government. I don't think this is necessarily a bad thing. Others disagree. Then again, there's the 10th Amendment to the Constitution, and the last piece of the Bill of Rights: "The powers not delegated to the United States by the Constitution, nor prohibited by it to the States, are reserved to the States respectively, or to the people." That can be interpreted in any number of ways, and has been. Does it mean the federal government can only do things expressly described in the Constitution? Does it mean anything not addressed in the Constitution is up to the states? Does it create wiggl room for interpreting the Constitution, or take it away? Some people would tell you they are sure it means one thing or another, and others would simply disagree.

## KEY TERMS

**Articles of Confederation**: The original constitution of the United States, ratified in 1781, which was replaced by the US Constitution in 1789.

**Block Grant**: Funds given by the federal government to state or local governments for general purposes with few restrictions.

**Checks and Balances**: A system that allows each branch of government to limit the powers of the other branches to prevent any one branch from becoming too powerful.

**Commerce Clause**: A clause in the Constitution (Article I, Section 8, clause 3) that gives Congress the power to regulate interstate commerce.

**Concurrent Powers**: Powers shared by both the federal government and state governments.

**Confederation**: A union of sovereign states, united for purposes of common action often in relation to other states.

**Cooperative Federalism**: A concept of federalism where national, state, and local governments interact cooperatively and collectively to solve common problems.

**Diffusion**: The process of spreading policy ideas from one city or state to others.

**Dual Federalism**: A system of government in which both the states and the national government remain supreme within their own spheres, each responsible for some policies.

**Elastic Clause**: Another name for the necessary and proper clause of the Constitution (Article I, Section 8, clause 18), which allows Congress to pass laws needed to carry out its enumerated powers.

**Federalism**: The division of power between a central government and regional governments.

**Federalist Papers**: A collection of 85 articles and essays written by Alexander Hamilton, James Madison, and John Jay promoting the ratification of the United States Constitution.

**Judicial Review**: The power of the courts to declare laws unconstitutional.

**Necessary and Proper Clause**: A clause in the Constitution (Article I, Section 8, clause 18) that allows Congress to make all laws which shall be necessary and proper for carrying into execution its powers.

**New Federalism**: A political philosophy of devolution, or the transfer of certain powers from the United States federal government back to the states.

**Publius**: The pseudonym under which Alexander Hamilton, James Madison, and John Jay wrote the Federalist Papers.

**Republic**: A form of government in which power resides in elected individuals representing the citizen body and government leaders exercise power according to the rule of law.

**Shay's Rebellion**: An armed uprising in Massachusetts (1786-1787), which highlighted the weaknesses of the Articles of Confederation and led to the drafting of the Constitution.

**Supremacy Clause**: A clause in the Constitution (Article VI, clause 2) establishing that federal laws and treaties are the supreme law of the land, taking precedence over state laws.

**Unfunded Mandate**: A regulation or policy imposed by the federal government on state and local governments without adequate federal funds to carry out the policy.

**Unitary Government**: A system of political organization with a central supreme government which holds the authority over and makes the decisions for subordinate local governments.

# CHAPTER 8

# THE DECLARATION OF INDEPENDENCE AND THE UNITED STATES CONSTITUTION

The United States political culture resulted from the influence of English political culture and Western philosophical tradition. Since the United Colonies of America were English provinces, England has historically played an essential role in shaping American economics and culture. The ultimate political enforcer in Colonial English America was the British monarchy, which based its legitimacy on kings' divine rights. The English King was God's legitimate representative on Earth.

Since the independence period, the United States has developed a new political culture that still serves as inspiration for the rest of the world. At the time, there was no model to follow for the United States Founders. The process of writing the constitution required creativity, originality, and clarity. The Founders chose Thomas Jefferson to write the United States Declaration of Independence. The ideas of John Locke served as an inspiration to write the political document. Both legally and politically speaking, the national constitution was the founding document for the United States democracy.

# THE ROOTS OF THE UNITED STATES POLITICAL CULTURE

As a former colony, the nation was a political subject of the ruling country—England. America was economically dependent on England, and the United Colonies had cultural ties to it as well. The economic relationship between the mother country and its colonies was called *mercantilism*. England provided protection and settlement costs to the colonists. The colonies sent prime resources and cuts of the profits from their trade back to the mother country. The center of power denied colonists access to the lucrative markets in which England competed.

The ultimate political enforcer in Colonial English America was the British monarchy. England followed the *divine right of kings*, which had its roots in a political culture that understood the power to be vested in the king because he was God's legitimate representative on Earth. This situation put a significant burden on the colonists to produce a counternarrative to justify political independence that did not make them all sinners. As the American colonists began to consider themselves a separate cultural and political entity, the idea of struggling for independence started to look like a desirable and viable option for some American-born Englishmen.

More than anything, the Americans developed a new way of looking at the world during the independence days. The social contract theory was essential to the development of the United States as an independent country. This theory principally emerged and took shape from the writings of the British philosophers Thomas Hobbes and John Locke. In a *social contract*, power is to be held by all citizens, each of whom gives up some of their rights to the government in exchange for the right to use safely and securely the power citizens retained.

The recently-formed government based its legitimacy on the consent of those governed. If the government did not adequately protect and guarantee their remaining rights, subjects had the right to rebel and establish a new government. A government that does not secure the remaining rights of citizens lacks legitimacy.

British political philosopher Thomas Hobbes believed that free men had the right to subject themselves to a ruler who would protect them. The government was an all-powerful entity, and its subjects had no right to push back against its power. On the other hand, John Locke believed that the social contract was conditional upon rights' protection. Governed subjects could revoke the social contract if the government failed to safeguard their rights.

Of all the political thinkers who influenced American beliefs about government, the most relevant was assuredly John Locke, who wrote nearby in time that the founders of the United States were contemplating independence. The ideas of Locke were hugely popular in the United Colonies of America. When discussing the influences of the political philosophy of John Locke, one should start by analysing and focusing on the theory of natural law and rights. However, one should consider that the natural law concept existed long before Locke and was an integral principle of his philosophical theories. The natural law is a way to express universal moral truths that apply to all people. Universal moral law likely served as a preceding influence of the United States Constitution.

In many more than one pamphlet, the United States writers and thinkers cited Locke on natural rights and the social and governmental contract as well; they referred to Montesquieu and Delolme on the character of British freedom and the institutional prerequisites for its fulfilment; Voltaire on the evils and disasters of clerical oppression; Beccaria on the change of criminal law; Grotius, Pufendorf, Burlamaqui; and Vattel on the laws of nature and nations, and the standards of civil government. The pervasiveness of such citations is, on occasion, astonishing.[45]

The most significant early contrast was between natural and generally applicable laws and those conventional, which operated only in those

---

[45] Bailyn, Bernard. *The Ideological Origins of the American Revolution*, 1967. Massachusetts: Belknap Press.

places where specific particular customs existed. Simply put, this is a contrast between a universal moral right and a law created by society depending on culture and historical tradition. This distinction is known as one of the main differences between natural law and positive law.

Natural law also differs from divine law. Divine law is from the Christian tradition and customarily referred to those laws that God had directly revealed through visionary prophets and other enlightened writers. One can discover natural law by reason alone. Natural law applies to all people. On the contrary, one can get in touch with divine law only through God's special revelation, and it is only applicable to those whom the revelation God disclosed. For Locke, the biblical law did not apply to the modern human being[46].

## THE DECLARATION OF INDEPENDENCE

The Founders chose Thomas Jefferson to write the *Declaration of Independence.* The ideas of John Locke served as an inspiration to write the document. Locke, born in 1632, is among the most influential political philosophers in history. In the *Two Treatises of Government*, Locke supported the claim that men are by nature free and equal against those that said that God had made all people naturally subject to a divinely-legitimate monarch. He argued that humans have natural rights, such as the right to life, liberty, and property.

The rights to life, liberty, and property are universal and natural. These rights have a foundation independent of the cultural and consuetudinary law built on any particular society's traditions. Locke stated that all men are naturally free and equal as part of the justification for understanding the legitimate political government that results from the social contract. This social contract is a condition in which people in the state of nature conditionally transfer some of their rights to the government,

---

[46] For an in-depth analysis of Locke's influence in United States independence, see Bailyn.

which subjects expect to provide stable and comfortable enjoyment of their lives, liberty, and property.

The Declaration of Independence is a political document about changing the rules about what makes power legitimate and who should reasonably hold it. The historical record represents the social contract between the government and the U.S. people. By relying on the social contract, the Declaration of Independence stated that Americans had *inalienable rights* that subjects could not give up to the government.

One should acknowledge that the American Constitution created the modern notion of citizens distinct from subjects. Even if related, both terms are not equivalent. The United States constitution writers laid blame on George III for breaking a political contract he barely understood. This incident was one of the main circumstances that legitimated the Americans' rebellion. It also attempted to convince the leaders of other colonial powers like Spain and France that they had nothing to worry about since supposedly they were not tyrants like George, King of Great Britain, and Ireland. Not every person in the new country was a citizen with full political rights. The task of creating a new government was not as easy as they had hoped, and it took more than one try to get things done right.

## THE UNITED STATES CONSTITUTION

The Constitution is the framework for the legal system of the United States. Depending upon the constitution's definition and since some Nation-States do not have a formal central constitution like the United States, one can argue that the United States Constitution is the oldest codified constitutional text still in use today. The United States Constitution is divided into Articles and Amendments. Congress Representatives have updated the American Constitution over the years, and courts continue to argue the text's applications. Both legally and politically speaking, the national constitution was the founding document for the United States democracy.

The Preamble of the United States Constitution—the document's famous first fifty-two words— introduces everything to follow in the Constitution's seven articles and twenty-seven amendments. It proclaims who is adopting this Constitution: "We the People of the United States." It describes why the country adopts the Constitution—the purposes behind the enactment of America's governing charter. Furthermore, it explains the principles adopted, as the United Constitution, a single authoritative written text, serves as the land's fundamental law.

While accurate, the word "preamble" does not quite capture the full importance of this provision. "Preamble" implies that these words are merely an opening rhetorical flourish or frill without meaningful effect. To be sure, the "preamble" usefully conveys the idea that this provision does not itself confer or delineate powers of government or rights of citizens, outlined in the substantive articles and amendments that follow in the main body of the constitution's text.

## THE ARTICLES OF CONFEDERATION

Before the Civil War, the two leading and legislative power-affecting doctrines of American Constitutional Law were the Doctrine of Vested Rights and the Police Power Doctrine, both complementary to each other. The first one presumably flourished before the rise of the Jacksonian Democracy style in the United States. The Doctrine of the Vested Rights is the more fundamental doctrine[47].

The United States Constitution has a foundation in the Articles of Confederation. The founders' primary duty was to write a constitution or political rulebook that would determine who would have power, how that power would be limited, and how the new government functioned. The first constitution has been historically known as the *Articles of Confederation*. Because the states viewed themselves as sovereign, they

---

[47] Corwin, Edward. "The Basic Doctrine of American Constitutional Law." *Michigan Law Review*, vol. 12, no. 4, 1914, pp. 247–276. *JSTOR*, www.jstor.org/stable/1276027.

decided to limit their new constitution to a "firm league of friendship" amongst states rather than a complete union entity. This change was about the establishment of a *United States Confederation*. Economic troubles, drought, and crop failures meant that there were heavy demands for relief from state governments.

The Articles of Confederation provided new restrictions on the government's power. The national government was not allowed to take some measures under the Articles of Confederation, such as draft soldiers' power. Drafting soldiers allowed for a robust military force; whoever, not allowing a draft made it challenging to coordinate a response to a threat from a foreign power. The Articles of Confederation stopped citizens' taxation, making the Federal government dependent on the states for funds. The Articles could not regulate interstate commerce; consequently, it left the states to create their own markets, economic rules, and more. Furthermore, the Articles forbid establishing a central monetary system and having different currencies in each state.

The last draft of the Articles of Confederation, which framed the new country's government's basis, was acknowledged by Congress in November 1777 and submitted to the states for endorsement. It would not become the tradition that must be adhered to until every one of the thirteen states had endorsed it. Within two years, all except for Maryland had done so. Maryland contended that all domains west of the Appalachians, to which a few states had laid case, should instead be held by the public government as open land to help every state. When the remainder of these states, Virginia, surrendered its property claims in mid-1781, Maryland affirmed the Confederation Articles. Half a month later, the British capitulated. Americans aspired their new government to be a republic, wherein people, not a monarch or ruler, held power and chose agents to oversee as per law and order.

Many feared that a country as large as the United States would not be managed successfully as a republic. Those voices also stressed that even an administration of delegates elected by the people might become too powerful and overbearing. Subsequently, public administrators created a confederation as an entity in which independent, self-governing states form a union to act together in defense areas. Unfortunate of supplanting one abusive public government with another. Nonetheless, the Articles of Confederation's composers made collusion of sovereign states held together by a feeble focal government.[48]

The result of the problems with the Articles led to economic problems. When economic chaos arose, so did Shay's Rebellion. Shay's Rebellion was a march of angry farmers demanding debt relief in western Massachusetts. This rebellion drove some of the founders to meet in Annapolis in 1786 to discuss fixing the dysfunctional Articles. Later, some at the gathering in Annapolis decided the Articles were too broken to fix, and thus they decided to create a whole new Constitution instead.

## THE CONSTITUTIONAL CONVENTION

The drafting of a new national constitution began with the Constitutional Convention of 1787. The most significant fracture came between two groups, the first known as the Federalists and the second as the Anti-Federalists. The Federalists were those who wanted a more robust national government. The prospect of a stronger government less threatened the Federalists because they mainly were representatives of large states who felt they could control national government power. Over time, they were known as the Federalists because they preferred to get rid of the Articles' confederal system, where the states ultimately held power and moved to a federal system, where power would be shared between states and national government.

There were multiple plans put forth at the Constitutional Convention as proposals for the new government. One plan put forward was a bicameral legislature by Virginia. The *Virginia Plan* was a comparatively strong but limited government whose signature institution would be a *bicameral legislature* (meaning it would have two chambers). The

---

[48] Corwin, 33-44.

representation in both chambers would be based on population and taxes paid. On the other hand, the Anti-Federalists were against a robust national government on principle and out of fear. They would have preferred to tweak the Articles to make them more valuable and practical. Mostly, representatives of smaller states feared a more robust government would roll over them, and the big states would always get their way. The *New Jersey Plan* wanted a slightly upgraded Articles of Confederation—a single chamber of the legislature where every state cast one vote, with a weak executive and a nonexistent court system, but some additional powers for the national government.

The solution to this political crisis was the agreements on compromises. The Great Compromise was "great" because it effectively worked to bring the two sides together. However, it was more remarkable for the Federalists than the Anti-Federalists since the outcome exceeded its initial expectations. The Federalists truly benefited from the negotiation results. The Compromise the two groups agreed on called for a bicameral legislature that split the difference between the two political sides. Parliamentary representation was based on the state's population in the House of Representatives. Every state received two members, regardless of population, in the Senate.

The result of the Great Compromise was the *Three-Fifths Compromise* indicates that, when determining representation, the population count would be made "by adding to the whole Number of Free persons … three-fifths of all other persons." Both the Great Compromise and the Three-Fifths Compromise reduced the national government's popular control by countering it with state control and significantly empowering smaller, rural states.

The concerns of southern states to boost their power vis-a-vis the north had another lasting effect on the United States Constitution: we do not elect the United States president by direct popular vote. Instead, we have the Electoral College. In this settlement, the states had more power to choose the president. The number of electors a state gets in the Electoral College (that is, the number of votes that a state can cast for president) is determined by the total number of representatives that that state has in both houses. The South fought a direct popular presidential election because actual population totals would have determined the presidency in some cases.

## BASIC CONSTITUTIONAL PRINCIPLES

The American founders had created a document that was path-breaking in its innovative approach to human governance. Several nations have throughout the years used the United States Constitution as an inspiration, but at the time, there was no model for the American founders to follow. The writers of the national constitution were original and have inspired other states throughout history. *James Madison* was the genius behind the United States Constitution. His fundamental idea was to design a system that takes human nature *as it is* (self-interested, greedy, and ambitious), not as you want it to be. James Madison wanted to create an internal mechanism based on the idea that human nature will produce fair laws and public policy because of it, not despite it.

Basic principles of the United States provided by the national constitution are to have separation of powers[49], checks and balances, and federalism. The United States Constitution gives the three branches of government their own powers, shared powers, and checked powers. In some countries, these functions are not separated (i.e., a *parliamentary system*).

Separation of powers is the government's division vertically into three branches: legislative, executive, and judicial. This power division gives each layer and branch independent status with some of its constitutional power.

The founders thought a presidential system would better protect against abuses of power. In the United States, we have a presidential system: the executive and the other two branches are constitutionally distinct.

---

[49] On the separation of powers in the United States constitution, see Corwin.

The three are given their own powers according to the United States Constitution. Checks and balances give each layer and branch just enough power over the others in its system that their jealousy will guard against the others' over-reach. Simply put, the legislative branch is the lawmaking component, the *executive branch* is the law-enforcing component, and the judicial branch is the law-interpreting component. Federalism divides the government horizontally into layers: national and state.

## CONSTITUTIONAL POWERS

The United States Constitution provides powers to the Federal government and the states. The constitutional provisions fostered federalism's development. Article I Section 8 (*enumerated powers*) spells out exactly what Congress (and hence the national government) is allowed to do, including coining money and managing interstate commerce.

The *necessary and proper clause* coming at the end of the enumerated powers indicates Congress can do anything "necessary and proper" to carry out its duties suitably. The United States constitution's necessary and proper clause defines the Congress's authority to exercise the necessary and proper powers it needs to carry out its designated functions. This power or clause of the United States Constitution also goes by a similar name, *the elastic clause,* because it stretches the national government's authority to include or imply anything written in the United States Constitution's text. In practice, this clause generally strengthens the national government at the expense of state power.

The *Tenth Amendment to the United States Constitution* indicates that any powers not explicitly given to the national government are reserved to the states. It ultimately depends on what the Court says, and the Court changes its mind repeatedly. Who gets the advantage? It is pretty much a tie; the balance of national state power again depends on judicial interpretation.

In Article VI of the Constitution, the *supremacy clause* states that the constitutional text itself and national laws made under it are the land's law.

This clause found in the Constitution defines the national government's authority. The supremacy clause says that the national government's authority prevails over state or local government claims provided that power was given to the federal government. This idea found in the United States Constitution provides the federal government's implied powers, and when laws between States and Federal governments clash, the Federal Government's laws are supreme and take priority over the state's laws. Who gets the advantage? If national law clashes with state law, national law almost always wins if the federal government chooses to impose its will.

The founders were well aware of the tension between the states themselves as a threat to national stability. The United States Constitution's framers developed a formal way to balance federal vs. state rights. The *Constitution's full faith and credit clause* (Article IV, Section 1) says that the states have to respect the other states' legal proceedings and public acts. An example of the full faith and credit clause includes one's driver's license, which must be accepted across state lines as a valid form of identification. The *privileges and immunities clause* (Article IV, Section 2) indicates a state cannot deny a citizen of another state the rights its citizens enjoy.

The balance has changed over time, but the national government has often gained power at the states' expense. Battles over federalism are typically fought in the states, except for the Civil War. The history of federalism proves that national and state governments have periodically checked each other over time.

## KEY TERMS

**Articles of Confederation**: The first constitution of the United States, creating a loose confederation of sovereign states with a weak central government.

**Bicameral Legislature**: A legislative body with two chambers, typically a lower house and an upper house.

**Checks and Balances**: A system that ensures no single branch of government becomes too powerful by giving each branch some degree of oversight and control over the others.

**Constitutional Convention of 1787**: The meeting in Philadelphia where the United States Constitution was drafted, replacing the Articles of Confederation.

**Divine Right of Kings**: The belief that monarchs derive their authority directly from God and are accountable only to Him.

**Electoral College**: The body of electors established by the United States Constitution to elect the president and vice president.

**Federalism**: The division of power between national and state governments.

**Great Compromise**: The agreement during the Constitutional Convention that created a bicameral legislature with representation based on population in one house and equal representation in the other.

**John Locke**: An influential English philosopher whose ideas about natural rights and government by consent inspired the American Founders.

**Natural Law**: The concept of a universal moral law that applies to all humans and is discoverable through reason.

**Necessary and Proper Clause**: A clause in the United States Constitution granting Congress the authority to pass all laws necessary and proper to carry out its enumerated powers.

**Preamble**: The introductory statement of the United States Constitution that outlines the reasons for its adoption and the purposes it serves.

**Separation of Powers**: The division of government responsibilities into distinct branches to limit any one branch from exercising the core functions of another.

**Shay's Rebellion**: A 1786 uprising of Massachusetts farmers protesting economic injustices and prompting calls for a stronger national government.

**Social Contract Theory**: The philosophical idea that individuals consent to form a government that will protect their rights in exchange for some relinquishment of their freedoms.

**Supremacy Clause**: A clause in the United States Constitution stating that federal law takes precedence over state law when the two conflict.

**Thomas Jefferson**: The principal author of the Declaration of Independence and the third president of the United States.

**Three-Fifths Compromise**: A compromise where each enslaved person would be counted as three-fifths of a person for purposes of representation and taxation.

**Virginia Plan**: A proposal at the Constitutional Convention for a strong central government with a bicameral legislature based on population.

# CHAPTER 9

# CIVIL LIBERTIES

What is the difference between civil rights and civil liberties? It is the word *civil*—having to do with the non-political life of citizens—that gives the phrases *civil rights* and *civil liberties* specific and different meanings. In democracies and other non-authoritarian societies where, at least some political power is held by citizens, both civil liberties and civil rights are essential to operational societies. Civil liberties are individual rights that come from the *limitation of* government power. Civil rights *empower the government* to give us group rights. You could say civil liberties are about equal protection *from* the law and civil rights are about the equal protection *of* the laws.

So, what do civil liberties and civil rights actually mean in order to differentiate from one another? Civil liberties are the individual freedoms that limit government. These rights are guaranteed by the Bill of Rights and the text of the Constitution itself. Some others, like the right to privacy, come from Supreme Court decisions that have interpreted the Constitution. Civil rights are the freedom of groups to fully participate in the public life of a nation. These groups are defined by some particular characteristic—like race, gender, or sexual orientation—that is beyond their members' control. Rather than limiting government, the protection of civil rights often *empowers the government* to act.

## RIGHTS EQUAL POWER

Giving citizenry rights empowers the people. Rights confer power on people and limitations on government. When a person has the ability to claim a right, it makes one a citizen, not a subject. The ability to deny rights gives citizens power over each other. The ability to use government to fight back against those who would deny their fellow citizens rights is also a form of power.

## WHERE DO OUR RIGHTS COME FROM?

If we believe we have rights because the government, the Constitution, the Bill of Rights or any other amendments grant them to us, then those rights can also be taken away. These rights differ from natural rights, which are the inalienable rights conferred by "Nature and Nature's God" that no government can take away.

The rights of American citizens provided by the Constitution and the Bill of Rights are limited in two main ways. First, they become limited when they clash with other people's rights. Second is when they conflict with collective societal values. Solving rights conflicts often involves compromise. These conflicts are resolved by different aspects of government such as Congress, the President and the bureaucracy, the courts, and the people.

## THE BILL OF RIGHTS

The Bill of Rights established the fundamental constitutional rights afforded to every American. These important rights are included in the Bill of Rights. These rights are:

- Amendment 1: Establishment clause, free exercise of religion, free speech, free press, right to assemble.
- Amendment 2: Right to bear arms necessary for a well-regulated militia.

- Amendment 3: You can't be forced to house soldiers during peace.
- Amendment 4: No unreasonable searches and seizures.
- Amendment 5: Grand jury indictment for capital crimes; no double jeopardy, self-incrimination, or deprivation of property without due process of law.
- Amendment 6: Right to a speedy trial and counsel.
- Amendment 7: Jury trials for civil cases where the value in controversy is over $20.
- Amendment 8: No cruel or unusual punishment or excessive bail.
- Amendment 9: The rights listed in the Constitution does not limit the possession of other rights.
- Amendment 10: All rights not given to the national government are reserved to the states.

The founders struggled with having a Bill of Rights. Alexander Hamilton argued in *Federalist* #84 that a Bill of Rights might be redundant, because the founders' intent was to create a government that was already powerless to do the things the Bill of Rights ruled out. All of the founders feared a powerful government; they just differed on ways to limit it. The Federalists thought they had created internal mechanisms—separation of powers, checks and balances—that would keep the government from over-reaching. The Anti-Federalists wanted to spell out restrictions on the government—limiting powers the Federalists didn't think the Constitution conferred.

The Bill of Rights limited the national government's power. On its face, the Bill of Rights applies to the national government and specifically to Congress. But most Americans don't interact with the federal government or commit federal crimes. States may have their own Bill of Rights within their own state constitutions, but states are not required to guarantee these rights and there are no regulations about what their state constitutions should cover.

The power of the states is checked or held accountable by the federal government. Americans are not helpless if a state denies them a basic right. The Fourteenth Amendment was originally drafted and intended to stop southern states from denying former slaves their citizenship rights after the Civil War. Using a process called incorporation, the Court was able to fold the national right into required state protections via the Fourteenth Amendment. Language in the Fourteenth Amendment can be interpreted to mean that no state can deny a citizen any of the rights the federal government guarantees. With incorporation, the Supreme Court expanded the national power at the expense of the state, changing the balance of federal power.

## CIVIL LIBERTIES—UNDERSTANDING THE FIRST AMENDMENT

The basic civil liberties of Americans include all the rights the founders felt were necessary to keep the states in check. The most important of those rights they packed into the First Amendment, because they wanted to indicate their primary importance. The reason that this amendment covers so many rights is that, for the founders, these were all fundamental to a fully functioning democracy.

The First Amendment prohibits Congress from establishing a religion or interfering with the exercise of religion, abridging the freedom of speech or the press, or interfering with the right of the people to assemble. These prohibitions have been made applicable to the states through the Fourteenth Amendment. The freedoms, however, are not absolute and encompass different boundaries that have been established by judicial interpretation.

## FREEDOM OF RELIGION

Freedom of religion was important to the founders. The founders' main task was to write a constitution, or rulebook, that would determine how the new government was to function, who would have power, and how that power would be limited. The Articles of Confederation gave the foundational importance to the writing of the Bill of Rights because religious freedom was at the forefront of the founders' minds. Many of the original colonists had fled England to avoid an established church in the first place.

The First Amendment has two clauses that establish freedom of religion. The First Amendment provides "Congress shall make no law respecting an establishment of religion or prohibiting the free exercise thereof".

### *Establishment Clause*

First, the Establishment Clause was designed to limit Congress and ensure that Congress shall make no law respecting an establishment of religion. The role of the state is to accommodate all religions. Unfortunately, this first amendment guarantee can be divisive. Accommodationists are people who want to support "all" religions equally. This is opposed to separationists: people who want a separation between church and state. Americans and, indeed, members of the Supreme Court, are divided on whether we need to keep church and state entirely separate, or whether it is okay to allow some state recognition and support for religion as long as it accommodates all religions. What is a constitutional issue—how far church and state can be intermingled—has become a cultural clash that it is almost impossible to solve to everyone's satisfaction.

The first step is to determine if the law has a religious preference. When determining if a law or government program violates the Establishment Clause and includes a preference for some religious sects over others, the law or program will be subject to a compelling interest analysis and ask if it is narrowly tailored to promote a compelling interest. In *Board of Education v. Grumet*, the Supreme Court struck down a state law that created a public school district whose boundaries were intentionally set to match the boundaries of a particular Jewish neighborhood. Since the government had no other interest rather than one that was furthered by "religious favoritism", the Court held it failed to exercise governmental authority in a religiously neutral way.[50] Therefore, if there is a preference and the law is not crafted in a religiously neutral way, it will receive the compelling interest test.

Secondly, if there is no religious preference, and the compelling interest test is not used, then the law is subject to the Lemon Test. The Lemon Test was established in *Lemon v. Kurtzman* to provide a constitutional understanding on how much the government can establish a religion. The law or program will be valid under the Establishment Clause if it:

1. Has a secular purpose

2. Has a primary effect that neither advances nor inhibits religion; and

3. Does not produce excessive government entanglement with religion.[51]

"Secular", as opposed to sacred, means not having a religious, spiritual or temporal basis. If the government maintains a holiday-Christmas Times display that does not appear to endorse one religion and includes holiday decorations, such as a Christmas tree or a Santa Claus figure, the court will hold that the display has a secular purpose based on the history of government recognition of holidays.[52]

If the law advances or inhibits a particular religion or specific religious group, then that law will be invalid. But if a law favors or burdens a larger segment of society that happens to include religious groups, it will generally be upheld. For example, the IRS may provide deductions and other financial benefits to churches and other religious donations because the primary effect of the benefit does not only include religious

---

[50] *Board of Education v. Grumet*, 512 v. 687 (1994).
[51] *Lemon v. Kurtzman*, 403 U.S. 602 (1971).
[52] *County of Allegheny v. ACLU*, 492 U.S. 573 (1989).

organizations- but it also applies to all charitable organizations that happen to include religious groups.[53]

It is hard for the Court to decide what "excessive entanglement" means. Excessive entanglement can mean too much government involvement. There are times when government action can cross paths with private religions. It becomes excessive when government action crosses into religious action that they can run afoul of other people's actions or the state's obligation to exercise its police power to protect the health, well-being, and security of all citizens. For example, if a public school allows members of the public and private organizations to use school property when classes are not in session and a religious organization utilizes the space and the meetings are not run by school personnel, there is no excessive government entanglement.[54] The government was not a significant actor.

## FREE EXERCISE CLAUSE

The freedom from an establishment of a religion afforded the free exercise of religion for the founders. Because the government cannot establish one or more religions means people have the freedom to practice any religion. The Free Exercise Clause states that Congress shall make no law... prohibiting the free exercise thereof.[55] The trouble with those words spelling out religious freedom protection is that they contain an inherent contradiction. Any effort to establish one of the founders' denominations as the official state religion would have doomed the new country from the start. When political differences are reinforced with religious differences, every conflict is infused with profound meaning and compromise is impossible. When a government can put the power of an Almighty behind its laws, it is very hard to resist it if it over-reaches.

---

[53] *Hernandez v. Commissioner of Internal Revenue*, 490 U.S. 680 (1989).
[54] *Good News Club v. Milford Central School*, 533 U.S. (2001).
[55] U.S. Const. Amend I.

The Free Exercise Clause prohibits the government from punishing, denying benefits to or imposing burdens on someone on the basis of the person's religious beliefs. For many years the Supreme Court had suggested that the government had to show it had a compelling reason to infringe on religious practice. But in 1990 it reversed course and put the burden of proof back on religious groups to show that the state regulation has violated the groups' rights. However, the test for such impermissible government action remains unclear as the Court has never found an interest that was so compelling that it would justify punishing or regulating a religious belief.

The Court has directed that the Free Exercise Clause prohibits the government from punishing conduct merely because it is religious or displays religious belief.[56] A law that is designed to suppress actions only because the actions are religiously motivated is not a neutral law and would be invalid. A city law that prohibits a precise type of animal slaughtering for a particular religion violates the Free Exercise clause because the law was not neutral and did not prohibit all animal slaughtering.[57]

But the states can prohibit or regulate conduct in general, and this is true even if the prohibition or regulation happens to interfere with a person's religious practices. The Free Exercise Clause does not require exemptions from criminal laws or other regulations. A law that regulates conduct of all persons can be applied to prohibit the conduct of a person despite the fact that his or her religious beliefs prevent him or her from complying with the law. For example, the prohibition against the use of peyote was permissible if it applied generally to all persons, even if individuals require use of peyote during religious ceremonies.[58]

But what is a religious belief?

The Supreme Court has not defined or laid out elements for what constitutes a religious belief. However, it has made clear that religious

---

[56] *Employment Division v. Smith.*

[57] *Church of the Lukumi v. Babalu Aye, Inc. v. Hialeah*, 508 U.S. 520 (1993).

[58] *Employment Division v. Smith.*

beliefs do not require recognition of a supreme being[59] and need not arise from a traditional, or even an organized, religion.[60]

## WHY FREEDOM OF EXPRESSION IS A BIG DEAL

As important to the founders in limiting government as freedom from an established religion was freedom of expression. Freedom of expression includes speech, press, and freedom of assembly, the right to join together with other persons for expressive or political activity. While freedom of speech and press are mentioned in the First Amendment, freedom of association is not mentioned but is still protected by the First Amendment. The freedom of speech protects the free flow of ideas, a most important function in a democratic society. A regulation or law that tries to forbid speech of specific ideas (content regulation) is more likely to violate the free speech doctrine. It is usually unconstitutional for the government to prohibit speech based on its content. In *Brandenburg v. Ohio*, the Court held that the government could not prohibit political speech, or speech with political content, unless it is linked to immediate lawless behavior[61]. However, conduct regulation, which is content-neutral and regulates how the speech is conducted, is more likely permitted (*i.e.*, law prohibiting billboards for purposes of traffic safety).

Speech and communication, and its conduct from which it is expressed, can take many forms and, if that conduct is intended to express an idea, can still be protected under the First Amendment much like content speech. In *Masterpiece Cakeshop v. Colorado Civil Rights Commission*, a cake shop owner refused to sell a wedding cake to a same sex couple, claiming, in part, requiring him to create the cake would violate his First Amendment right to free speech by compelling him to exercise his artistic talents to express a message with which he disagreed.

---

[59] *Torcaso v. Watkins*, 367 U.S. 488 (1961).
[60] *Frazee v. Illinois Department of Employment Security*, 489 U.S. 829 (1989).
[61] *Brandenburg v. Ohio*, 395 U.S. 444 (1969)

The Court did not rule on the speech claim but agreed with the Court of Appeals holding that preparing a wedding cake is not a form of protected speech or would force the cake shop owner to adhere to and express an ideological point of view. In their concurring opinion, Justices Kagen and Breyer, note and insinuate that cake making is certainly a conduct for which speech is expressed, which is generally permitted. However, the Justices noted that "the Court has recognized a wide array of conduct that can qualify as expressive, including nude dancing, wearing a military uniform and conducting a silent sit-in" and cake making also be a type of protected speech conduct if it intends to express an idea. Here the Justices suggest that conduct, like making a cake, can be protected speech if the cake maker uses his artistic talent of cake making as an expression of value, or opinion. [62]

Freedom of expression is important predominantly for the right to criticize the government. Denying free speech sets a dangerous precedent—if we can stop our opponents from speaking out today, they might stop us from speaking out tomorrow. So, if free speech is so important, why do we ever limit it?

The Supreme Court has at various times ruled that speech (and symbolic speech) can be limited. As indicated above, very few restrictions on the content of speech are tolerated. The Court allows them only to prevent grave injury. The following is a list of the reasons for which the Court has allowed content-based restrictions on speech:

- For purposes of national security during war (sedition)
- Because it is obscene
- Speech that is inherently likely to incite immediate physical retaliation (fighting words)
- Because it maliciously damages a reputation (libel when printed; slander when spoken)

---

[62] *Masterpiece Cakeshop v. Colorado Civil Rights Commission*, 138 S. Ct. 1719 (2018).

To determine what is unprotected speech, the Court has come up with a series of tests, many of which have introduced even more ambiguity. The clear and present danger test was meant to distinguish speech that was immediately harmful from that posed only a remote threat.[63] The imminent lawless action test protected speech unless it was directed to producing or inciting imminent lawless action and is likely to produce or incite such action.[64] The *Miller* test defines standards for obscenity and asks whether the work lacks "serious literary, artistic, political, or scientific value".[65] The prior restraint test prohibits censoring and refusing to allow the publication of something, even though it very well might fail one of its tests after publication. The Supreme Court has been fairly steady on its refusal to engage in prior restraint.[66] Only a national emergency could justify such censorship.

## ELECTRONIC COMMUNICATION MAKES IT VASTLY MORE COMPLICATED.

In addition to the wide variety of types of speech discussed above, electronic communication can also be a type of speech. The question as to whether media companies can limit access to the internet is evolving. The role of net neutrality is the way the Internet works now on the principle that service providers cannot speed up or slow down access for customers or make decisions about the content they see or the apps they download. The Supreme Court is constantly, and likely indefinitely, interpreting the Free Speech Clause to keep up with new types of speech created through new technology.

---

[63] *Scheneck v. United States*, 249 U.S. 47 (1919).
[64] *Brandenberg v. Ohio*, 395 U.S. 444 (1969).
[65] *Miller v. California*, 413 U.S. 15 (1973).
[66] *Near v. Minnesota*, 283 U.S. 697 (1931)

## CIVIL LIBERTIES—UNDERSTANDING DUE PROCESS RIGHTS

What are due process rights? Due process rights are the rights that give Americans some protections against being railroaded into jail by the police and the courts, especially for political purposes. The founders devote half the Bill of Rights to this subject to protect the citizens from a police state. A chief fear of the founders was a government so strong that its leaders could use the police power and the judicial system for political purposes. These protections provide that the government shall not take a person's life, liberty, or property without due process of law. Due process contemplates fair procedures, which at least require at least an opportunity to present objections to the proposed action to a fair, neutral decision maker, like a judge. There are two separate clauses protecting due process: (1) The Due Process Clause in the Fifth Amendment (applies to the federal government) and (2) The Due Process Clause in the Fourteenth Amendment (applies to state and local governments).

## WHAT DO THE DUE PROCESS RIGHTS INCLUDE?

Article I provides that Congress cannot suspend habeas corpus, pass a bill of attainder, and pass an ex post facto law. Congress cannot suspend a person's right to be brought before a judge. The writ of habeas corpus is the right from unlawful imprisonment and includes the right to be brought before a judge and informed of the charges and evidence against you. The due process rights of people cannot be violated by acts of Congress unduly targeting them by passing a bill of attainer. A bill of attainder is a law directed at an individual or group that accuses and convicts them without a trial. The due process of people is so important that Congress was precluded from making laws to incriminate people for actions previously committed. An ex post facto law is a law that makes a criminal act (not civil regulation, such as denial of a professional license) illegal that was innocent when done, or "after the fact", hereby not allowing an accused to make an informed decision about the legality of his or her actions before he or she acts.[67] The right to be brought before a judge, informed of the law and charges and receiving a trial, ensures a due or appropriate judicial process before a conviction.

Due process rights include civil liberties. The exclusionary rule prohibits evidence from being introduced at a criminal trial if it was obtained by violating your civil liberties protected under the Constitution. The main purpose of the exclusionary rule is to deter the government, usually the police, from violating a person's civil liberties and constitutional rights. If the government cannot use evidence obtained in violation of a person's rights, it will be less likely to infringe on the person's rights.

The right to self-protection in a police arrest is guaranteed under the Fifth Amendment which provides that no person "shall be compelled to be a witness against himself...".[68] This has been interpreted to establish a guarantee against compelled incrimination. *Miranda* rights come from the case that established that you have the right to be told that you possess these rights and guarantees.[69] Miranda rights are a set of warnings that must be given to an accused person that is in custody prior to any police interrogation. In order for the accused statement's to be later admissible in court, the accused must be clearly informed that: (1) he or she has the right to remain silent, (2) anything he or she says can be used against him in court, (3) he or she has the right to an attorney, and (4) if he or she cannot afford an attorney, one will be appointed.

While the above are some examples, additional civil rights and liberties include a right to be told why you are being arrested, a right to not be tried twice for the same crime, a right to an attorney and the right to resist questioning.

---

[67] U.S. Const. Art. I §9 prohibits the federal government and U.S. Const. Art. I §10 prohibits the states from passing ex post facto laws.

[68] U.S. Const. Amend. V.

[69] *Miranda v. Arizona*, 384 U.S. 436 (1966).

# CIVIL LIBERTIES—UNDERSTANDING THE RIGHT TO PRIVACY

What is the right to privacy? While one can argue that the founders created a limited government and never intended it to be powerful enough to infringe on the private lives of Americans, none of them thought it a serious enough threat to put it into the document itself. The right to privacy is a judicial creation of the Supreme Court in the 1965 case of *Griswold v. Connecticut.*[70] In this case the Court declared that the Constitution does guarantee a "zone of privacy" within a "penumbra" of existing fundamental constitutional guarantees and amendments. Since there was no actual right to privacy mentioned in the Constitution or any of the amendments, the justices "found" such a right to be implied in the Bill of Rights. These specific rights for privacy emanated from:

- The First Amendment protection of one's beliefs and speech
- The Fourth Amendment protection against unreasonable searches and seizures
- The Fifth Amendment protection against self-incrimination
- The Ninth Amendment's promise that one's rights weren't limited to the ones enumerated in the document

The Supreme Court extended this right to privacy marriage, sexual relations, abortion, childrearing and LGTBQ rights in later decisions. The right to privacy has become controversial because, through constant interpretation of the Constitution, the Court creates new rights not explicit in the Constitution. The disagreement arises because the precedent set in *Griswold* was the basis for the landmark, and most controversial, decision in *Roe v. Wade*, which held the right to privacy includes the right to abortion with some limitations.[71] Although contraception

---

[70] *Griswold v. Connecticut*, 381 U.S. 479 (1965).
[71] *Roe v. Wade, 410 U.S. 113* (1973).

may not be all that controversial when considered today (unless we are talking about the provision of health care), abortion still definitely is decades after the *Roe* decision.

The conflict over the right to privacy brings us back to Hamilton's *Federalist* #84. Underlying this controversy is an interesting constitutional issue: whether the Constitution should be read literally as the founders wrote it or whether it can be read flexibly in the light of contemporary circumstances. The first position is exactly the argument that Hamilton feared would be made if a Bill of Rights were to be attached to the Constitution. The right to privacy has become a target of those who argue that position.

The method in which the court systems interpret the Constitution can be either strict constructionists or judicial interpretivists. Strict constructionists are scholars and judges who believe that the Constitution should be read just as it was written. Judicial interpretivists are those who believe that the founders could not have anticipated all the changes that make the world today different from theirs and, therefore, that judges should read the Constitution as the founders would write it in light of modern-day experience. Strict constructionists generally interpret the Constitution to limit rights to privacy, while judicial interpretivists recognize the evolving right to privacy as implied in the Constitution.

The method in which a justice interprets the Constitution determines how rights are created from the constitution. The political significance of this argument today can give people new civil rights and liberties or take them away. Since individual interpretations of the Constitution have such clear policy implications, Supreme Court confirmation hearings have often become battlegrounds as well. Reproductive rights are not the only ones that fall under the right to privacy. Supporters of LGBTQ rights tried to use the right to privacy to fight laws that criminalized homosexual behavior but were initially unsuccessful. Slowly, the Court recognized the LGBT community has some protections under the right to privacy by holding unmarried couples (largely LGBTQ couples since same sex marriage was illegal at the time) had the same right to obtain contraception as married couples.[72] The movement has had setbacks in 1986 when the Court held that the Constitutional guarantees don't prohibit states from criminalizing sex between people of the same sex. In *Bowers v. Hardwick*, the Court held that the right of privacy recognized in cases such as *Griswold* and *Roe* does not prevent the criminalization of homosexual conduct between consenting adults. [73] The opinion of the Supreme Court pendulum swung again in 2003 and reversed their prior decision and held that the due process clause gave people "the full right to engage in private conduct without government intervention...[and there is] no legitimate state interest which can justify its intrusion into the individual's personal and private life."[74]

A landmark decision in 2015 held that the fundamental right to marry under the right to privacy is guaranteed to same-sex couples in *Obergefell v. Hodges*.[75] While the law is slowly moving in the direction to eventually provide full equal protection for the LGTBQ community, it is likely that real change will be incremental, and the movement has a long way to go.

Recently, the Supreme Court overturned Roe v. Wade. *Dobbs v. Jackson Women's Health Organization, 597 U.S. ___ (2022)* Supreme Court case that reversed *Roe v. Wade* and *Planned Parenthood of Southeastern Pennsylvania v. Casey*, the decisions that originally asserted the fundamental right to an abortion prior to the viability of the fetus. *Dobbs v. Jackson* states that the Constitution does not confer a right to abortion, and the authority to regulate abortion is "returned to the people and their elected representatives."

The overturning of Roe v. Wade last summer dramatically changed the landscape for people seeking reproductive care. It has impacted other

---

[72] *Eisenstadt v. Baird*, 405 U.S. 438 (1972).

[73] *Bowers v. Hardwick*, 478 U.S. 186 (1986).

[74] *Lawrence v. Texas*, 539 U.S. 558 (2003).

[75] *Obergefell v. Hodges*, 576 U.S. 644 (2015)

aspects of American privacy as well. Since the Dobbs decision, concerns about data privacy have grown. Research has shown that mainstream period tracking apps have faulty or weak security. A person's browser history, search history, location and private messages can be used by law enforcement or private citizens to pursue people who are suspected of having or aiding an abortion. There are cases in which American prosecutors have used text messages and online research as evidence against women facing criminal charges related to the end of their pregnancies. In Nebraska, a woman was charged with helping her teenage daughter end her pregnancy at about 24 weeks after investigators uncovered Facebook messages in which the two discussed using medication to induce an abortion. The landscape of privacy is changing.

## KEY TERMS

**Bill of Rights**: The first ten amendments to the United States Constitution guaranteeing certain fundamental rights and protections to individuals.

**Civil Liberties**: Individual rights that limit government power, guaranteed by the Bill of Rights and the Constitution.

**Civil Rights**: The freedom of groups to fully participate in the public life of a nation, often empowering the government to act and protect these groups based on characteristics such as race, gender, or sexual orientation.

**Compelling Interest Test**: A standard of review used by courts to determine if a law that affects constitutional rights is necessary to achieve a compelling government interest and is narrowly tailored to achieve that interest.

**Establishment Clause**: A clause in the First Amendment that prohibits Congress from making laws respecting the establishment of religion, ensuring the separation of church and state.

**Exclusionary Rule**: A legal principle that prohibits the use of evidence obtained in violation of a person's constitutional rights in a criminal trial.

**Free Exercise Clause**: A clause in the First Amendment that prohibits Congress from making laws that interfere with the free exercise of religion.

**Habeas Corpus**: The right to be brought before a judge and informed of the charges and evidence against you, protecting against unlawful imprisonment.

**Incorporation**: The process by which the Supreme Court has applied the protections of the Bill of Rights to the states using the Fourteenth Amendment.

**Lemon Test**: A three-pronged test established in Lemon v. Kurtzman to determine if a law violates the Establishment Clause by assessing whether it has a secular purpose, its primary effect neither advances nor inhibits religion, and it does not produce excessive government entanglement with religion.

**Miranda Rights**: Warnings that must be given to an accused person in custody before any police interrogation, informing them of their rights to remain silent, to an attorney, and that anything they say can be used against them in court.

**Natural Rights**: Inalienable rights that are conferred by "Nature and Nature's God" and cannot be taken away by any government.

**Prior Restraint**: A legal doctrine that prohibits the government from censoring or preventing the publication of speech before it occurs.

**Rights**: Powers or privileges granted to individuals either by an agreement among people or by law.

**Secular Purpose**: The requirement that a law must have a non-religious, temporal purpose to pass the Lemon Test.

**Strict Constructionists**: Judges or scholars who believe that the Constitution should be interpreted as it was originally written, without inferring additional rights or meanings.

**The Right to Privacy**: A judicially created right implied in the Bill of Rights, protecting individuals from government intrusion into personal matters such as marriage, sexual relations, and childrearing.

**Due Process Rights**: Protections against arbitrary deprivation of life, liberty, or property by the government, ensuring fair procedures.

# CHAPTER 10

# CIVIL RIGHTS IN AMERICA

Not all people have always had equality under the law in the United States of America. The dilemma of equal protection is vital to ensure that some people in America do not have more rights afforded them than others. Discrimination occurs when the government treats its citizens differently and usually takes the form of denying a benefit or imposing a burden or penalty on a group of persons simply because of a societal dislike for that social class. The deal is to know what kinds of discrimination are permitted and what kinds are not.

Slavery abolitionists and women's rights, and African American civil rights movements set a precedent in American political history. Three civil rights amendments to the United States Constitution, the Fifteenth, Nineteenth, and Twenty-Sixth— prevent both the states and the federal government from abridging citizens' right to vote based on race, sex, and age. Their tactics to engage people around spreading their ideas and their tricks to influence public opinion and the policymaking process still serve as inspiration these days. The rights gained have significantly improved the quality of life for many in America, especially for minorities. Boycotting and desegregation practices are still prevalent among human rights activists.

## INTRODUCTION TO CIVIL RIGHTS IN AMERICA

Civil rights are constitutionally supported, guaranteeing that government officials treat citizens equally and base their decisions on merit rather than race, gender, or other personal characteristics. In the United States of America, it is unlawful for a school or university to discriminate against a student based on its identity and background. In the 1960s and 1970s, many states still had separate schools where only students of a certain race or gender could study and afford a career. Over time, the courts ruled that these policies violated students' civil rights who could not be admitted because of those discriminatory rules.

Although the United States Constitution, as written in 1787, did not formally include a *Bill of Rights*, the idea was proposed and discussed. United States Constitution framers decided to dismiss the bill during the final week of the Constitutional Convention. They dismissed it because there were more important issues to address since the union was still weak and national unrest was still likely to happen. Besides, they perceived that they already had appropriately covered rights concerns in the American Constitution's main body.

The United States' founding principles are liberty, equality, and justice. Throughout its history as an independent country, not all its subjects have enjoyed equal access to rights and opportunities, nor have they been considered citizens by law. Discrimination can take many forms, from *segregation to forced mass sterilization policies*, based on sex, income, race, ethnicity or country of origin, religion, sexual orientation, or physical or mental abilities. Federally-funded sterilization programs took place in 32 states continuously through the 20th century in America; for around 70 years, California led the country in the number of sterilization procedures performed on men and women. For much of United States history, most of its people have been deprived of civil and fundamental rights, and sometimes of citizenship itself.

The struggle for equality and civil rights for all continues today since many subjects still encounter prejudice, violence, injustice, and negative stereotypes that lead to exclusion, discrimination, and marginalization.

## CONSTITUTIONAL SOURCE

*The Equal Protection Clause of the Fourteenth Amendment* only applies to the states and provides that "[no state shall] deny any person within its jurisdiction the equal protection of the laws".[76] There is no equivalent counterpart in the United States Constitution applying to the federal government. Therefore, the language of the Fourteenth Amendment is limited to state action.

Nevertheless, the Supreme Court has held that the federal government's grossly unreasonable discrimination violates the *Due Process Clause of the Fifth Amendment*, where the language applies to the federal government. Thus, there are two equal protection guarantees for each state and federal government. While the protections stem from different constitutional sources, the Court applies the same standards in interpreting those protections and determining appropriate discrimination.

When the Court tries to answer what is permitted governmental discrimination, it applies three different standards based on the classification of persons involved: (1) *suspect classifications or fundamental rights*, (2) *quasi-suspect classification*, and (3) any other classification of persons.

## DISCRIMINATION BASED ON SUSPECT CLASSIFICATIONS

The Supreme Court has held that specific kinds of government actions that discriminate against individuals are inherently suspect and, therefore, must automatically be subject to the strictest judicial scrutiny. This stipulation means the government must have a valid reason to discriminate and has the burden of proof, or the party must prove that their actions are constitutional. The Court determined that there are generally four suspect classifications of people: race, religion, national origin, and alienage. However, this is not a complete list, and as the law develops, the

---

[76] For more information, see the Constitution of the United States, Amend. XVI, Sec. 1.

current classifications could be modified, and they may later add more classifications.

Suppose a law or governmental action discriminates against persons that belong to a suspect classification. In that case, the Court will review the law under the most rigorous review called strict scrutiny. Strict scrutiny means asking if the law is necessary to achieve a compelling state interest. If strict scrutiny is applied, the law or government action will be struck down unless the government proves and demonstrates to the Court the crucial or necessary reason for the discriminatory action to accomplish a vital or compelling governmental interest or result.

Instances whereby the government classifies or uses an individual's race and national origin when applying the law, have been closely reviewed by the Court over the last century. During World War II, Franklin Roosevelt issued an executive order requiring people of Japanese descent, two-thirds of whom were citizens, to be relocated and placed in internment camps, where they stayed until the order was suspended in 1944. The order was challenged on equal protection grounds and reached the Supreme Court in 1944. In *Korematsu v. United States*, the Supreme Court decided that laws that treat people differently because of race are highly suspicious, making race a suspect classification.[77] In the majority opinion, Former Associate Justice of the Supreme Court of the United States Hugo Black declared "all legal restrictions which curtail the civil rights of a single group are immediately suspect. That is not to say that all such restrictions are unconstitutional; it is to say that courts must subject them to the most rigid scrutiny. Pressing public necessity may sometimes justify the existence of such restrictions; racial antagonism never can".

Since the government action, the executive order has used individual's race and national origin; the Court had to apply *strict scrutiny* when asking if the action was constitutional. In Korematsu, it was the only

---

[77] See Kenney, Karen L, and Friedman, Richard D. *Korematsu V. the United States: World War II Japanese-American Internment Camps*. Minneapolis: ABDO Pub, 2013. Print..

clear racial discrimination case upheld despite applying strict scrutiny. The Court found placing the Japanese Americans in the camps was necessary to achieve *national security's compelling interest*. The Court held there was a compelling state purpose in national security. However, this holding was vital because it set a precedent and legal standard of review that legislators have used to evaluate laws that had discriminated against based on race and national origin.

Becoming a suspect class sounds like a good thing since it means that laws that discriminate against one's group get the strictest level of scrutiny. Nevertheless, it has proven to be a double-edged sword for racial groups because it tends to strike down laws that discriminate against one and laws that discriminate in one's favor. The efforts that groups have had to gain higher levels of scrutiny applied to the laws that treat them differently have been grueling. Moreover, even when the outcome is successful and discriminatory laws get annulled, only de jure discrimination formally is ended, while de facto discrimination may still be prevalent.

In United States constitutional law, when a court finds that a law infringes a fundamental right, it will also apply the strict scrutiny standard to hold it until the government can demonstrate that the law or regulation is necessary to achieve a *compelling state interest*. The United States Constitution protects certain fundamental constitutional rights and civil liberties.[78] If rights are denied to everyone, it is a substantive due process problem. If they are denied to some individuals but not to others, it is an equal protection problem. In either case, the standard of strict scrutiny will be applied.

Various privacy rights, including marriage, sexual relations, abortion, and childrearing, are fundamental rights. Thus, regulations affecting these rights are reviewed under the strict scrutiny standard and upheld only if necessary to protect a compelling interest.

---

[78] Even if lawyers and political scientists use to make a distinction between civil liberties and civil rights, they have interpreted the United States Constitution to protect both.

## DISCRIMINATION BASED ON QUASI-SUSPECT CLASSIFICATION

Laws that discriminate according to gender do not get the same level of scrutiny applied to race and other suspect classifications. *Quasi-suspect classifications* are based on gender and legitimacy (such as legitimate and illegitimate children), and representatives review them with a less rigorous analysis. When analyzing government action based on quasi-suspect classifications, the Court will apply the intermediate standard and strike down the law or government action unless it is substantially related to a significant government interest. As with strict scrutiny, *intermediate scrutiny* also places the burden of proof on the government.

First, when a law creates a gender classification, intermediate scrutiny will apply. As stated in *United States v. Virginia*, "parties who seek to defend gender-based government action must demonstrate an exceedingly persuasive justification for that action." (Ginsburg and Supreme Court Of The United States). *The important governmental interest* used to justify discrimination based on gender must be genuine, meaning it has to be reliable and cannot be overly broad or generalized. When, in *United States v. Virginia*, a state military school's policy of admitting only men was challenged, the state attempted to justify it, claiming that it offers a diversity of *educational approaches*. Also, that females would not be able to meet the male-only military school's physical requirements.

The Supreme Court found these arguments unconvincing. There was no evidence that that the single-sex school was established or maintained with a view of fostering diversity of educational opportunities, and there was some evidence that some women could meet the school's physical requirements. The state's argument of a vital governmental interest was not genuine and had no evidence to prove their claims were valid.

Intermediate scrutiny is not as hard to overcome as strict scrutiny. Therefore, there are more examples of where the Court has upheld classification or discrimination based on gender. A state law that excluded normal pregnancy and childbirth from state disability benefits was upheld that the law did not create a classification based on gender. The program's purpose was to create classifications based on the risk of disability, and normal pregnancies did not create such a risk.[79]

The Court has also reviewed discrimination against men. Laws punishing males but not females for statutory rape were upheld because the Court found the classification to be substantially related to the vital interest of preventing minors' pregnancy.[80] While other laws that preferred males over females to act as an administrator of an estate[81] or only authorize wives to be eligible to receive alimony[82] were struck down because there was no substantial relationship to a significant government interest.

## DISCRIMINATION BASED ON OTHER GROUPS' CLASSIFICATIONS

All other classifications are reviewed under the rational basis standard and will be upheld unless they bear no rational relationship to any conceivable legitimate government interest. Nevertheless, the classification will not meet the standard if the government has no interest in discriminating against a group of persons other than a societal fear or dislike of them. The understanding is that for any class of persons that is not a suspect or quasi-suspect class defined by the Court, then the rational basis standard will apply.

---

[79] For more information, see Stewart, Potter, and Supreme Court Of The United States. *U.S. Reports: Geduldig v. Aiello, 417 U.S. 484.* 1973. Periodical. Library of Congress, www.loc.gov/item/usrep417484/.

[80] See Rehnquist, William H, and Supreme Court Of The United States. *U.S. Reports: Michael M. v. Sonoma County Superior Court, 450 U.S. 464. 1980.* Periodical. Retrieved from the Library of Congress, www.loc.gov/item/usrep450464/.

[81] See Supreme Court Of The United States. U.S. Reports: Reed v. Reed, 404 U.S. 71. 1971. Periodical. Retrieved from the Library of Congress, www.loc.gov/item/usrep404071/.

[82] See Brennan, William J., Jr, and Supreme Court Of The United States. *U.S. Reports: Orr v. Orr, 440 U.S. 268. 1978.* Periodical. Library of Congress, www.loc.gov/item/usrep440268/.

The Court has held that several classifications are not suspect. Age is not a suspect class. Thus, government action based on age will be upheld if the classification has a rational basis. Laws that force police officers to retire at age 50, even though physically fit as a young officer, or judges to retire at age 70 do not violate the *Equal Protection Clause*. Mental disabilities are also not suspect classifications. The Court struck down a zoning ordinance that prohibited a group of mentally disabled persons from sharing a residential home because the only reason to deny them the benefit was their mental condition. The government has no legitimate interest in prohibiting mentally disabled persons from living together.[83]

Utterly because a law or governmental action results in discrimination is not sufficient to trigger strict or intermediate scrutiny or the rational basis test, the government's law or action must be intentional. The intent is shown in three different ways: (1) *facial discrimination*, (2) *discriminatory application*, or (3) *discriminatory motive*. Once the Court has determined that there was an intent to discriminate, the Court will then apply and look at the law through one of the strict standards of review.

*Facial discrimination* is when a law includes classifications that make evident social distinctions based on race and gender on its "face" or within its terms. In *Strauder v. West Virginia*, the Supreme Court considered a law that provided that only white males can serve as jurors[84]. In such cases, the Court can then apply the appropriate standard of review for racial and gender classifications. Another indicator of facial discrimination is *de jure discrimination*, which is discrimination by laws. De jure segregation, or legalized segregation of Black and White people, was present in almost

---

[83] See White, Byron Raymond, and Supreme Court Of The United States. *U.S. Reports: Cleburne v. Cleburne Living Center, 473 U.S. 432. 1984.* Periodical. Library of Congress, www.loc.gov/item/usrep473432/.

[84] See Strong, William, and Supreme Court Of The United States. U.S. Reports: Strauder v. West Virginia, 100 U.S. 303. 1879. Periodical. Library of Congress, www.loc.gov/item/usrep100303.

every aspect of life in the South during the Jim Crow era: from public transportation to cemeteries, from prisons to health care, from residences to libraries. Under segregation laws that, on their face, created racial classifications, Black and White people were to be separated, purportedly to minimize violence. De jure segregation, or "Jim Crow," lasted from the 1880s to 1964. *Jim Crow laws* were efficient in perpetuating the idea of "white superiority" and "black inferiority."

In contrast, *de facto discrimination* results from life circumstances, habits, customs, or socioeconomic status. De facto segregation is the direct manifestation of de jure segregation. While the Court eventually held laws that segregated races were unconstitutional, it could not change its people's hearts and minds. If people did not want to be in the presence of another ethnicity or race, they could certainly make this a reality. So, de jure segregation was implemented by law, de facto segregation, shared understandings, and personal choice.

Second, *discriminatory application* applies when a law appears neutral and fair on its face but is applied differently to different groups of people and cultures. If the persons challenging the governmental action can prove that the government officials applying the law had a discriminatory purpose, representatives will likely annul the law. In *Yick Wo v. Hopkins*, a law prohibited people from operating a laundry mat in wooden buildings but gave local governmental officials discretion to grant exceptions[85]. At that time in history, the laundry mats in that area were owned almost exclusively by people of Chinese descent. The governmental officials only ended up granting exceptions to non-Asian laundromat owners. The law had a discriminatory application based on the suspect classification of race and national origin and was annulled.

Sometimes, a law or government action will appear neutral and fair on its face and its application but will have a discriminatory impact on a

---

[85] For more information and insights, see Matthews, Stanley, and Supreme Court Of The United States. *U.S. Reports: Yick Wo v. Hopkins, 118 U.S. 356. 1885.* Periodical. Library of Congress, www.loc.gov/item/usrep118356.

particular class of persons. Such law will be found to involve a prohibited classification (and be subject to the level of scrutiny appropriate to that classification) only if a court finds that the law-making body enacted the law for a discriminatory purpose. It can be challenging to prove that the government had a discriminatory purpose when passing a law. In *McCleskey v. Kemp*, the statistics and historical facts showing that black defendants in capital cases are much more likely to receive the death penalty than white defendants in similar cases. However, the statistical evidence was not enough to prove that the state had a discriminatory motive or purpose when convicting the black defendants. Moreover, the convictions, the governmental action were upheld. It takes more than statistical evidence to prove a discriminatory purpose.

It is important to remember that the Equal Protection and Due Process Clauses only prohibit state or government action. Furthermore, while private actors are not subject to the *Equal Protection Clause*, they may be subject to other laws preventing discrimination. For example, the federal Age Discrimination in *Employment Act* prohibits age discrimination for people who are age 40 or older. Similar laws prohibit workplace discrimination based on disability, race and national origin, genetic information, pregnancy, religion, and sex. These laws were passed by Congress and enforced by the *Equal Employment Opportunity Commission.*

## THE CASE OF RACE

It is essential to understand the origins of discrimination to understand the journey and development of civil rights. Why do some people call slavery America's original sin? The narratives that white slave-owners used to justify slavery created an image of an inferior race that required white mastery. These tales established a set of stereotypes of African Americans that continue to haunt the nation. Researchers have evidenced stereotypes' lingering effects in the relatively recent cases and development of law discussed above. While slavery has not been prevalent in the United States for over a century, racial stereotypes are still prevalent today.

As slavery persisted in the country's beginnings, the landmark decision in *Dred Scott v. Sandford*[86], which held African Americans were not citizens and could not be free, increased tensions between the North and South and helped incite the anti-slavery movement. The Supreme Court came up with the principle of separate but equal. This decision created a two-class system in America. The Civil War did not settle the issue of slavery in the United States. The American Civil War (1861–1865) was fought mainly over slavery, and even the conclusion of that event did not put the issue to rest. Immediately following the war and the passage of the *Thirteenth Amendment* of the United States Constitution banning slavery, white southerners tried to seize back the power they had lost, bypassing state and local laws.

The laws passed after the Civil War limited the rights of African Americans. The arena of national legislative politics was closed to African Americans after the North turned to its own affairs following the Civil War Amendments' passage. Black codes were known as state and local laws that denied freed blacks the right to vote, go to school, and own property. The era of Jim Crow laws began. To shut down the black codes, the Northern-dominated Congress passed the Fourteenth and Fifteenth Amendments that granted citizenship and the right to vote to African Americans. *Jim Crow laws* were passed by white southerners that tried to re-create the power relations of slavery by running around the amendments designed to give blacks citizenship rights. These were forms of de jure discrimination that created a segregated society.

While the Civil War attempted and failed to remedy the societal damage of slavery, Congress and the Supreme Court were also slow with their

---

[86]  See Taney, Roger Brooke, and Supreme Court Of The United States. *U.S. Reports: Dred Scott v. Sandford, 60 U.S. 19 How. 393. 1856.* Periodical. Retrieved from the Library of Congress, www.loc.gov/item/usrep060393a/.

efforts. Decades after the Civil War, in *Plessy v. Ferguson*[87], the Supreme Court still did not provide equal treatment of all citizens and came up with the principle of separate but equal use of public facilities by different races and put the seal of constitutional approval on segregation. This established a two-class system in America.

In the 1930s, the NAACP began to use a law school-centered strategy to undermine Plessy slowly. The separate but equal view held a standard that separate facilities were legal if they were equal. Of course, this was not equal at all. This circumstance gestured that the courts would not be a profitable arena for blacks to fight in either. In 1910, African Americans who refused to accept the Jim Crow second-class citizenship organized the National Association for the Advancement of Colored People.

The NAACP's calculation was that to most Americans, law schools would be a less threatening area for desegregation than primary education, but one where the justices of the Supreme Court were particularly well suited to find arguments against segregation to be persuasive. In Brown v. Board of Education, the Court finally reversed its prior ruling, holding that segregation itself was unequal and the separate but equal doctrine that had prevailed in the legal community for more than half a century was unconstitutional.[88]

Even after the Brown decision, the right to equality was fought with boycotts to address systematic discrimination. One year after the Brown decision, when Rosa Parks refused to vacate her bus seat for a white man in Montgomery, Alabama and launched the bus system boycott, African Americans realized that their purchasing power could be a considerable

---

[87] See Supreme Court Of The United States. *U.S. Reports: Plessy v. Ferguson, 163 U.S. 537. 1895.* Periodical. Retrieved from the Library of Congress, www.loc.gov/item/usrep163537/.

[88] See Warren, Earl, and Supreme Court Of The United States. *U.S. Reports: Brown v. Board of Education, 347 U.S. 483. 1953.* Periodical. Library of Congress, <www.loc.gov/item/usrep347483/.

political weapon[89]. This circumstance was to be followed by the quick realization that television's new technology could bring their plight out of isolation in the South to the whole country's attention.

The battle for equality was also fought with public opinion. The civil rights movement was fought in the arenas of public opinion and, finally, in Congress. In 1964 and 1965, civil rights legislation, initiated by President John Kennedy and then pushed through Congress by President Lyndon Johnson after Kennedy's assassination, removed most of the legal barriers to integration. Southern Congress members staged a filibuster to prevent a vote on the Senate's legislation, voting against their party's president. Most notably, the Civil Rights Act of 1964 prohibited segregation in public places based on race, religion, or national origin. It also created the Equal Employment Opportunity Commission that enforces laws that prohibit discrimination in the workplace. The civil rights movement was the combination of all these strategies used to alleviate African Americans' plight.

Did the civil rights movement eradicate de facto discrimination as well as de jure? One irony of all the legislative changes was that it ended the de jure discrimination in the South but pointed out the shortcomings of legal change as a method to redress de facto segregation in the North. Segregation in the North arose from long-term economic patterns and demographic changes that left African Americans in the city centers and succeeding waves of newly assimilated white immigrants in the suburbs. De facto discrimination cannot be remedied by fixing laws. It requires an effort to fix the outcomes, which strikes many Americans as fundamentally unfair. Despite the hard-won changes in laws, demeaning racial narratives were still woven into the American story and still determined how African Americans were treated and fared in rules and institutions based on white privilege.

[89] See Krutz, Glen S. *American Government 2e.*, 2019. Internet resource. especially chapter 5, for an in-depth analysis on how boycotts were used to address systematic discrimination in the United States.

Does the United States still have a race problem? Racial discrimination endures as one of American politics' defining issues, especially as demographic change forces whites to grapple with sharing minority status with other racial groups. Systemic racism is built into the American system to give whites preference and stacks the deck against people of color. The battle for equal rights does not end with African Americans. People of color who have had to fight for equal treatment by the law also include Native Americans, Latinos, and Asians. The assimilation of European immigrants has traditionally been about their ability to fit in; the assimilation of people of color has depended on the willingness of the white population to give up racist narratives to accept them.

The government has a compelling interest in remedying past discrimination against a racial or ethnic minority. Thus, if a court finds that a governmental agency has engaged in racial discrimination, it may exercise affirmative action, a race-conscious remedy to help end the discrimination and ease the effects. A remedy of this type is permissible under the *Equal Protection Clause* because it is narrowly tailored to further the compelling interest to eliminate discrimination. For example, when it has been proven that a public employer engaged in persistent racial discrimination, a court may order relief that establishes a goal for hiring or promoting minority persons to eliminate the effects of the past discrimination.

## THE CASE OF GENDER

*The women's rights movement* began in Seneca Falls in 1848. Sexism, like racism, is pervasive, often unrecognized, and has deep cultural roots. The women's rights movement is commonly dated from the Seneca Falls (NY) Convention of 1848, where the first woman's rights convention was held. The widely accepted narrative that kept wealthy white women out of public life was that they were too good and pure for the rough and tumbled corruption of public life. As with the racial equality movement, the women's suffrage movement was also gradual and spanned several decades.

Women fought for equality across all levels of government. On the western frontier, women worked side by side with men to carve a life out of the wilderness. The state-level effort promised more but slower success for women's rights. By 1912, women could vote in states that accounted for 74 electoral votes for the presidency. The *Nineteenth Amendment (1920)* gave women the right to vote. More equal rights would have required the passage of the *Equal Rights Amendment.* It was never ratified by the states but still discussed in current political platforms.

Modern legislation has called for equality for women. The *Lilly Ledbetter Fair Pay Act of 2009* requires equal pay for equal work. Women often make less money than men for the same work. The glass ceiling is the concept that women are still a minority in places where power is wielded. *Cultural attitudes* toward women are changing (e.g., the #MeToo movement) and will continue to change.

## SEXUAL ORIENTATION AND GENDER IDENTITY

Unlike race and gender, the movement for equal protection for LGBTQ (lesbian, gay, bisexual, transgender, and queer or questioning) is still in its beginnings. It has only gained momentum in the last couple of decades. The movement seeks to accomplish what the race and gender movements have only recently achieved- guarantees for federal and state civil rights and protections against discrimination.

The Court addressed the first step in considering LGBTQ rights in *One, Inc. v. Olsen*, which primarily expanded the right of free speech by establishing that material published for a gay audience was not inherently obscene.[90] The movement had had setbacks in 1986 when the Court held that the *14th Amendment's Due Process guarantee* does not prohibit states from criminalizing sex between people of the same sex. The opinion of the Supreme Court pendulum swung again in 2003 and reversed their

[90] See Supreme Court Of The United States. *U.S. Reports: One, Incorporated, v. Olesen, 355 U.S. 371. 1957.* Periodical. Library of Congress, www.loc.gov/item/usrep355371/.

prior decision and held that the due process clause gave people "the full right to engage in private conduct without government intervention… [and there is] no legitimate state interest which can justify its intrusion into the individual's personal and private life". (Kennedy and Supreme Court of The United States, Lawrence et. al. Texas)

A landmark decision in 2015 held that the fundamental right to marry under the right to privacy is guaranteed to same-sex couples in *Obergefell v. Hodges*. While the law is slowly moving toward providing complete equal protection for the LGBTQ community eventually, real change will likely be incremental. The movement still has a long way to go.

## KEY TERMS

**Abolitionists**: Individuals who advocated for the end of slavery.

**Bill of Rights**: The first ten amendments to the United States Constitution, guaranteeing specific freedoms and protections to citizens.

**Black Codes**: State and local laws that denied freed blacks the right to vote, go to school, and own property after the Civil War.

**Boycotting**: The act of refusing to purchase, use, or participate in something as a way of protesting.

**Civil Rights**: Rights that protect individuals' freedom from infringement by governments, social organizations, and private individuals.

**Civil Rights Act of 1964**: A landmark piece of legislation that prohibited segregation in public places and banned employment discrimination.

**De Facto Discrimination**: Discrimination that occurs in practice but is not necessarily ordained by law.

**De Jure Discrimination**: Discrimination that is enshrined in law and official policy.

**Due Process Clause**: Clauses in the Fifth and Fourteenth Amendments to the United States Constitution that provide legal protections against arbitrary denial of life, liberty, or property by the government.

**Equal Employment Opportunity Commission (EEOC)**: A federal agency that enforces laws against workplace discrimination.

**Equal Protection Clause**: A clause in the Fourteenth Amendment to the United States Constitution that mandates equal protection under the law to all people within a state's jurisdiction.

**Fifteenth Amendment**: An amendment to the United States Constitution that prohibits the federal and state governments from denying a citizen the right to vote based on race.

**Fourteenth Amendment**: An amendment to the United States Constitution that grants citizenship and equal civil and legal rights to all people born or naturalized in the United States, including former slaves.

**Glass Ceiling**: A metaphorical barrier preventing women and minorities from rising to the highest ranks in a corporation or organization.

**Intermediate Scrutiny**: A standard of review used by courts to evaluate laws that involve quasi-suspect classifications, such as gender.

**Jim Crow Laws**: State and local laws that enforced racial segregation in the Southern United States.

**Lilly Ledbetter Fair Pay Act of 2009**: A law that aims to address wage discrimination, making it easier for workers to sue for pay discrimination.

**National Association for the Advancement of Colored People (NAACP)**: An African-American civil rights organization in the United States, formed in 1909.

**Nineteenth Amendment**: An amendment to the United States Constitution that prohibits the states and the federal government from denying the right to vote to citizens of the United States on the basis of sex.

**Plessy v. Ferguson**: A landmark 1896 Supreme Court decision that upheld the constitutionality of racial segregation under the "separate but equal" doctrine.

**Quasi-Suspect Classification**: Categories, such as gender and legitimacy, that are subject to intermediate scrutiny in legal reviews of discriminatory laws.

**Rational Basis Standard**: A standard of review used by courts to evaluate laws that classify people into groups that are not considered suspect or quasi-suspect.

**Strict Scrutiny**: The highest standard of review used by courts to evaluate the constitutionality of laws, typically applied to laws that affect fundamental rights or involve suspect classifications such as race.

**Suspect Classifications**: Categories of people who have historically been discriminated against and are therefore given heightened protection under the law, including race, religion, national origin, and alienage.

**Thirteenth Amendment**: An amendment to the United States Constitution that abolished slavery and involuntary servitude, except as punishment for a crime.

**Twenty-Sixth Amendment**: An amendment to the United States Constitution that prohibits the states and the federal government from using age as a reason for denying the right to vote to citizens who are at least 18 years old.

# CHAPTER 11

# THE LEGISLATIVE BRANCH

To successfully prevent the national government, or any group within it, from becoming exceedingly powerful, the United States Constitution divided the government into three branches with different powers and attributions. Congress can pass laws, but its power to do so can be checked by the United States president, who can veto potential legislation so that it ultimately cannot become a law.

Most of Congress's work activities and work take place in *l*egislative committees. The House of Representatives has 20 permanent committees. The Senate has 21, and there are four joint committees with members from both chambers. These congressional committees have purview over specific issues, and they identify potential issues that could be subject to legislative review. Some areas in which these committees' jurisdiction include agriculture, foreign affairs, budgets, and finance. House members from states with significant sectoral interests, such as agriculture, will likely seek these specific committees' positions.

To sit in the United States Congress, almost every member has to run for election and beat their opponent. The Seventeenth Amendment outlines how representatives should fill a vacancy caused by death, resignation, or removal from office.

## WHAT IS THE LEGISLATIVE BRANCH?

The legislative branch is one of the three branches of the United States government as outlined by the Constitution. The legislative comprises the two chambers of Congress, the House, and the Senate. The legislative government branch produces the laws, declares war, and regulates taxes, among other duties.

One hundred elected representatives, two from each state, compose the United States Senate. It is the Senate's upper chamber and has more powers than the House, such as the power to impeach the United States President and confirm Cabinet positions, Supreme Court Justices, and other positions. Since it has more specific powers and fewer members than the House, politicians have a more sought-after position. Citizens elect Senators to six-year terms with elections staggered, so approximately 1/3 of the Senate is up for election every even-numbered year.

The House of Representatives is the lower chamber of Congress, and it has 435 elected members. Unlike the Senate, the House is divided proportionally based on the population size of each state. The seven states with the lowest population have only one representative, while the most populous state, California, has 53 representatives in the House. The House also has powers that are unique to it, including impeaching federal officers and electing a United States President in the event of an Electoral College tie. A *Representative* serves a shorter term than a Senator, only two years, and is up for election every even-numbered year.

## HOW THE CONSTITUTION ESTABLISHED CONGRESS

The Constitution outlines the role of Congress in Article I. Article I, Section I, states:

> "All legislative Powers herein granted shall be vested in a Congress of the United States, which shall consist of a Senate and House of Representatives."

One of the key design elements from the Founding Fathers was making Congress bicameral. A bicameral legislature is a legislative body that has two chambers. When discussing the government's structure under the United States Constitution, the delegates from Virginia called for a bicameral legislature consisting of two Houses. Delegates from small states objected to the Virginia Plan, which ultimately prevailed.

Another proposal, the New Jersey Plan, called instead for a unicameral legislature with one House, in which each state would have one vote. Consequently, smaller states would have the same power in the national legislature as larger states. Notwithstanding, the larger states argued that they should be allotted more legislators to represent their interests because they had a more significant population. (Corwin, 48)

The two chambers of Congress in the United States were created with different characteristics to represent different interests to protect any region or state from getting too much power. Each state has equal representation in the Senate, while in the House, states with a higher population have more seats and thus more voting power. The House of Representatives has developed a more robust and structured leadership than the Senate. Because its members serve two-year terms, they regularly answer their constituency's demands when running for election or reelection. Even House members of the same party in the same state will occasionally disagree on different issues because of their specific districts' particular interests. The House can be highly partisan at times. In contrast, members of the Senate are furthest from the demands and scrutiny of their constituents. Because of their longer six-year terms, they will likely see every House member face their constituents' multiple times before they have to seek reelection.

The foundation of Congress and the Constitution's contents resulted from the bitter battle between Federalist and Anti-Federalist factions. The Federalists supported a strong federal government, while the Anti-Federalists wanted more power in the states' hands. In the Constitution's passage, the Federalists ultimately prevailed, but Congress's structure was a source of compromise. While not all Anti-Federalists agreed between the House's proportional representation and the Senate's equal representation, they also created state legislatures to compromise with Anti-Federalists.

Another compromise to Anti-Federalists was who elected members of the Senate. While the voting public elected members of the House, state legislatures initially elected their state's senators. This setting gave the state legislatures more power over federal policy. State legislatures elected senators until the Seventeenth Amendment's ratification in 1913, which changed senators' election to a popular vote by voters in the state.

The Senate and the House were made with two different structures so that they would represent different constituencies. Each member of government has a *constituency*, the individuals and groups whose interests the elected official represents. Senators represent their whole state when they go to Congress, and until 1913 they were closely tied to political interests in their state's legislature. Each House member represents a district in their state. For example, California has 53 distinct districts. Under this original design, representatives were supposed to represent the people and their opinions, while senators were representatives of their state and legislature.

The two chambers of Congress also have different qualification requirements and restrictions. A senator has to be at least 30 years old, a United States citizen for at least nine years, and be a resident of the state they are running to represent. A representative only has to be 25 years old, be a United States citizen for seven years, and live in the state they politically represent.

## HOW CONGRESS DOES ITS JOB

To adequately perform the duties given to Congress by the Constitution, the legislative body's structure has various leadership roles. Throughout United States history, the division of power for congressional leadership positions has evolved. Partisanship, narrow margins between the two parties, and the rise in leadership positions' power have marked and shaped modern congressional politics. The Speaker of the House and the Senate majority leader, the majority party's congressional leaders, have all-powerful tools at their disposal to conveniently punish party members who defect on a particular vote.

Most of Congress's work activities and work take place in *legislative committees*. The House of Representatives has 20 permanent committees. The Senate has 21, and there are four joint committees with members from both chambers. These congressional committees have purview over specific issues, and they identify potential issues that could be subject to legislative review. Some areas in which these committees' jurisdictions include agriculture, foreign affairs, budgets, and finance.

Initially, Senate committee membership was determined either by a vote by the full Senate or appointments by the committee's presiding officer. In 1846, the Senate changed its rules on committee appointments to streamline the process. Today, each party's leadership determines Senate committee membership and submissions to the floor for approval. Similarly, in the House, Democratic and Republican leadership determine which representatives to submit for committee membership approval. This situation gives each party's leadership significant power to keep incoming and incumbent Congress members in line with the respective party's vision.

In Congress, four main types of committees perform different roles and specialize in specific public policy areas. Standing committees are permanent as laid out in the House and Senate rules that have specific legislative jurisdiction. In this type of committee, members review and recommend legislative measures and monitor government agencies relevant to their jurisdiction. The Senate has 16 standing committees with 67 subcommittees, and the House has 20 standing committees with 97 subcommittees.

Select or special committees are established for a limited time, often to conduct investigations or research. If an emerging issue does not fall under a standing committee's purview or crosses multiple committees' jurisdiction, a select committee will be set up. While they put these committees in place for a limited time, they can renew them by their respective chambers, and sometimes they become permanent standing committees.

Conference committees are used to reconcile bills passed in both the House and the Senate. The conference committees are appointed on an ad hoc basis when a bill passes the House and Senate in various forms. Congress members sometimes skip these committees in the interest of expediency, in which one of the chambers relents to the other.

Lastly, joint committees are composed of members of both the House and the Senate. Joint committees are permanent and mainly perform housekeeping duties or conduct studies rather than doing legislative work. Leadership on these committees alternates between the Senate and the House.

The most influential role in the Senate is the Speaker of the House. This position was established in Article 1 Section II of the Constitution, but the office's power has grown significantly in the modern era. The Speaker is the House's presiding officer, the lower chamber of Congress's administrative head, and the majority party's head in the House. The Constitution does not call for the Speaker to have a partisan role, but the role has developed significantly over the years. The Speaker of the House is also third in line for the presidency.

The leader of the majority party in the Senate is known as the *Senate Majority Leader*. Unlike the Speaker of the House, the United States Constitution does not set this position. They are the majority party's head in the Senate and derive their power from their party and various Senate precedents. While the Senate Majority Leader does not enjoy as much formal power as the House's Speaker, they serve as the chief spokesperson for their party in the Senate. The leader of the party with fewer members in the Senate is known as the Senate Minority Leader. The Constitution established the Vice President as President of the United States Senate.

## CONGRESS'S ROLE IN THE SYSTEM OF CHECKS AND BALANCES

The Founding Fathers established the federal government as a system of checks and balances so no single branch of government, person, or political interest would become too powerful. The framers of the Constitution created such a system to satisfy the concerns of those who feared an overly strong central government. In this vein, Congress plays a crucial role and has some power over the executive and judicial branch, and vice versa.

Congress has three keyways to check the executive branch, and they give the legislative branch power to balance the President's power. The first and most important is *congressional oversight*. This provision refers to Congress's powers to oversee the executive branch and numerous federal agencies. Congress can review and keep an eye on various federal programs, administrative activities, and policies. The power to create an investigative committee, hold legislative hearings, and set budgets also fall under this category. The Constitution does not explicitly state that Congress has these powers; instead, these powers have been built up over time under the principle of implied powers.

One of the most visible powers of Congress in the modern presidency has been the power of impeachment. Congress has the sole power to impeach a government official and remove them from office. The House has the power to impeach government officials. The Senate can take up the House's impeachment, hold a trial, and vote in the Senate to convict and remove the impeached official from office. The Constitution explicitly gives Congress the power to impeach federal officials, and it also gives the legislative branch the power to bar impeached and convicted officials from running for office.

The House has passed articles of impeachment 21 times, three times against a sitting president. Presidents Andrew Johnson, Bill Clinton, and Donald Trump have all been impeached by the House, and the Senate later acquitted all. President Richard Nixon resigned in 1974 rather than face certain impeachment and a likely conviction in the Senate after the Watergate scandal. President Donald Trump is the only federal official to be impeached twice, and he was acquitted both times. Of those impeached, only eight officials were found guilty by the Senate and removed from office.

## HOW FEDERAL IMPEACHMENT WORKS

Impeachment is the process of bringing charges against a government official for wrongdoing. A trial may be held, and the official may be removed from office. The Constitution gives Congress the power to impeach federal officials. An official can be impeached for treason, bribery, and "other high crimes and misdemeanors."

1. The House of Representatives brings articles (charges) of impeachment against an official.
2. If the House adopts the articles by a simple majority vote, the official has been impeached.
3. The Senate holds an impeachment trial. In the case of a president, the U.S. Supreme Court chief justice presides.
4. If found guilty, the official is removed from office. They may never be able to hold elected office again.
5. If they are not found guilty, they may continue to serve in office.

The final important check Congress has on the executive branch is advice and consent, the Senate's role of confirming presidential appointments, including Supreme Court appointments, Cabinet officials, and ambassadors. The Constitution only grants this power to the Senate and not the House, and it is outlined in Article II Section 2 Clause 2. Initially, the Founding Fathers disagreed about the Senate's role in advising the President on nominations. In modern American politics, this power mostly plays out in high-profile congressional hearings with a majority of senators needed to approve appointments. A two-thirds majority of the Senate is also required to approve international treaties signed by the President.

Not only does Congress check and balance the power of the executive branch, but they also have powers to do the same with the judicial branch. Some of these powers are also within the above powers to check the executive, such as approving or denying judicial appointments and impeach and remove federal judges from office.

One of the leading powers that Congress has to check the judicial branch's power is to amend the Constitution. As the highest court in the land, the Supreme Court takes cases and gives rulings based on the justice's interpretation of the legislation or executive order constitutionality. As the federal courts use the Constitution as the basis for their legal rulings, the ability to amend the Constitution through the legislative process is one of Congress's most important powers.

Congress also has significant organizational power over the judicial branch. The United States Constitution grants Congress the power to determine how many Supreme Court Justices sit on the court and establish inferior courts. The Constitution only required the Supreme Court, but Congress has established a vast and powerful judicial branch with many inferior federal courts. Congress established the district courts system in the Judiciary Act of 1789. Today, there are 94 district courts in the country. Congress also established the 13 courts of appeals.

Furthermore, Congress can also pass laws that circumvent the courts' rulings. While one has traditionally assumed that the Supreme Court has the final say on applying the law regarding new legislation, congressional overrides have become more common in the modern era. William Eskridge Jr. and Matthew Christiansen found that congressional overrides grew dramatically between 1967 and 1990. While they have decreased after the Clinton impeachment, they remain a relevant tool for Congress to override the judicial branch.[91] Former Supreme Court

---

[91] Eskridge and Christiansen state that, before 1975, the United States Congress regularly overrode Supreme Court decisions interpreting federal statutes, but this mostly was an occasional phenomenon. The big turning point in United States history of statutory overrides was the 94th Congress (1975-1976), where the post-Watergate representatives overrode twenty Supreme

Justice Ruth Bader Ginsburg asked Congress to override the Supreme Court's ruling in 2013 and said, "Congress has, in the recent past, intervened to correct this Court's wayward interpretations of Title VII."[92]

While Congress has significant power to check the executive and judicial branches, these two branches also have been granted the ability to check and balance the legislative branch. The President's most important check on Congress is the power to veto legislation, thus directing the legislative agenda. However, this power is not ultimate, and Congress can reject a presidential veto by a two-thirds vote. The judicial branch primarily checks Congress's power through judicial review. One of the Supreme Court's primary roles is to review the legality of legislation passed by Congress.

## HOW CONGRESS MAKES THE LAW

How does Congress go about performing its most important duty, making laws through passing legislation? Both the Senate and House are constrained by the Constitution and norms that have been built up over time. Political interests may influence Congress members, who also have different commitments to their state or district's particular interests. Specifically, in the House, where representatives face reelection every two years, Congress members are constrained by electability concerns. With all this said, Congress is the place all new federal legislation has to go through, and it performs an essential role in American democracy.

Congress members are often drafting and working on bills for years before they reach the floor of Congress, and many bills go through a long and arduous process before they become the law of the land. Bills do not necessarily originate from Congress members, as political interest groups,

---

Court decisions. Amid political polarization, the 1990s was the golden age of overrides. Eskridge Jr., William N., and Matthew R. Christiansen. "Congressional Overrides of Supreme Court Statutory Interpretation Decisions, 1967-2011." *Texas Law Review*, vol. 92, 2014, doi:https://digitalcommons.law.yale.edu/cgi/viewcontent.cgi?article=5895&context=fss_papers.

[92] For more information, *see* Supreme Court. Vance v. Ball State University. 24 June 2013.

think tanks, policy groups, and more pitch ideas to congresspeople regularly. Whether a member of Congress presents himself with a bill or ideates and finetunes the whole piece of legislation, the next step for a bill is to be introduced in either Congress's chamber.

The bill's sponsor is the representative or Senator who first brings the bill to Congress. In addition to the bill's primary sponsor, other senators and representatives who sign on supporting the legislation in this early phase are cosponsors.

Next, the bill is sent to a relevant committee or multiple committees if the bill spans multiple jurisdictions. The committee then assigns the bill to a subcommittee, where representatives kill most legislation. Here the senators or representatives on the committee discuss and hold hearings on the bill and either decide to kill the bill through inaction or make amendments to the bill and send it to the floor for a chamber-wide vote.

If the bill makes it to a vote in the House or Senate for a debate and vote, a simple majority supporting it will send it to the other chamber for approval. The two chambers have some minor differences in how a bill comes out of committee and debating on the floor. In the House, the House Committee on Rules decides for approval before representatives can debate it on the House floor. A bill in the Senate will be put to open debate, but it can be subject to a *filibuster*.

Unlike the House, which got rid of the filibuster in 1842, the Senate filibuster allows a senator as much as they want to slow down a bill's passage and take floor time away from it. The practice is a Senate rule and not in the Constitution, and it has become increasingly used in the modern era. The longest filibuster by a single senator was Strom Thurmond's unsuccessful 24 hour and 18-minute attempt to stop the 1957 Civil Rights Act. Thurmond also participated in a 60-day filibuster by multiple senators attempting to stop the 1964 Civil Rights Act. The only way to stop a filibuster is by *cloture*, a vote that requires 60 senators.

Once sent to the other chamber, it faces a similar cycle where relevant committees hold hearings on the bill and make potential amendments before approving it or killing the bill. A bill can pass one chamber of Congress but be voted down or killed through inaction, and both chambers have to agree on the final version of the bill. Once both the House and the Senate approve a bill, they send it to the President for signature and approval. A president can either sign the bill, approve it, make it law, or veto it. United States presidents have historically used the line-item veto and signed statements to influence the laws they will sign. While a presidential veto will often kill the legislation, Congress can override a veto if two-thirds of each chamber votes to override the President.

While this is the standard procedure for a bill to become a law, there are multiple ways that congressional leadership or a congressperson can bypass committee hearings to fast-track legislation through various congressional rules not outlined in the Constitution. If a Congress member asks for unanimous consent to put a bill on the agenda and nobody votes against it, a bill can bypass committees. The Senate Majority Leader can also use Senate Rule XIV to bypass committee hearings.[93]

There are also ways for the Senate to bypass the traditional rules around the filibuster by using reconciliation. While bills in the Senate require a 60-vote supermajority to avoid a filibuster, the Senate can use reconciliation to pass legislation by a simple majority on bills related to spending, revenue, and the federal debt limit. The Senate can do this three times a calendar year, one per subject.

Another modern development in Congress is *omnibus legislation*; unrelated legislation packaged together for a single vote. Due to their large size

---

[93] On pieces of noncontroversial legislation, Senate leaders and representatives might use one of two informal processes called clearance and hotlining to determine the feasibility of expeditious or immediate consideration of a measure. The process of passing noncontroversial measures may include bypassing a Senate committee or truncating committee action, even though a committee might well have played a key role in the development of the measure sought to be passed or in the measure's clearance. For more information, *see* Koempel, Michael L. "Bypassing Senate Committees: Rule XIV and Unanimous Consent." *Congressional Research Service*, fas.org/sgp/crs/misc/RS22299.pdf.

and scope of multiple subjects, many congresspeople do not have enough time to read and understand the bill. In modern politics, this creates what is known as "pork," unrelated and sometimes controversial spending that gets attached to bills that will quickly pass. For example, many criticized elements within the various stimulus package deals during the coronavirus pandemic as senators filled omnibus bills with unrelated spending.

## HOW CONGRESS IS CHALLENGED AND HOW CONGRESSPEOPLE REPRESENT VOTERS

Modern Congress is shaped and constrained by the Constitution, the precedence set over hundreds of years, and present-day political realities.

First, in that list, the Constitution contains the foundation for Congress, both its powers and limitations. The founding fathers shaped the legislative branch's structure after the Constitution's predecessor, the Articles of Confederation, left the then unicameral legislature with some shortcomings. As it lacked power and was challenging to have all the relevant members meet with an impending war with Britain looming, the Founding Fathers saw it necessary to change Congress while submitting it to a system of checks and balances.

While the Constitution set the Congress foundations, the political body has gone through many changes since its inception. As the country has expanded, so has Congress, making the balance of power between big and small states all the more delicate to balance. The country's demographics have changed immensely since the Constitution called for proportional representation in the House of Representatives; one should before calculate by counting each slave as three-fifths of a person for population counts.

This situation leads to the modern political constraints that Congress has. The body is supposed to represent everyone in the country. With diverging political interests and growing corporate power, Congress members are beholden to a wide variety of political groups.

As a rule of thumb, Congress has to answer three constituencies: the voters who elected them, the nation, and their party. In Congress, the people who elect congresspeople all reside in the same state. These politicians are supposed to focus on the *representation* of this group mainly. This political representation means a congressperson has to look out for the constituents' interests in their state or district. Each state is divided into *congressional districts* by their state legislatures. Each member of the House of Representatives represents one of these congressional districts.

In modern politics, congresspeople attempt to represent their constituents in several ways. The first form is *policy representation*, the passing policy that will benefit the people's interests in their constituency. A particular policy proposal may be prevalent in a congressperson's constituency, and voting for its passage is a form of political representation. Secondly, members of Congress often represent their district or constituency by *allocative representation*. These conditions work by a congressperson securing funds for allocating to their district or state that will materially benefit their voters. In section 11.5, "pork" is mentioned, and this is one of the most prominent forms of allocative representation. This obligation also works through *earmarks*, providing taxpayer dollars to projects related to a specific district. Congresspeople also represent their constituents by doing *casework* and solving problems faced by people living in their district and through *symbolic representation*, representing the district and its people at public events.

Congress also passes legislation that impacts the nation as a whole. By the process of *national lawmaking*, Congress passes legislation meant to benefit the entire country. However, it is often perceived as real contractions between the national interest and a congressperson's district or state's interests. Nationally popular legislation can be hamstrung by individual congress people's decision to vote against the popular will in favor of constituents in their district. The tension between national and local interests is inherent in Congress's structure. In case a congressperson does not represent their constituents' interests, they enjoy an *incumbency advantage*. The sitting congressperson is more likely to be elected under these conditions.

Senators and representatives are also beholden to their political parties. Many United States Founding Fathers opposed political parties at the outset of the nation, and President George Washington did not belong to a party. The Constitution does not mention political parties at all. In the Federalist Papers, Founding Fathers James Madison and Alexander Hamilton wrote about the dangers they perceived in political parties. Nevertheless, the pipedream of non-partisan politics quickly dissipated, and parties formed on Federalist and Anti-Federalist lines. While the American political party system has been through multiple iterations, a two-party system has reigned after Washington's presidency.

While the Founding Fathers were concerned about political parties, Congress was established without considering the implications of a two-party partisan system. Throughout the history of Congress and the United States, there have been ebbs and flows in *partisanship*. If a politician is notably partisan, they will fall in line with the direction of his party. If political parties differ on significant, key issues, *political polarization* leads to high levels of partisanship. They perceived that the public's increasing polarization levels were also prevalent within the political parties and Congress. In *hyper-partisanship times*, party members stick strictly to their party line, leading to a *gridlock* in the legislative branch. If there is a divided legislative branch, where each party controls one chamber, and parties have high partisanship and polarization levels, legislators can pass very scarce meaningful legislation through Congress.

The Pew Research Center found in 2014 that Democrat and Republican voters had become significantly more polarized in previous decades.[94] Beginning in the 1980s and escalating since then, the Democratic and Republican parties began to polarize in Congress. The

---

[94] *See* Pew Research Center, for an insightful analysis of this trend. Republicans and Democrats seem to be more divided along ideological lines, and partisan antipathy is deeper and more extensive than at any point in the last two decades. Political Polarization in the American Public. Pew Research Center, 12 June 2014, www.pewresearch.org/politics/2014/06/12/political-polarization-in-the-american-public/

moderate members in each party started diminished, while more ideologically motivated candidates began to win election to the House and later the Senate. Consequently, the Democrats in Congress generally turned more liberal, and the Republicans became more conservative than before. The moderates from each party, who had earlier been able to work together, were politically edged out. It became more likely that the party opposite the President in Congress might be more willing to question his initiatives, whereas, in the past, it was uncommon for the opposition party to publicly stand against the United States president in foreign policy affairs.

If the legislative branch is divided or the President is from a different party than both chambers, Congress often has to rely more on *bipartisanship* to pass legislation. The two parties often work together to craft legislation and compromise on issues. However, bipartisanship does not solve all the tension and constraints within Congress. Local versus national interests still would play a significant role. All in all, the different levels of representation and how Congress is organized play crucial constraints on Congress's ability to pass sweeping legislation.

## ELECTIONS

To sit in Congress, almost every member has to run for election and beat his opponent. The Seventeenth Amendment outlines how representatives should fill a vacancy caused by death, resignation, or removal from office should. In the House, a special election always has to be held when a vacancy occurs. However, the Constitution leaves vacancies in the Senate to state legislatures, so some states' governors are required to appoint someone to fill a Senate vacancy rather than hold a special election.

Other than the difference when a vacancy occurs, Senate and House elections also have other distinctions. Senate elections are more straightforward as every state receives two senators, and these borders do not change. Every six years, a senate seat is up for election, so a sitting senator or a challenger has plenty of time to prepare for an election. In the House, they regularly redraw districts to reflect demographic changes as each district has to have about the same number of residents living in the area. Representatives are also up for reelection every two years, so they often have to campaign and raise money more regularly.

One of the most critical determinants of House elections is how districts are drawn and redrawn. The districts are drawn based on pre-set rules and political lines. Districts are drawn based on United States Census results held every ten years, mandated by Article I, Section 2, of the United States Constitution. The Constitution sets out that Congress members will use this data every ten years to finalize *congressional apportionment*, dividing up to the now 435 seats in the House.

The number of representatives may fluctuate based on state population. For the 2016 and 2020 presidential elections, there were 538 electors in the Electoral College, and a majority of 270 electoral votes were needed to win the presidency. Once the President of the Senate has read the electoral votes during a special joint session of Congress in January, the presidential candidate who received the majority of electoral votes is officially named President of the United States.

While the Census might seem apolitical, it often becomes a politicized and controversial topic. If someone does not return their census form, he will not be counted. Republicans have long attempted to exclude undocumented immigrants from the Census,[95] and President Donald Trump pushed hard to include a citizenship question on the 2020 Census. The Democratic Party has pushed statistical estimation to represent better who lives in each district, including undocumented immigrants, which

---

[95] One should also consider that, weeks before the 1980 census formally began, the Federation for American Immigration Reform launched its campaign to exclude unauthorized immigrants from population counts, *See* Lo Wang, Hansi. "Immigration Hard-Liner Files Reveal 40-Year Bid Behind Trump's Census Obsession." *National Public Radio*, 15 Feb. 2021, www.npr.org/2021/02/15/967783477/ immigration-hard-liner-files-reveal-40-year-bid-behind-trumps-census-obsession.

would theoretically benefit the Democrats. If a state increases its population relative to other states, it will increase its share of seats in the House and political power.

## REDISTRICTING AND GERRYMANDERING

There are other manners in which the two parties attempt to tip the congressional district system in their favor. *Redistricting* is one of the most politicized ways that the House's make-up is determined, which is the process of redrawing congressional district lines based on the Census results so that all districts remain about equal in population. Every ten years, the state legislature has the final say on how they will redraw districts, and in the end, the majority party in the state legislature has the most significant say. This provision makes state legislatures quite influential in determining the look of Congress. These districts are subject to *gerrymandering*, a highly politicized process that redistricts the congressional lines to benefit one party over another. This situation leads to bizarre congressional districts drawn to include voting populations that the majority party in the state legislature believes will benefit their party. The name gerrymandering originates from Massachusetts Governor Elbridge Gerry, who redrew a district in 1812 to resemble a salamander.

Historically, *gerrymandering* has been used in the United States to change districts' racial composition to marginalize racial minorities. This process of racial gerrymandering was made illegal in the Voting Rights Act of 1965. However, the Supreme Court had to intervene in several cases in the 1990s to overturn *redistricting* and drawing on racial lines. Now districts are often redrawn to benefit one party, known as partisan gerrymandering. Some have argued that this is an extension of racial gerrymandering and still marginalizes racial minorities and other groups. The Supreme Court has ruled that this type of gerrymandering is a political question with a 5-4 ruling on a conservative-liberal line.

## DOES CONGRESS LOOK LIKE AND REPRESENT AMERICA?

While anyone over a certain age and a United States citizen can run for Congress, there are high barriers to running and winning a successful campaign. In 2016, the average winning Senate campaign spent $10.4 million, and the average winning House campaign spent $1.3 million.[96] While this money often does not come from the candidate's wealth, it often means a politician has to appeal to monied interests, including either the Republican or Democratic Party, to have political success. Although about 40% of Americans identify as political independents[97], there is very little room for citizens who do not want to run in either party to succeed at the national level.

Outside of money spent on a political campaign, other factors determine who runs and wins Congress seats. Incumbents have typically enjoyed an advantage electorally. Thus, *open seats* without an incumbent are much more desirable. Congress elections also often are impacted by presidential elections to be held in the same year. Suppose a Republican wins the presidency by a large margin. In that case, Republicans running for the Senate and House may enjoy the *coattail effect*, which boosts their chances of winning thanks to a solid presidential campaign from the candidate in their party. After two years in office, the President's party quite frequently will be subject to a *midterm loss* and see their seats in Congress diminished.

And how about the representation of the American electorate? Does Congress look like the voters who elect them? Throughout history, Congress

[96] For more information on current spending by campaigns in the United States, *see* Kim, Soo Rin. "The Price of Winning Just Got Higher, Especially in the Senate." *OpenSecrets*, 9 Nov. 2016, www.opensecrets.org/news/2016/11/the-price-of-winning-just-got-higher-especially-in-the-senate/.

[97] Significantly more U.S. adults continued to identify as political independents (42%) in 2018 than as either Democrats (30%) or Republicans (26%). *See* Jones, Jeffrey M. "Americans Continue to Embrace Political Independence." *Gallup*, 7 Jan. 2019, news.gallup.com/poll/245801/americans-continue-embrace-political-independence.aspx.

and the American government have had shallow *descriptive representation* levels, how much the legislature looks like the population. While this representation has increased since the times in which only white land-owning males in government, Congress does not have a high descriptive representation level. The 117th Congress is the most racially and ethnically diverse in history, but it is still 77% white[98], which is a percentage significantly higher than that of the general population (60% white). Furthermore, only a handful of congresspeople are not college graduates, despite only 22.5% of Americans above 25 finishing four years of college.[99] Congress is also significantly wealthier than the general population, and only 3% of congresspeople are immigrants despite the United States having the highest immigrant population in the world at 47 million people.

[98] Among today's United States senators and representatives, the overwhelming majority of racial and ethnic minority members are Democrats (83%), while 17% are Republicans. See Schaeffer, Katherine. "Racial, Ethnic Diversity Increases Yet Again with the 117th Congress." Pew Research Center, 28 Jan. 2021, www.pewresearch.org/fact-tank/2021/01/28/racial-ethnic-diversity-increases-yet-again-with-the-117th-congress/. .

[99] See the official release of the US Census for more information Bureau, US Census. "U.S. Census Bureau Releases New Educational Attainment Data." The United States Census Bureau, 30 Mar. 2020, www.census.gov/newsroom/press-releases/2020/educational-attainment.html#:~:text=In%202019%2C%20high%20school%20was,from%2029.9%25%20to%20 36.0%25

# KEY TERMS

**Advice and Consent**: The Senate's role in confirming presidential appointments.

**Allocative Representation**: Securing funds for specific districts.

**Articles of Confederation**: The predecessor to the United States Constitution.

**Bicameral Legislature**: A legislative body with two chambers.

**Casework**: Solving problems faced by constituents.

**Checks and Balances**: System to prevent any single branch from becoming too powerful.

**Committee**: Groups in Congress that review and recommend legislative measures.

**Conference Committee**: Reconciles bills passed in both the House and Senate.

**Constituency**: Individuals and groups whose interests elected officials represent.

**Constitution**: The document outlining the structure and powers of the U.S. government.

**Descriptive Representation**: How much the legislature looks like the population.

**Filibuster**: A Senate rule allowing extended debate to delay a bill's passage.

**Gerrymandering**: Redrawing district lines to benefit a particular party.

**House of Representatives**: The lower chamber of Congress.

**Impeachment**: The process of bringing charges against a government official.

**Joint Committee**: Permanent committees with members from both the House and Senate.

**Judiciary Act of 1789**: Established the district courts system.

**Legislative Branch**: One of the three branches of the U.S. government responsible for making laws.

**Majority Leader**: The head of the majority party in the Senate.

**Oversight**: Congress's power to oversee the executive branch and federal agencies.

**Partisanship**: Strict adherence to a political party's policies.

**Pork**: Unrelated spending attached to bills.

**Proportional Representation**: Allocation of seats based on population size.

**Redistricting**: The process of redrawing congressional district lines.

**Senate**: The upper chamber of Congress.

**Seventeenth Amendment**: Outlines how to fill vacancies in Congress.

**Speaker of the House**: The presiding officer of the House of Representatives.

**Standing Committee**: Permanent committees with specific legislative jurisdiction.

**Symbolic Representation**: Representing constituents at public events.

**Unicameral Legislature**: A legislative body with one chamber.

**Voting Rights Act of 1965**: Made racial gerrymandering illegal.

# CHAPTER 12

## THE EXECUTIVE BRANCH

What is an executive, anyway? By definition, the Executive is one who has the power to carry out plans, strategies or laws. In some countries around the world, the chief executive is a prime minister. The United States does not have a prime minister, and instead the United States chief executive is a president. The executive branch is led by the President who is the leader of the entire federal bureaucracy system. The Federal bureaucracy is the vast network of departments, agencies, boards, and commissions that constitute the Federal government. In the United States, these agencies include the FBI, CIA, EPA, and so forth. The president is only the head of the federal bureaucracy and not the legislative branch of government, unlike a prime minister who typically has more control over legislation. The executive branch in the United States is tasked with carrying out and enforcing the law as stipulated in the Constitution. In addition to the President, the Vice President and the Cabinet are tasked with aiding the President.

## THE JOB OF THE AMERICAN PRESIDENT

The American President has specific job descriptions and powers and authority that are granted to the office. The key elements of the

President's job description are codified in the Constitution and have been granted to the office through Congress and the Courts. The United States Constitution originally limited the power of the Executive Branch, but throughout the history of the American presidency, the power of the President has been significantly expanded. Yet still, the Constitution gives the president less power than many other chief executives around the world. One of the president's most important powers is executive privilege. Executive privilege allows the president to keep certain documents that concern the executive branch or national security confidential.

According to the Constitution, the president must meet certain requirements and conditions in order to serve. The Constitution also lists several restrictions upon the office. The President of the United States must be:

- At least 35 years old
- A natural-born citizen of the United States
- A United States resident for at least 14 years
- Chosen by the Electoral College to serve a four-year term
- Succeeded in the event of death or incapacity by the vice president, elected at the same time
- Removed from office only for "high crimes and misdemeanors" by the House and the Senate
- Unable to receive "emoluments" (that is, profit beyond their normal salary) from the country or any of the states

The job of the American president has been significantly modified through the years despite the formal powers granted by the Constitution remaining the same. Several amendments have modified presidential power and each of these amendments to the constitution have addressed changes in society.

The different amendments of the constitution have contributed to defining the roles of the Presidency. The most important amendments to the office of the president have been the Twelfth, Twentieth, Twenty-Second, and Twenty-Fifth Amendments.

When the Twelfth Amendment was passed, it limited and changed how the President and Vice President were elected by the Electoral College. During the first years of our nation, the two candidates who received the most votes in the Electoral College would serve as President and Vice-President. The Twelfth Amendment states that the President and Vice President would be voted in distinct ballots rather than the second-place in the Electoral College presidential election being selected as the Vice President. The change was made to limit the chance of a President and Vice President being elected from different parties. Additionally, under this amendment, the President and Vice President are not allowed to be residents in the same state. In 2000, the Twelfth Amendment became a point of contention in the election of President Bush and Vice President Cheney. Bush was the Governor of Texas and Cheney had lived in Texas for five years while maintaining a residence in Wyoming[100].

The Twentieth Amendment set the official start and end date for a term in office for the President, Vice President, Senate, and House of Representatives. After the amendment, the President and Vice President's term begins and ends on January 20 at noon. Newly elected Senators and Representatives begin their term on January 3, which gives the incoming Congress the power to break a deadlock in the event of a tie in the Electoral College, rather than the outgoing Congress. This section of the amendment served to limit the "lame duck" session, or the time in between presidential terms. It also set out that the vice president takes over if the president dies before taking the oath.

In an effort to limit the power of a popular politician, Congress approved the Twenty-Second Amendment to create term-limits for the President. The amendment was a direct response to President Franklin Delano Roosevelt who served four terms and enjoyed high levels of

[100] Maravilla, Christopher Scott. "That Dog Don't Hunt: The Twelfth Amendment after Jones v. Bush." *Pace Law Review*, vol. 23, no. 1, 2002, pp. 214–270.

popularity leading the country out of the Great Depression and through World War II. The Twenty-Second Amendment implemented a two-term limit for any president. Roosevelt is the only American president to serve more than two terms after President George Washington established a two-term norm as the first President of the country.

The impeachment process to remove the President or Vice President from office is mostly laid out in Articles I and II of the Constitution. The Twenty-Fifth Amendment created a mechanism for the president to be removed without impeachment. The vice president and a majority of the cabinet or Congress can remove a president if they determine the president is unable to perform their job. Near the tail end of President Donald Trump's first term in office, several Democratic Representatives called on Vice President Mike Pence to invoke the Twenty-Fifth Amendment to remove Trump from office[101]. The amendment also outlines presidential succession, stating, "In case of the removal of the President from office or of his death or resignation, the Vice President shall become President."

## THE PRESIDENTIAL JOB

The Presidential Succession Act of 1947 delineates additional detail on who does the president's job when he cannot, and it fundamentally changed the Presidential Succession Act of 1886. In the wake of President Roosevelt's death in office in 1945, his successor, President Harry Truman, sought to change the line of presidential succession. Under this act, the Speaker of the House and the president pro tempore of the Senate were made third and fourth in line for the Presidency, respectively, after the Vice President. The new act changed succession and moved members of the President's cabinet further down the line of succession, thus not allowing a President to appoint their own line of succession.

---

[101] Cicilline, David N. *Cicilline, Lieu Lead Judiciary Committee Dems Urging Pence to Invoke 25th Amendment.* cicilline.house.gov/press-release/cicilline-lieu-lead-judiciary-committee-dems-urging-pence-invoke-25th-amendment.

In order to govern and lead the country, the president relies on their cabinet, an advisory group to the President composed primarily of the heads of the major departments of the federal bureaucracy and the vice president. Each cabinet member carries out elements of the President's agenda. The President's cabinet has 23 members, including the vice president, 15 department heads, including the Attorney General, Secretaries of State, Treasury, and Defense, and seven other cabinet-level members. The Cabinet does not possess any collective executive power, and they have to be submitted to the Senate for approval by a simple majority. While the Cabinet-level positions need to be approved by the Senate, the president can remove Cabinet members at their discretion.

So as no single entity or branch gets too much power, the executive branch exists in a system of checks and balances, and the role of the executive is to make sure that Congress and the Judicial Branch do not usurp more power over other branches of government. In theory, the president has been given just enough legislative and judicial power to hold the other branches in check. While the system is built on checks and balances, the president is the leader of the county and serves as both the head of state and head of government.

In countries with two separate heads of state and government, the head of state is a largely ceremonial, apolitical role that rallies the country together. This can be done through the moral or historical influence of the office. The head of government is a partisan role, as in the United States, the President serves as the head of the president's political party. Each president utilizes this role differently. A president's talents might suit them better for one or the other of these tasks, for example President George Washington is considered by many to be a great statesman. America, unlike some other countries, has one person, the President, do both jobs.

The Constitution gives the president a limited number of powers, and they are all in Article II, but it grants the president three main executive powers. The president is the chief executive, the commander in chief, and the chief foreign policy maker. As the Chief executive, the president is head bureaucrat, making sure the laws are enforced. One of the president's most important powers in this role is appointment power. The President has the power to nominate ambassadors to foreign countries, public Ministers, Supreme Court Judges, and various other bureaucrats. As a check on the President's power, some of these nominations have to be approved by the Senate, for example Supreme Court Justices.

The president also serves in the position of commander in chief. In the United States, the commander in chief is the civilian head of the armed forces of the United States. The President's exact powers within this role have been hotly contested throughout American history. The President is the commander in chief, but they are not legally allowed to declare war on another country without the approval of Congress. So, the President cannot unilaterally declare war, but if Congress approves a war resolution, the President is considered the head of the operation.

The president is also the chief foreign policy maker. As the chief foreign policy maker, the president negotiates treaties with the approval of two-thirds of the Senate. The president also receives ambassadors and represents the United States on the global stage. While Article II of the Constitution grants the president only the limited power to receive foreign ambassadors, this clause is cited to justify the president's powerful and much broader role in foreign affairs.

The president also has a unique power afforded to the office to issue executive agreements. An executive agreement is an agreement issued by the president with other countries that enter the countries into binding international obligations. These executive agreements describe how the president will abide by an agreement and can terminate with a new president. An executive agreement is not a treaty, and it is often implemented to circumvent other country's laws regarding the signing of a treaty.

While the president's main responsibilities are related to the office's executive power, the president also has powers of legislative authority. These legislative powers are part of the checks and balances built into the American system. Every year, the president offers the State of the Union address. The Constitution says that the president will regularly inform Congress of the state of the union and recommend the measures he considers useful or necessary. While it is not constitutionally required to be a speech, President Woodrow Wilson began the tradition in 193 of addressing Congress and the American people in an annual address.

One of the President's most well-known powers over legislation is the veto. The Presidential veto in the Constitution gives the president the option of refusing to sign a bill that Congress has passed. This is a power given to the executive branch in line with the model of checks and balances. There are two types of veto, a direct veto when the President formally sends back the bill with objections, and a pocket veto where the President simply allows the 10-day review period to elapse, leaving the space for the President's signature blank. While the presidential veto is powerful, it can be overridden by Congress. Two-thirds of the Senate and House are required to overturn a presidential veto. Only 4% of all presidential vetoes have been overturned.

Congress has the legislative power to write and pass laws, but when a president wants to create policy that is not passed as law, the president can issue an executive order. An executive order is what presidents can issue to fill in details and enforce the laws passed by Congress. These powers direct the federal bureaucracy to act in a particular way. Executive orders can be overturned by the Judicial branch if they are found to be unconstitutional. Executive orders can also be cancelled or revoked by the President, so when a new President is elected, they often review the executive orders of their predecessor. While executive orders are not mentioned in the Constitution, they have become an integral part of a president's power. Before 1900, executive orders were informal and often not made public, nonetheless nearly every president has made some kind of declaration that can be considered an executive order. Modern presidents have issued many more executive orders than their predecessors. Three presidents, Theodore Roosevelt, Calvin Coolidge, and Franklin Delano Roosevelt, issued over 1,000 executive orders during their time in office. More recent presidents have often issued several hundred executive orders.

The president has strong powers of judicial appointment. With appointment power, the president can appoint judges, with the advice and consent of the Senate, to the entire federal judiciary. Some of the judicial posts that the president can appoint include the solicitor general, Supreme Court justices, courts of appeals judges, and district court judges. The solicitor general is the legal officer who argues cases before the Supreme Court when the United States is a party to that case, as it often is. The president also has removal power. While not in the Constitution, the Supreme Court has ruled in several cases that the president has the sole power to remove some federal appointees. The most important case was *Myers v. United States* in 1926 in which the Supreme Court ruled the president has sole removal authority of federal appointees, except for federal judge appointments.[102]

The president also has the power of the pardon. The pardon power of the president means the president can pardon those accused or convicted of federal crimes. The Constitution grants the president the power to pardon. In recent years, many presidents have issued pardons near the end of their terms, and these pardons have caused a great deal of controversy.

## HOW THE AMERICAN PRESIDENCY HAS CHANGED

The job of the president has become more involved as America itself has become larger and more complex. Citizens' expectations of the presidency have grown over time, but the job's formal powers outlined in Article II of the Constitution have not. The Twenty-Second Amendment is the only constitutional change to affect presidential powers, and it limited them by imposing term limits. The founders envisioned a presidency with limited powers; however, many presidents expanded the office's informal powers, and the formal powers have been broadly interpreted to increase presidential power. Through this process, the presidency has shifted from

---

[102] Supreme Court of the United States. *Myers v. United States*. Oyez, www.oyez.org/cases/1900-1940/272us52.

a traditional presidency to a modern presidency. The traditional presidency was consistent with the founders' intentions for a president, with the Constitution's limited powers as the groundwork for the president's powers. There are 19 powers given to the national government from the constitution, and these powers are known as delegated powers. The delegated powers are the explicit forms of power the constitution gives to the federal government. In Article I, Section 8, the itemization of powers to the United States Congress includes functions such as commerce, taxation, and declaration of war. In Article II, Section II, the president is delegated powers, including those noted previously (commander-in-chief powers, pardon powers, treaty-making powers, etc.).

The presidency also has inherent powers that have built up over time. Inherent powers are powers that were not explicitly laid out but rather were implied in their constitutional duty to take care that the laws be faithfully executed. The inherent powers are given to the federal government so that they can operate the federal bureaucracy systems and government according to new laws that have been passed. Examples of inherent powers given to the federal government include the federal government's oversight of food production and the environment in the form of the FDA and the EPA. The government can use their powers to revise warnings and lists to the American citizens regarding food poisoning health matters and environmental impact issues. There are other certain powers not given to the federal government that were thus reserved for the states by the Tenth Amendment.

These powers not explicitly given to the presidency in the constitution are therefore retained for the individual states. These *Reserved Powers* are powers listed in the Tenth amendment to the constitution, and it says that the states retained government authority not explicitly granted to the national government. Some of these reserved state powers include public education, public health, commerce within the state, organizing state elections, prisons and police, other issues regarding arrests and incarcerations, highway and road maintenance, and many more. When the constitution allows for powers to be shared between the national and state governments, these powers are known as concurrent powers. A concurrent power is known as the power shared by the national government and the state government such as taxation, and the minimum wage.

The executive branch changed significantly and became much more powerful with President Franklin Delano Roosevelt's New Deal. The limited vision of the executive changed with the stock market crash of 1929 and subsequent economic collapse known as the Great Depression. President Roosevelt's New Deal created a variety of jobs programs and turned the government into a much larger employer to help people out of the Great Depression and build the country's infrastructure. The wide-reaching social program built infrastructure, public works, and art, created social insurance programs like Social Security to ensure that a safety net existed for the elderly, disabled, and orphaned, and it reformed the financial system to prevent another repeat depression in the future. The New Deal also signaled the birth of the modern presidency, and with this the modern presidency grew the role of the president as compared to the traditional presidency.

After the growth of the modern presidency with FDR, the government grew at all levels. Though presidential candidates started promising to do more and more, the formal powers of the office as outlined in the Constitution stayed the same. The presidency had to find ways to expand its power and influence through more informal channels. It did this through the power to persuade and convince Congress to support the executive office plans. This could be done by going directly to the people, known as going public. The president's increasing capacity to talk to citizens through the media made this method particularly successful. FDR began having "fireside chats" to talk to the American people informally and discuss the state of the nation.

## PRESIDENTS, POPULARITY, AND CONGRESS

To be effective, presidents need to have some level of popularity with the public. This is a minimum requirement to be elected; but it may not be sufficient to make a successful presidency. What factors make a president popular? The president often suffers from steadily declining popularity after an initial peak when they take office. Almost all presidents go through a period called the Honeymoon period. This Honeymoon period is the first 100 days of a presidency, when the press is likely to be most kind and the majority of the public is giving the new president the benefit of the doubt. Not all presidents do enjoy a honeymoon. Factors like the state of the economy and external events like wars and natural disasters can influence how popular a president is.

A president's popularity is often split between political parties, with the president enjoying the most popularity within their own party. Due to the polarization within American politics, the president's approval is often tied in with how popular their political party is at the moment. This limits how the president can cooperate effectively with Congress, and it can help or hinder how real legislative change occurs because these changes require congressional cooperation. If there is a majority in at least one house that is different from the president's party, then the current government is known as a divided government and the power of the president can be significantly hindered. In many divided governments, Congress chooses not to work with the president or the president's legislative liaison. The congressional liaison is a presidential appointee whose chief job is to coordinate with Congress on behalf of the president to find points of potential agreement and create a legislative agenda.

## KEY TERMS

**Cabinet**: A group of advisors to the President, primarily composed of the heads of major federal departments and the Vice President.

**Chief Executive**: The President's role as head of the federal bureaucracy, responsible for enforcing laws.

**Chief Foreign Policy Maker**: The President's role in negotiating treaties, receiving ambassadors, and representing the U.S. internationally.

**Commander in Chief**: The President's role as the civilian head of the armed forces.

**Concurrent Powers**: Powers shared by both the national government and state governments, such as taxation and minimum wage laws.

**Constitution**: The foundational legal document outlining the structure, powers, and functions of the U.S. government.

**Electoral College**: The body that elects the President and Vice President of the United States.

**Executive Agreement**: An agreement made by the President with other countries that binds the countries to international obligations without Senate approval.

**Executive Branch**: The branch of government responsible for carrying out and enforcing laws, led by the President.

**Executive Order**: A directive issued by the President to the federal bureaucracy to implement or interpret federal statutes.

**Executive Privilege**: The President's power to keep certain documents and communications confidential, particularly those related to national security.

**Federal Bureaucracy**: The network of departments, agencies, boards, and commissions that make up the federal government.

**Inherent Powers**: Powers not explicitly stated in the Constitution but implied through the President's duties.

**Legislative Powers**: Powers related to law-making, such as the veto and the ability to recommend legislation to Congress.

**Presidential Succession Act**: The law detailing the line of succession beyond the Vice President in case the President is unable to serve.

**Reserved Powers**: Powers not explicitly granted to the federal government by the Constitution and therefore reserved for the states.

**Twelfth Amendment**: An amendment that changed how the President and Vice President are elected, ensuring they are from the same political party.

**Twentieth Amendment**: An amendment that set the start and end dates for the terms of the President, Vice President, and Congress.

**Twenty-Second Amendment**: An amendment that established a two-term limit for the Presidency.

**Twenty-Fifth Amendment**: An amendment that provides the procedures for replacing the President in the event of death, removal, resignation, or incapacitation.

# CHAPTER 13

# THE JUDICIAL BRANCH

The judiciary is an integral part of checks and balances between different branches of government. Alexander Hamilton wrote an essay advocating for the ratification of the United States Constitution called the Federalist Paper No. 78. Here, Hamilton described what the newly created judicial branch would look like, and that the judiciary would be the weakest and thus the "least dangerous branch" of government. Through time, the power of the judiciary has changed. The judiciary is the branch of government that interprets and applies the law and solves disputes involving citizens and other government actors.

The courts have changed in their capacity to influence both branches of government. The judiciary has become an enormously powerful branch through *the power of the pen*. The Constitution does not explicitly state that the Supreme Court may determine the constitutionality of an act of the other branches of government. However, judicial review of other branches of the federal government was established in *Marbury v. Madison* when the Court claimed this power for itself.[103] The Court held that American courts have the power to strike down laws, statutes, and some government actions that they find to violate the Constitution of

---

[103] *Marbury v. Madison*, 5 United States 137 (1803).

the United States. *Marbury v. Madison* gave the Supreme Court (itself) the ultimate power of deciding what the Constitution means.

## KINDS OF LAWS

The United States is a democracy. In a democracy, laws rule. The rule of law is a system in which laws are known in advance, they apply the same way to everyone, and if we feel they have been applied unjustly we can appeal to a higher authority. The laws we notice most limit our behavior and stop us from acting on impulses that are damaging to other people. Laws make collective life possible and even comfortable.

There are different types of laws in the United States judicial system. There are substantive laws, and these laws govern how members of a society are to behave. Substantive laws are a body of rules that define what we can or cannot do. When determining what a person cannot do, thereby limiting their freedom, criminal laws are a form of substantive law that prohibit behavior that makes collective living difficult or impossible. Engaging in a prohibited behavior is considered a crime and subject to a legal punishment. A crime is an action that breaks criminal law. When regulating interactions between people or organizations, it is a civil law. Civil laws are laws that regulate interactions between individuals or other private parties, such as a corporation. When an action between individuals causes harm against another person it is a tort, which is an action that violates a civil law.

Substantive laws are contrasted with procedural law, which is the set of procedures for making, administering, and enforcing substantive law. Procedural laws define how the laws are used, applied, and enforced. Court procedures were founded from the United States Constitution's Fifth and Fourteenth Amendment's guarantee of due process which both state no one shall be "deprived of life liberty or property without due process of law"[104]. Due process requires the government to abide by fair procedures before depriving a person of life, liberty or property.

---

[104] United States Const. Amend. X and XIV.

# FORMS OF LAW

What form do laws take? Laws originate from different places and different entities have authority to create them. The form of laws and how they are interpreted are important to the judicial system. Constitutional laws are established by federal and state constitutions. This body of laws establishes the legal infrastructure of our governments. Constitutions set the framework for the court systems, determine how the three branches of federal government relate to each other and shape the relationship between the federal and state governments. More notably, constitutional law determines how the game of politics is played. Much of constitutional law has grown from federal and state supreme court rulings interpreting their respective constitutions. Constitutional law, and most other court rulings, create case law or common law that can be binding precedent. Precedents are a series of court rulings of similar issues and facts. These rulings create an authority for courts to apply the same law to future cases that have similar issues or facts.

Unlike case law that was developed by court rulings, statutory laws are laws that are made by legislatures. Statutory law is written law passed by a legislative body of local, state or federal government and codified in statute- which means law that is arranged and numbered into a systematic code. Administrative law is the body of law that governs the activities of administrative agencies of government. Executive-level governmental agency action can include rule-making, adjudication, or the enforcement of a specific regulatory agenda. Administrative law is considered a branch of public law. Examples of federal administrative law are the regulation of civil aviation, planes, and pilots to protect public safety through the Federal Aviation Administration.

Finally, executive orders are rules that also have the full force and effect of law and are issued by the executive branch, such as the President of the United States or the Governor of a state. They are issued based on authority granted to the President or Governor in their respective constitutions and must be consistent with that authority.

## THE AMERICAN LEGAL SYSTEM

Legal systems around the world are different. American legal systems are heavily influenced by political culture. The United States system, in particular, can be adversarial and litigious.

The United States system is adversarial in nature. The adversarial system or adversary system is a legal system used in common law countries where two advocates represent their parties' case or position before an impartial person or group of people, usually a judge or jury, who attempt to determine the truth and pass judgment accordingly. An adversarial system is a system that is primarily concerned with the legal process being fair and resulting in just judgment. This type of system is different from an inquisitorial system. An inquisitorial system is a legal system in which the court, or a part of the court, is actively involved in investigating the facts of the case. This is distinct from an adversarial system, in which the court's role is primarily that of an impartial referee between the prosecution and the defense. An inquisitorial system is a system in which the truth is the goal, and if it requires that the judge leave his or her neutral perch to ask questions and investigate, so be it.

The United States legal system is a litigious system. Litigation refers to the process of resolving disputes by filing or answering a complaint through the public court system. A litigious system is a system in which citizens prefer to settle their differences in court. As discussed above, if the issue of the case is one of criminal law, the two parties will be the state and the defendant where the state is charging the defendant for violating a criminal law. If the issue of the case is based on civil law, the two parties will be private individuals alleging harm was caused to one or both parties.

## THE CRIMINAL JUSTICE SYSTEM

The criminal justice system focuses on justice. Through the process of adjudication, the truth can be discovered, and justice served by providing a formal judgment in a disputed matter. If there has been a mistake in the trial, an appeal can be filed, which is a process brought by a petitioner if that party believes there has been a procedural error or that the judge has applied the law incorrectly.

A right given in criminal trials in the United States is a right to a jury trial. The right to a jury trial in criminal cases is found in both Article III[105] and the Sixth Amendment[106]of the Constitution. If you are accused of a serious offence that carries a potential sentence of more than six months' imprisonment, you are guaranteed a trial by a jury of your peers[107]. Jury duty is a collective action problem—we all want to share in the outcome, but many of us try to get out of providing the effort that makes that outcome possible.

### Equality and the Criminal Justice System

One of the hallmarks of American political culture is that everyone should be treated the same. But the procedural value that everyone be treated the same is often not the way things actually work in America. The equality for all people, regardless of race, gender and class has not always existed. Even though the Constitution established the equal protection clause which provided in part that "[no state shall] deny any person within its jurisdiction the equal protection of the laws,"[108] the judiciary did not originally interpret this to mean equal protection for black Americans. From its beginnings, the United States has had what amounts to separate criminal justice systems for black and white Americans. America has had stronger punishments for those of color. An example of this was the case of Emmett Till. Till, a 14-year-old boy, was caught and lynched in Mississippi in 1955 for allegedly offending a white woman who later

---

[105] United States Const. Art. III, § 2 provides "The trial of all Crimes, except in Cases of Impeachment, shall be by Jury".

[106] United States Const. Amend. XI provides "In all criminal prosecutions, the accused shall enjoy the right to a speedy and public trial, by an impartial jury."

[107] *United States v. Nachtigal*, 507 United States 1 (1993).

[108] United States Const. Amend. XIV, § 1

admitted she lied. The white men who killed Till were acquitted by a white jury.

The role that justice has served white and African Americans has developed inconsistently since the inception of the nation. There are dual narratives about who are the "good guys." African Americans and whites have developed very different narratives about the role the criminal justice system plays in their lives.

Racial profiling has prevented African Americans from receiving equal access to justice. Racial profiling is a violation of civil rights in which police target people because they fit the mental image of what a criminal looks like. Obviously, it is not possible to have a stereotype based on race, gender, or class of a person and profile them as a police target. This difference in the application of the law is racism. Racism isn't just what you say, it is also an acceptance of different rules of treatment according to race built into the norms of the system. In the criminal justice system, the issue is *equal treatment*. In the civil justice system, the issue is *equal access*.

## THE CONSTITUTION, CONGRESS, AND THE DUAL COURT SYSTEM

The founders wanted to avoid having a national court system and chose to root the court system under the foundation of Federalism. Because the question of whether there would be a national court system with jurisdiction over the states was such a hot-button issue, the authors of the Constitution tended to gloss over it.

### Article I Courts

Only the actions of Article III courts are the subject of this chapter, but it is important to note there are two types of federal courts. Article I courts are created by Congress in order to implement its various legislative powers. For example, the United States Tax Court has jurisdiction over federal income tax subject matters. Judges of such Article I courts do not have a life tenure or protection from salary decreases. Article I courts are sometimes vested with administrative as well as judicial functions, and the congressional power to create such "hybrid" courts has been sustained by the Supreme Court.[109]

### Article III Courts

Article III of the United States Constitution states that the "judicial Power of the United States, shall be vested in one supreme Court, and in such inferior Courts as the Congress may from time to time ordain and establish."[110] What this means is that the Constitution provides for one Supreme Court and lower courts established by Congress as necessary. Although Congress has the complete power to set the jurisdictional limits of the federal courts, it is still bound by the standards of judicial power set forth in Article III as to subject matter, parties, and the requirement of "case or controversy" (discussed later). Therefore, Congress cannot require the federal courts to perform nonjudicial functions.

What are lower courts? Most court systems have an entry-level court to which you first bring your case or in which you are first tried before a jury. If you lose this entry level court case, you have a right to appeal, which is to ask a higher or appeals court to ensure that everything was handled properly and to review the process.

### Federal Judges

The Article III constitutional section also authorizes Congress to appoint federal courts judges for life terms. This means these judges can only be removed through a vote of impeachment, so they hold their jobs as long as they behave themselves. To be a judge in the federal court system, the Constitution requires judges to be appointed according to certain

---

[109] *Glidden v. Zdanok*, 370 United States 530 (1962).
[110] United States Const. Art. III, § 1.

procedures but sets forth no specific required qualifications to serve as a judge. There are no age, citizenship, or other requirements. The Constitution specifies only that the judges shall be appointed by the president, with the advice and consent of the Senate. The judiciary is the only unelected branch of the government.

In order to protect federal judges from political interference or pressures, they receive a salary that cannot be reduced during their lifetime terms. The Constitution gives federal judges this protection so that they can make fair and trustworthy decisions on cases without worrying their decision will be publicly or politically unpopular. Judges can, however, be removed from office only if impeached and convicted by the House of Representatives and the Senate, a process that has resulted in only 15 impeachments and eight convictions in more than 200 years.

## FEDERAL COURT SYSTEM

The federal court system is three-tiered. First, the lowest level of the federal judiciary hierarchy consists of 94 federal district courts. Each state has at least one federal district court located within its borders, while the largest states have four. Federal district courts will hear the case first because district courts have original jurisdiction. At this level, the court will consider and rule on all the facts of the case during a trial. Each federal district court has a United States attorney that are government attorneys that represent the United States in criminal and civil cases. United States attorneys are appointed by the president and approved or affirmed by the Senate for four-year terms.

Next, once a case is decided by the federal district courts, it can be appealed and heard by the federal Courts of Appeals. These courts are arranged into 12 circuits. These circuits are large super districts that encompass several of the district court territories. Each circuit has its own Court of Appeals. The 12th circuit covers just Washington, D.C., and hears all appeals involving government agencies. Cases are heard in the circuit that includes the district court where the case was heard originally.

The sole function of these courts is to hear appeals from the lower federal district courts if the losing party believes the law was applied incorrectly and to review the legal reasoning behind the decisions reached there. This is referred to as appellate jurisdiction. These courts do not hold trials and generally do not consider the facts of the case. The decisions in the courts of appeals are made by a rotating panel of three judges who sit to hear the case. The judges rotate in order to provide a decision-making body that is as unbiased as possible. Having all the judges present (*en banc*) gives a decision more legitimacy and sends a message that the decision was made carefully.

The third and highest tier of the federal court system is the United States Supreme Court, which is discussed below. The judicial ideology is important for the courts because it can sway important legal concepts in the public policy of the United States, such as abortion rights. Judicial ideology varies by the president who nominates a justice. These days, an increasingly important qualification for the job of federal judge is the ideological or policy positions of the appointee. The Senate confirmation process has become more rancorous. The nomination process has been more important to conservatives than to liberals.

## STATE COURT SYSTEM

State court systems are different from federal court systems. Each state establishes their own state courts through state law or their constitution. Therefore, the structures of state court systems vary from state to state. Each state has a tiered system that has a highest court for appeals, which is often, but not always, called a state supreme court. State courts have jurisdiction over state law subject matter and interpret their respective state law and constitutions.

State courts judges are chosen differently than the federal court judges and, again, the procedures are established by state laws. State judges are chosen through three different methods: Appointment by the governor, election by the state legislature, and election by the state population as a whole. The state election of judges can be controversial. Critics argue that judicial elections can create a conflict of interest because few people are able to cast educated votes in judicial elections. There is a further problem that the political nature of elections and campaigning may influence judges' rulings.

## THE SUPREME COURT

The Supreme Court is the highest court of the land. In the United States Judiciary, the top player is the Supreme Court. The founders wanted the Supreme Court to be above politics. The President is not seen going to the Supreme Court, and the Supreme Court Justices are not seen visiting the president in order to keep a perceived bias from occurring. The Supreme Court is still a POLITICAL institution. The very reasons that the founders could not be frank about their plans for the Court in the Constitution shows just how politically volatile the whole institution was. As discussed above, the primary job is to determine if laws are permitted under the United States Constitution and provide judicial review of those laws.

The political nature of the Supreme Court can influence laws, freedoms, and civil rights for all Americans for generations. The Supreme Court is political in three respects: (1) How justices are chosen, (2) How the justices make decisions, and (3) The impact of those decisions on all the rest of us.

It is very difficult to get on the Supreme Court. The president appoints Supreme Court justices, and the Senate approves or affirms the nomination of the president. The president and the Senate consider the merit and demographics of the nominee, but mostly the appointing entities are fixated on ideology. Supreme Court justices have always been attorneys, had extensive careers in the legal field and have overwhelmingly been white males. In 1967, Justice Thurgood Marshall became the first African American Supreme Court Justice. And shortly thereafter in 1981, Sandra Day O'Connor became the first woman appointed.

The type of justice appointed to the Supreme Court can either be someone who is a judicial interpretivist or a strict constructionist. A Judicial interpretivist is one who believes that the founders could not have anticipated all the changes that make the world today different from theirs and, therefore, that judges should read the Constitution as the founders would write it in light of modern-day experience. A strict constructionist is a scholar and judge who believes that the Constitution should be read just as it was written. This is a political hot-button issue now because, until Justice Antonin Scalia's death in 2016, there was a 5-4 majority who were sufficiently committed to interpretivism that they supported the right to privacy and the case that was based on *Griswold, Roe v. Wade* (1973).

## FEDERAL COURT JURISDICTION

Jurisdiction is the authority of the court to hear the case. The federal courts have jurisdiction over all cases involving a federal question, or subject matter jurisdiction, that seeks to answer a question based on federal law or the United States Constitution. Any subject matter involving the federal government or foreign governments would also be within the jurisdiction of federal courts. Federal courts also have diversity jurisdiction where the disputes are between two parties that are from different states. Additionally, courts have diversity jurisdiction to resolve disputes between two different state governments. If Tennessee and Arkansas are disputing rights to Mississippi, the case would be heard in federal court.

Even if a federal court has subject matter or diversity jurisdiction, it still might refuse to hear a case. Whether the court will hear the case (*i.e.*, whether the case is justiciable) depends on whether a case or controversy is involved, and whether the other elements of jurisdiction are met. Article III, Section 2 of the United States Constitution also requires federal courts to decide questions that arise out of actual disputes or real cases and controversies.[111] Therefore, federal courts cannot issue advisory opin-

---

[111] United States Const. Art. III, § 2.

ions in cases involving challenges to governmental legislation or policy whose enforcement is neither actual nor threatened. Although, some state supreme courts do have the judicial power to issue advisory opinions.

A party to a case is generally not entitled to review of a law before it is enforced. Therefore, a federal court will not hear a case that is not ripe (case is brought too early). This means the party must have been harmed or there is an immediate threat of harm. A federal court will also not hear a case that has become moot (case is brought too late). A "real, live controversy" must exist "at all stages of review", not merely when the complaint is filed.[112]

A person who brings a case to federal court must also have standing and show he or she has a concrete stake in the outcome of the controversy. This means the party bringing the action must show an actual injury or harm done and a causal connection between the injury and the conduct complained of (*i.e.,* the injury is traceable to the challenged conduct of the defendant and not another third party). Generally, people do not have standing to challenge the way the government spends tax dollars simply because the person bringing the action is a taxpayer, because their interest is too remote, and the person has not suffered an injury-in-fact.

## THE POLITICS OF MAKING A DECISION

Getting a case to the Supreme Court may seem very political and, because the decisions of the Supreme Court affect every American and the Court hears a small majority of the applications it receives, it can be difficult to get your case before the Court. In fact, the Court accepts 100-150 of the 7,000 cases that it is asked to review each year.[113] If four of the nine justices agree to hear the case, then the case will be heard. The court can decide to hear a case or not and is generally under no obligation to approve or deny an application to hear the case.

---

[112]   *De Funis v. Odegaard*, 416 United States 312 (1974).

[113]   https://www.uscourts.gov/about-federal-courts.

There are a couple ways that the parties can get their cases heard before the Supreme Court. If a party is not satisfied with a lower court decision and wants to get before the Supreme Court, the party can ask the court for review or certiorari. In law, certiorari is a court process to seek judicial review of a decision of a lower court or government agency. Certiorari comes from the name of an English prerogative writ, issued by a superior court to direct that the record of the lower court be sent to the superior court for review. Writs of certiorari are pleas from a party who lost in a lower court who believes there is a procedural or legal problem with the previous verdict. Most cases come before the Supreme Court through writs of certiorari.

When a party who is not a party to a lawsuit would like to influence the court to hear a case, the party may write an amicus curiae brief. Amicus curiae briefs, also known as "friend of the court" briefs, are submitted by concerned groups. They are someone who is not a party to a case who assists a court by offering information, expertise, or insight that has a bearing on the issues in the case. The decision on whether to consider an amicus brief lies within the discretion of the court. The phrase amicus curiae is legal Latin.

When a case goes before the Supreme Court that involves the United States and not two private parties, it is led under the solicitor general, who is a lawyer of the federal government and supervises the litigation.

Once the Court decides to hear the case, the parties submit written arguments with a brief, which is a summary of the argument and states the reasons the Court should rule in their favor. Next, the lawyers for each party will present oral arguments before the Court, where the justices are able to ask questions. Often, the justices have already reviewed the briefs before the oral arguments and can express how he or she is leaning when asking questions. The justices then meet in private conference to discuss the case and make their decisions.

If a case is to be won by any party, it must receive majority opinion of the court, which is the opinion of at least five Supreme Court justices. Usually, one justice is tasked with drafting the majority opinion that represents the views of the other justices. The opinion will state the decision and the reasoning for the decision and sets a precedent for lower courts to follow. Sometimes the Supreme Court will issue concurring opinions written by justices who agree with the majority opinion but for different or extra reasons. A dissenting opinion is written by justices who disagree with the opinion and want to be on the record even though the dissenting opinion is not considered a binding precedent that lower courts are required to follow.

## IMPORTANT SUPREME COURT DECISIONS

Some important Supreme Court decisions over the past 200+ years have provided integral interpretations of the rights guaranteed, although not always explicitly, under the United States Constitution. The judiciary is tasked with interpreting exactly what this means and providing judicial review of laws that may violate these rights. Therefore, whenever the government seeks to regulate these rights or freedoms, the Court will weigh the importance of the right against the interest or policies sought to be served by the governmental regulation.

As discussed above, an important issue decided by the Court was that the Court should be the ultimate decider of what is constitutional in the United States federal government and the states. *Marbury v. Madison*[114] was a landmark United States Supreme Court case that established the principle of judicial review in the United States, meaning that American courts have the power to strike down laws, statutes, and some government actions that they find to violate the Constitution of the United States.

While the Constitution separates governmental powers among the branches of government, the United States Supreme Court interpreted and specified that the separation of powers doctrine specifically prohibits the legislature from interfering with the courts' final judgments in *Plaut*

---

[114] *Marbury v. Madison*, 5 United States 137 (1803).

*v. Spendthrift Farm, Inc.*[115] In this case, the legislature, through Congress, passed a law to provide a special motion for reinstating the cases dismissed as time-barred by Supreme Court rulings. The Court held the law providing for the reinstatement of dismissed cases violated the separation of powers doctrine- the legislature can't tell the judiciary what to do.

The Constitution also established the equal protection clause which provided in part that "[no state shall] deny any person within its jurisdiction the equal protection of the laws."[116] In 1896, the Supreme Court first dissected the meaning of the equal protection clause in *Plessy v. Ferguson.*[117] The Court reviewed a Louisiana law requiring railroads in the state to provide separate cars for white and African American passengers and upheld the constitutionality of the state-mandated racial segregation law for all public facilities as long as the segregated facilities were equal in quality, a doctrine that came to be known as "separate but equal". It took the United States sixty more years to reverse this decision and undo the damage done with the "separate but equal doctrine". *Brown v. Board of Education*[118] was a landmark decision of the United States Supreme Court in which the Court ruled that state laws establishing racial segregation in public schools are unconstitutional, even if the segregated schools are otherwise equal in quality.

The Court also declared that the Constitution required equal protection for women when it held that a state law that discriminated against women was unconstitutional in *Reed v. Reed.*[119]

Certain fundamental rights are protected under the Constitution. Various privacy rights, including marriage, sexual relations, abortion and childrearing, are fundamental rights. Modern rights to privacy guaranteed under the Constitution have been clarified by the Supreme Court.

---

[115] *Plaut v. Spendthrift Farm, Inc.*, 514 United States 211 (1995).

[116] United States Const. Amend. XIV, § 1.

[117] *Plessy v. Ferguson*, 163 United States 537 (1896).

[118] *Brown v. Board of Education*, 347 United States 483 (1954).

[119] *Reed v. Reed*, 404 United States 71 (1971).

In *Griswold v. Connecticut*, the Supreme Court established a "marital zone of privacy" and the fundamental right of a marital relationship protects couples right to buy and use contraceptives without government restrictions.[120] The Supreme Court has also held in *Roe v. Wade* that the right of privacy includes the right of a woman to have an abortion under certain circumstances without undue influence from the state.[121]

Another fundamental right is the freedom of speech, which provides that "Congress shall make no law ...abridging the freedom of speech."[122] The freedom of speech protects the free flow of ideas, a most important function in a democratic society. A regulation or law that tries to forbid speech of specific ideas (content regulation) is more likely to violate the free speech doctrine. It is usually unconstitutional for the government to prohibit speech based on its content. In *Brandenburg v. Ohio*, the Court held that the government could not prohibit political speech, or speech with political content, unless it is linked to immediate lawless behavior.[123] However, conduct regulation, which is content-neutral and regulates how the speech is conducted, is more likely permitted (*i.e.,* law prohibiting billboards for purposes of traffic safety).

While the Constitution remains largely unchanged and is the most important consideration when deciding a case and applying the facts to the law, the Court has recognized the law needs to be flexible and adapt to changing times. The Court has, and will continue to, overrule outdated precedents.

---

[120] *Griswold v. Connecticut*, 381 United States 479 (1965).

[121] *Roe v. Wade*, 410 United States 113 (1973).

[122] United States Const. Amend. I.

[123] *Brandenburg v. Ohio*, 395 United States 444 (1969).

## KEY TERMS

**Adversarial System**: A legal system where two advocates represent their parties' case before an impartial judge or jury, which attempts to determine the truth and pass judgment accordingly.

**Amicus Curiae Brief**: A "friend of the court" brief submitted by someone not a party to the case, offering information or expertise relevant to the case.

**Appeal**: A process by which a case is brought to a higher court for review of the decision made by a lower court.

**Article I Courts**: Courts created by Congress to implement its legislative powers, such as the United States Tax Court.

**Article III Courts**: Courts established under Article III of the Constitution, including the Supreme Court and lower federal courts, which have judges appointed for life.

**Certiorari**: A writ or order by which a higher court reviews a decision of a lower court.

**Civil Law**: Laws that regulate interactions between individuals or organizations, where violations are considered torts rather than crimes.

**Constitutional Law**: Laws derived from the federal and state constitutions, which set the framework for the organization of government and the relationship between the government and individuals.

**Criminal Law**: Laws that prohibit behavior deemed harmful to society, with violations punishable by the state.

**Dissenting Opinion**: An opinion written by one or more judges expressing disagreement with the majority opinion of the court.

**Diversity Jurisdiction**: Federal court jurisdiction over cases involving parties from different states or countries.

**Due Process**: Legal requirement that the state must respect all legal rights owed to a person, including fair procedures.

**Equal Protection Clause**: A clause in the Fourteenth Amendment of the U.S. Constitution stating that no state shall deny any person within its jurisdiction the equal protection of the laws.

**Executive Order**: A rule or order issued by the President or a state governor that has the force of law.

**Judicial Review**: The power of the courts to declare laws, statutes, and actions of the government unconstitutional, established by Marbury v. Madison.

**Litigation**: The process of taking legal action or resolving disputes through the court system.

**Majority Opinion**: The official opinion of the court, representing the views of the majority of judges.

**Original Jurisdiction**: The authority of a court to hear a case for the first time, rather than on appeal.

**Precedent**: A legal decision that serves as an authoritative rule for future similar cases.

**Procedural Law**: Laws that set the procedures for making, administering, and enforcing substantive laws.

**Solicitor General**: A legal officer who represents the federal government in the Supreme Court.

**Standing**: The legal right to bring a lawsuit, requiring that the party has suffered a concrete injury that can be addressed by the court.

**Statutory Law**: Written laws enacted by legislative bodies.

**Substantive Law**: Laws that define the rights and duties of individuals and collective bodies.

**Supreme Court**: The highest court in the United States, which has the ultimate authority in interpreting the Constitution.

**Tort**: A wrongful act or infringement of a right leading to civil legal liability.

**Writ of Certiorari**: An order by the Supreme Court to a lower court to send up the record of a case for review.

# CHAPTER 14

# PUBLIC OPINION

The media can influence the governmental implementation of public policies and the development of public opinion. Policymakers pay attention to both preferences and trends among the public. Preferences are not static and may not remain the same over time. Political involvement relies on how strongly people feel about current political issues. Public opinion polls track and affect election campaigns, the Electoral College and strategic campaign considerations, and the ultimate poll—choosing a president at the ballot box.

Opinions start to develop during childhood, and beliefs subjects acquire early in life are unlikely to change much as they age. The socialization process leaves citizens with attitudes and beliefs that create a personal ideology depending on attitudes and beliefs and prioritizing each belief over the others. To run a successful campaign requires understanding the nature of public opinion and its effects during elections. Campaign managers want to know how citizens will vote and persuade them. Candidates and elected public officials use polls' results to decide their future legislative votes, campaign messages, or propaganda.

# INTRODUCTION TO PUBLIC OPINION, CAMPAIGNS, AND ELECTIONS

Why does it matter what the American public thinks about political issues? In a federal constitutional democratic republic such as the United States, the national government, headed by the president, shares powers with the Congress and the judiciary as mandated by the Constitution. The federal government also shares some powers with state and local governments, again as prescribed in the Constitution. The American people elect their governmental representatives to serve their interests and influence the policymaking process.

Political office-seekers often use *public opinion polls* to determine voters' preferences on various issues, so they can tailor their campaign messages to secure the possible votes hopefully ascend to public office. They seek to persuade citizens during the *campaign.*

Public opinion is what the people may think on any given topic, especially on political issues for our purposes. In our representative democracy, there are two ways of determining what people may be thinking; first, by taking a headcount through polling, second, by asking them to vote in elections.

Polling public opinion is very different from "going to the polls" in actual elections. First, in a public opinion poll, for the sake of accuracy, those taking the poll sample respondents to create a group as representative of the voting public as possible during periods leading up to the actual casting of ballots. In elections, however, the voters take the lead and select whom they wish to lead their country, states, and localities.

Second, timing is a crucial element in polling. Researchers can conduct polls whenever an educational institution, marketing company, or media outlet has the time, money, and inclination to conduct them. Elections are different, as they are held on scheduled dates.

Third, polls are not binding on anyone, and one can pay them attention or choose to ignore them while elections are final. Still, public opinion polling and elections are essentially two ways of doing the same thing, finding out what people think at a specific point in time.

## THE QUALITY OF PUBLIC OPINION

Opinions start to develop during childhood, and beliefs subjects acquire early in life are unlikely to change much as they age.[124] The socialization process leaves citizens with attitudes and beliefs that create a personal ideology depending on attitudes and beliefs and prioritizing each belief over the others. To run a successful campaign requires understanding the nature of public opinion and its effects during elections.[125] Ideally, all citizens would be well informed about government, rules, and relevant political actors. They would also be tolerant of ideas other than their own and willing to compromise to further the collective interest, and happy to participate at various political levels and engage in civic activities. Subjects should receive their news from diverse sources to get in touch with different viewpoints and perspectives.

Most Americans do not always receive their news from high-quality sources, and while they may be theoretically tolerant, they are often less so in practice. Increasingly, some groups have come to view political compromise as a fundamental betrayal of their values. Additionally, United States elections tend to have meager voter turnout rates compared with other democratic countries. All of which leads people to a fundamental question about their government: Whose views should count?

One of the ideals of democracy is *tolerance*, which means that some people who vote in elections may not necessarily be the ones one would prefer. Some voters may even be pursuing a path of *rational ignorance*, that is, choosing not to be informed about politics because the payoff from participating feels too remote or the difference they make seems to be insignificant.

---

[124] *See* Krutz, Glen S. *American Government 2e.*, 2019. Internet resource. Accessed 9 Mar. 2021. Lau, Tim. Brennan Center for Justice, https://www.brennancenter.org/our-work/research-reports/citizens-united-explained, *Citizens United Explained*, accessed 19 March 2021.

[125] On the manufacturing of public opinion, see McNair.

Still, the country may be delivered from an ill-informed populace by specific shortcuts that can lead people toward rationality. Many citizens suffer from a phenomenon known as *online processing*, which is about ending the day with one's head full of opinions picked up on the fly with no clear idea of how one arrived at them. While people often have good reasons for holding their views, sometimes they process them too quickly and with insufficient information. People probably are not as ignorant as they sound. Moreover, they may find that others around can offer them clues as to the nature of things.

The *two-step flow of information* is a psychological process by which *opinion followers* look to opinion leaders for understanding and cues on how to vote[126]. Opinion followers are the vast majority of citizens. In contrast, *opinion leaders* usually prepare themselves through study and research to be well-informed and subsequently get involved in civic activities. Journalists often interview them on TV news and talk shows. Some subjects who receive some higher education may become opinion leaders themselves, providing cues and guidance to family members, friends, and members of groups to which one belongs.

Political parties and interest groups may provide subjects with a form of comprehension similar to the two-step flow, except that the opinion leader is not an individual but a group. Still, one should bear in mind that these shortcuts are not foolproof. There is no guarantee that these shortcuts will lead to decision-making that is, in fact, informed and smart.

## HOW TO KNOW WHAT AMERICANS THINK?

The science of public opinion polling has come a long way. According to The Gallup Organization, a Washington, D.C.-based analytics company

---

[126] See Zaller, especially chapter 9, to better understand two-sided and two-step information flows. Zaller, John. *The Nature and Origins of Mass Opinion*. Cambridge University Press, 2011.

founded in 1935, polls can accurately "tell what proportion of a population has a specific viewpoint."[127]

The modern science of public opinion polling is quite complex. Although statisticians have determined that a random sample of only 1,000 to 2,000 people can be very representative of a state or the country as a whole, modern polling consists of numerous methodologies, techniques, and considerations. Done correctly, this can be a fairly accurate gauge of what people are thinking. Scientific survey research involves random sampling of a population, and some fancy math to extrapolate those results to the public at large. A random sample means that everyone in the target population has an equal chance of being chosen. Survey research firms generate random lists of telephone numbers of voters in a state, district or even an entire country.

What you should look for in reports about survey research is:

1. a specified margin of error (you don't get one without doing the fancy math), and

2. the sample size. The margin of error is a way of judging how confident we are that the results of the survey are in range of what the entire population thinks. If this information is included in the survey, you have some assurance that it's a scientific survey, and not, say, one taken by a congressman by mass-mailing his district.

Legislators and members of Congress infrequently survey people back home, usually by doing a mass mailing to all the registered voters in the district. The problem with those sorts of surveys is that they are not random samples, but self-selecting samples. The only people who

---

[127] Even if polls tell one what proportion of the population has specific viewpoints and shares certain ideas, their purpose is not to change one's mindset. Social researchers are the ones who explain why people believe as they do and what to do about that. For more information, *see* Nielsen, Eric. What Is Public Opinion Polling and Why Is It Important?, *Gallup World Poll*, http://media.gallup.com/muslimwestfacts/pdf/pollingandhowtouseitr1dreveng.pdf, accessed 15 March 2021.

respond to such surveys are those with really strong feelings about an issue, and what we know about them is that there tend to be fewer of them than the mass of folks in the middle.

A *random sample* is a representative subset of a larger population in which everyone has an equal chance of being chosen, and no one group is over-represented. *Sample bias*, however, is when one part of the population has been accorded disproportionate weight. One of the most challenging parts of polling these days is persuading people who may be busy or distracted to offer their responses to questions. A *nonresponse bias* may occur in polls if a particular group is less likely to respond than another. To compensate for any sampling bias, polling companies may use a statistical process called *weighting*. Some groups are given more weight to make the results more accurately reflect what the wider public is thinking. Still, in the end, it is an inexact science, and no poll will be perfect.

One way of narrowing the sample is by taking *likely voter polls*, that is, by questioning people who are the most likely to vote in a forthcoming election. In this effort, pollsters may use *likely voter screens*, which are methods that attempt to weed out nonvoters. Furthermore, no matter what techniques pollsters use, polls' accuracy will always be problems, generally called *sampling errors*. Polls may also be skewed by house effects or how a pollster's results favor Democrats or Republicans. Thus, in light of all this, one finds that all polls will vary at least slightly. Sometimes, in an attempt by media outlets to arrive at more accurate results, methods may be used that pull together the results of several polls in what one calls *polling aggregators*.

Polling came into its own when enough Americans owned telephones to make spot digit dialing an effective way to draw a random sample. *Random digit dialing* was how pollsters could randomly sample Americans by calling them on their landlines. Different kinds of national polls measure where Americans stand on particular issues that are released periodically by major media organizations. *Tracking polls* show data movements over periods to detect changes in support for people or issues. They can be particularly helpful to those running for political office, enabling them to see how they are doing than their opponents.

Researchers take *exit polls* as people leave their places of voting immediately after casting their ballots. The raw data are sometimes leaked early, before the polls close, creating false expectations of who might win or even influence the eventual results. *Fake polls* are sometimes released to manipulate results, but they tell nothing about the real world. The upshot is that polls, in general, are notably informative if researchers conduct them scientifically, but any individual poll can suffer from sampling errors.

## HOW DO SUBJECTS FORM THEIR OPINIONS?

What elements may combine to shape one's political views when gathering and processing information? For one, a transfer of political attitudes, narratives, and beliefs from one generation to another, called *political socialization*, probably contributes to one's outlook. It helps create a stable, loyal citizenry who buys into the system's foundational values by bringing people together around shared values. Some of the socialization agents are families, schools, religious institutions, peer groups, and the media. *Patriotism*, or shared loyalty to one's country and its institutions, is also a potent socialization agent.

Still, some agents may socialize citizens to break into separate groups. Socialization works through a set of interests and values that tend to divide people according to ideologies. *Party identification*, or which political party one identifies with, is probably the most significant influence on one's opinions and votes. Party identification is not a randomly assigned feature to subjects. Data can reveal to researchers critical information concerning this vital component of political socialization.

Race and ethnicity play significant roles in determining party affiliations. Over time, the Republican Party has become whiter, and one sees that African Americans are far more likely to be Democrats, at about a ten-to-one ratio. So are Latinos and Asian Americans, both at two-to-one. There is also a clear *gender gap* in that women are more likely to be Democrats than are men, who are more likely to be Republicans. This situation is even more evident in the case of millennials than in previous generations. *Religion* may also play a role in party affiliation. White evangelical Protestants are much more likely to be Republicans, while Roman Catholics split along ethnic lines, and religiously unaffiliated people are predominantly Democrats. *Education* factors into party alliances, with more-educated voters moving in recent years toward the Democrats. The *location* has become another determinant factor nowadays, with Democrats tending to cluster in urban and, increasingly, suburban areas. Republicans, on the other hand, tend to live in outer suburban and rural areas.

The generations into which people of varying ages may fall also seem to influence how they vote. All the trends one has discussed here become increasingly more robust as the voter pool gets younger over time. Democrats are what journalist and data analyst Ron Brownstein[128] calls the *coalition of the ascendant*—that is, of the racial and ethnic groups getting more prominent and more visible. Republicans are becoming smaller and aging out, what Brownstein calls the *coalition of restoration*—a group composed of older, blue-collar, evangelical rural whites who want to "restore" the last century's social order. Brownstein's research suggests that without a change in the current trends, the parties' gulf will only widen when post-millennials begin to come of age in the next few years.

People may identify with a party initially because it takes policy positions that they agree with, but eventually, the party can become a kind of information shorthand for them. As Americans become more polarized, adopting "*Us vs. Them*" attitudes, voters are becoming less likely to leave their party's comfort zone to vote with the other.

If partisanship is remarkably important in shaping voters' opinions, do natural and practical concerns even matter? Well, some voters will

---

[128] *See* Brownstein, Ronald and National Journal. "The Clinton Conundrum." *The Atlantic*, 17 April 2015, www.theatlantic.com/politics/archive/2015/04/the-clinton-conundrum/431949.

not consider voting for a candidate who does not share their views on one issue that they consider to be fundamental, regardless of party. One refers to them as *single-issue voters*. A growing segment of voters, perhaps as much as thirty percent, eschew any party affiliations. Researchers call them *independent voters* or swing voters. The upshot is that whether one chooses to act on party cues or other socialization influences may depend on whether a particular candidate can motivate people to vote.

## THE ULTIMATE POLL IS VOTING IN ELECTIONS

The United States has one of the lowest voter participation rates among industrialized democratic nations. *Voter turnout* is the percentage of eligible voters who cast ballots, and efforts to legally limit who can vote are known as *regulating the electorate*. These efforts to determine who is allowed to vote, which reached a peak in the decades following the United States Civil War, are still alive and well, even resurging in recent years.

The voters who reliably tend to vote are older, whiter, wealthier, and more educated Americans. Younger voters, newer voters, people of color, single moms, and people lower on the socioeconomic scale are less likely to vote, and if they do, they are more likely to vote for the Democrats.

The voters who reliably tend to vote are older, whiter, wealthier, and more educated Americans. Younger voters, newer voters, people of color, single moms, and people lower on the socioeconomic scale are less likely to vote, and if they do, they are more likely to vote for the Democrats. Republicans reportedly want to make voting less open, and Democrats want to make it simpler for everyone. Republicans have expressed their concerns about voter fraud, specifically people who are not legal voters casting votes, so they want to tighten regulations.

The political stakes in regulating the electorate are high. The continuing battles about regulating the electorate are a political struggle over which party will have the advantage. Since about 2010, Republicans have found it easier to regulate folks out of the electorate than to reach out to groups that tend to vote against them.

The political stakes in regulating the electorate are high. The continuing battles about regulating the electorate are a political struggle over which party will have the advantage. Since about 2010, Republicans have found it easier to regulate folks out of the electorate than to reach out to groups that tend to vote against them.

So, if Americans stopped regulating the electorate, would the United States voter turnout rates increase? Studies show that voter turnout rates would probably increase if Americans decided to reduce the legal barriers to voting. Studies also show that voter fraud is not the problem that Republicans claim it is. Still, one would not achieve 100 percent turnout rates in the United States, as some potential voters have many personal reasons for not voting. They do not have time in their busy schedules to inform themselves enough to care about their voting issues. According to their mindset, their votes will not make a difference, and thus, they do not feel engaged or connected with American society. These citizens perceive there are no meaningful offers to choose from, or it may seem to them that all the available choices are corrupt.

Sometimes their parties do not engage in *voter mobilization*; they fail to make an effort to get out the votes of people who would support them. Encouraging party members to go to the polls can also be referred to as *get-out-the-vote (GOTV)* efforts. As one has seen above, this is a burden that tends to weigh more heavily on Democrats.

What difference does it make if people do not vote? People's decisions not to vote or their failure to exercise their rights affect the Democrats more than the Republicans, and not voting can reduce an elected government's legitimacy. An endorsement from the voters to govern is called an *electoral mandate*. The upshot is that voting is of great importance so that policymakers, politicians, and researchers account for everyone's policy preferences, and people can feel invested in their government's actions.

## TAKING A POLL

Most public opinion polls strive for accuracy, however achieving this goal is challenging. Political polling is a discipline that follows scientific principles. Polls are intricate and necessitate meticulous planning and attention from the design phase to the implementation phase. The polling tactics used by Mitt Romney's campaign are just one recent example of issues arising from polling techniques. Throughout our history, there have been numerous instances where polling firms have generated results that inaccurately forecasted popular sentiment as a result of inadequate survey design or flawed polling techniques.

In 1936, Literary Digest maintained its customary practice of conducting surveys among residents to ascertain the prospective winner of the presidential election. The magazine dispatched opinion cards to those who possessed a subscription, a telephone, or a car registration. Only a portion of the receivers returned their cards. What is the outcome? Alf Landon was projected to earn 55.4 percent of the popular vote; however, he ultimately garnered a mere 38 percent. Franklin D. Roosevelt secured re-election, highlighting the need to employ scientific methods when conducting surveys.

In the 1948 presidential election, Thomas Dewey was defeated by Harry Truman, even though polls indicated that Dewey had a significant lead and Truman was expected to lose. John Zogby, from Zogby Analytics, publicly forecasted that John Kerry would defeat incumbent president George W. Bush in the 2004 presidential election. However, his prediction turned out to be incorrect on election night. These examples are limited in number, yet each provides a distinct lesson. In 1948, pollsters did not conduct polling on the day of the election, instead relying on outdated data that did not account for a recent change in voter sentiment. Zogby's polls failed to accurately capture the preferences of probable voters and made erroneous predictions regarding voter turnout and candidate support. These instances emphasize the importance of employing scientific methodologies in conducting polls and exercising caution when presenting the findings.

The majority of polling firms hire statisticians and methodologists who are skilled in conducting surveys and evaluating data. Several prerequisites must be fulfilled in order to conduct a poll in a scientifically rigorous manner. Initially, the methodologists ascertain the target demographic, or specific group, of individuals they wish to conduct interviews with. For instance, in order to forecast the outcome of the presidential election, it is necessary to conduct interviews with individuals residing in various regions of the United States. To gain insight into the voting preferences of Colorado residents on a proposition, it is imperative that the sample population consists only of individuals who reside in Colorado. When conducting surveys on elections or policy topics, many polling organizations will exclusively interview respondents who have a track record of voting in past elections, as these individuals are more inclined to actually cast their votes on Election Day.

Politicians are more inclined to be swayed by the viewpoints of established voters rather than those of ordinary folks. After identifying the desired population, the researchers will proceed to construct a sample that is both random and representative. A random sample is a subset of individuals from a larger population, chosen in a manner that ensures every individual has an equal probability of being selected. In the initial stages of polling, telephone numbers of possible respondents were randomly chosen from different regions to prevent any regional bias. Although landline phones enable pollsters to attempt to assure randomness, the growing prevalence of cell phones poses challenges to this procedure. Cell phones, together with their corresponding numbers, are easily transportable and accompany the owner wherever they go. In order to avoid mistakes, surveys that involve recognized mobile phone numbers can employ zip codes and other geographical markers to mitigate regional bias. A representative sample is a subset of a population that has a similar demographic distribution to the entire population. For instance, approximately 51 percent of the population in the United States is comprised of females. In order to accurately represent the demographic distribution of women, any poll designed to gauge the opinions of the majority of

Americans on a particular issue should include a sample that somewhat over-represents women compared to men.

Pollsters endeavor to conduct interviews with a certain number of individuals in order to establish a statistically representative sample of the community. The sample size will fluctuate depending on the population size being surveyed and the desired level of precision the pollster aims to achieve. If the survey aims to ascertain the viewpoint of a state or group, such as the perspective of Wisconsin voters regarding modifications to the school system, the sample size may range from five hundred to one thousand respondents and yield results with a relatively small margin of error. In order to accurately gauge the national opinion of Americans, particularly regarding the White House's stance on climate change, it is imperative to increase the sample size of the survey.

The sample size differs among organizations and institutions due to variations in data processing methods. Gallup frequently conducts interviews with a sample size of only five hundred respondents, although Rasmussen Reports and Pew Research typically interview a larger sample size ranging from one thousand to fifteen hundred people. Academic institutions, such as the American National Election Studies, conduct interviews with more than 2,500 respondents.[34] Increasing the sample size enhances the accuracy of a poll as it reduces the likelihood of atypical replies and ensures a more representative portrayal of the overall population. Pollsters do not exceed the required number of respondents during interviews. Augmenting the quantity of respondents will enhance the precision of the poll. However, once the poll reaches a sufficient number of respondents to be statistically representative, further improvements in accuracy become negligible and are not economically viable. The accuracy of the poll will be seen in a reduced margin of error when the sample accurately represents the entire population. The margin of error is a numerical measure that quantifies the potential deviation between the poll findings and the true opinion of the entire population of citizens.

A poll becomes more predictive as the margin of error decreases. Significant margins of error pose a challenge. For instance, if a survey predicts that Elizabeth Warren is expected to secure 30 percent of the vote in the 2020 Massachusetts Democratic primary with a margin of error of +/-6, it indicates that Warren's actual vote share might range from as low as 24 percent (30 - 6) to as high as 36 percent (30 + 6). A smaller margin of error is very desirable as it provides us with a more accurate depiction of people's true opinions or future actions. Amidst the abundance of polls, how can one determine the reliability and predictive accuracy of a certain poll in reflecting the beliefs of a particular group? Initially, search for the numerical values. Polling firms demonstrate their scientific reliability by providing information such as the margin of error, polling dates, number of respondents, and demographic sampled. Has the poll been conducted recently? Does the question possess clarity and impartiality? Did the number of respondents meet the threshold required for population prediction? Is the margin of error minimal? When interpreting poll results, it is worthwhile to search for this vital information. While the majority of polling agencies aim to produce high-quality polls, there are other organizations that favor quick results and may prioritize immediate figures over random and representative samples. News networks frequently employ instant polling to promptly evaluate the performance of candidates in a debate.

## VIEWS ON POLITICAL MATTERS AND GOVERNMENTAL STRATEGIES

What is the perception of Americans toward their political system, policies, and institutions? The fluctuation of public opinion has been evident throughout the years. The fluctuations are influenced by various factors such as timing, events, and the individuals occupying significant positions of power. Occasionally, the majority of the general population shares common ideals, but frequently this is not the case. Where, then, do the opinions of the public align and diverge? First, let us examine the two-party system, followed by an analysis of viewpoints pertaining to public policy, economic policy, and social policy.

## TWO-PARTY SYSTEM

The collective sentiment of the general public has the potential to undergo substantial transformations as time progresses. Over the past two decades, public opinion on same-sex marriage and immigration has experienced significant and notable changes. The United States has historically operated under a two-party system. The presidency and seats in Congress are often won by Democrats and Republicans, with only a few outliers. Most voters tend to vote exclusively for candidates from the Republican and Democratic parties, even if there are third-party candidates on the ballot. However, citizens express their dissatisfaction with the existing party structure. Merely 33 percent of individuals classify themselves as Democrats, with a mere 29 percent identifying as Republicans, while 34 percent label themselves as independent. The Democratic Party's membership has remained relatively stable, while the Republican Party has experienced a decline of approximately 5 percent in its membership over the past decade. In contrast, the number of individuals identifying as independents has increased from 30 percent in 2004 to 34 percent in 2020.

Consequently, it is unsurprising that 58 percent of Americans believe that a third political party is necessary in the United States today. Certain fluctuations in party affiliation may be attributed to generational and cultural changes. The Democratic Party is more likely to receive support from Millennials and Generation Xers than to the Republican Party. According to a 2015 survey, 51 percent of Millennials and 49 percent of Generation Xers expressed their agreement, while just 35 percent and 38 percent, respectively, showed their support for the Republican Party. Baby Boomers, those born between 1946 and 1964, exhibit a little lower inclination compared to other demographic groups in supporting the Democratic Party, with only 47 percent reporting their allegiance to the party. The Silent Generation, which refers to individuals born in the 1920s to early 1940s, is the sole age group where a majority of its members express their support for the Republican Party.

The growing population of multiracial individuals with deep cultural ties may lead to another revolution in politics. Currently, approximately 7 percent of the population identifies as biracial or multiracial, and it is expected that this figure will increase in the future. The population of individuals who self-identify as both African American and White experienced a twofold increase between 2000 and 2010. In contrast, the population of individuals who self-identify as both Asian American and White expanded by 87 percent during the same period. According to the Pew study, a mere 37 percent of multiracial adults expressed support for the Republican Party, while a majority of 57 percent favored the Democratic Party. Furthermore, in the 2020 presidential election, the Democratic Party nominated Kamala Harris, who is of African American and Indian heritage, as their vice-presidential candidate, making her the first multiracial woman to hold this position in the country. As the demographic makeup of the United States evolves and new generations join the voting population, public concerns and expectations will also undergo transformation.

Politics fundamentally revolves on the equitable distribution of limited resources and the delicate equilibrium between individual freedoms and entitlements. Public policy frequently gets complex as politicians grapple with resolving issues within the country's constrained budget while accommodating diverse perspectives on the most effective approach to do so. Although the general population mostly remains silent, participating in public opinion polls or diligently voting on Election Day, there are instances when citizens express their views more vocally through protests or lobbying. Certain policy choices are made without soliciting public input if they maintain the current allocation of funds or defer to existing policies. However, policies that have a direct impact on individuals' financial situations, such as tax policy, might lead to a negative reaction from the public. Furthermore, policies that undermine civil liberties or deeply held values can result in even greater public unrest. Novel policies elicit comparable reactions from the public and bring about transformative shifts that some individuals find challenging. The approval of same-sex marriage created a conflict between individuals who wanted to uphold their religious convictions and those who wanted equal treatment under the law.

What is the public's stance on economic policy? Merely 27 percent of those questioned in 2021 held the view that the U.S. economy was in a commendable or satisfactory state. However, 53 percent stated that their personal financial circumstances were excellent or good. Although this may appear contradictory, it is a reflection of our tendency to pay more attention to external events rather than our own domestic affairs. Even if a family's personal finances are secure, its members will still be cognizant of acquaintances and relatives who are experiencing unemployment or home foreclosures. This knowledge will provide them with a more comprehensive and pessimistic perspective of the economy that extends beyond their personal financial situation.

In contrast to the widespread public endorsement of fiscal prudence and reductions in government expenditure a decade ago, the year 2019 witnessed a notable absence of public support for any form of budget cuts when queried about government spending or reductions in thirteen budgetary domains. In fact, there was a prevailing inclination towards augmenting expenditure in all thirteen areas. The majority of respondents, 72 percent, expressed their support for increased expenditure in the areas of education and veterans benefits. In contrast, only 9 percent of respondents favored cutbacks to education, and 4 percent favored cuts to veterans benefits. Even in sectors where a greater number of Americans desired reductions, such as aid to the unemployed (23 percent of respondents supported spending cuts), there was a larger faction (31 percent) in favor of increased spending, and an even larger group (43 percent) wanting spending to remain at its current level. A 2020 survey conducted by Pew revealed that the public's worry about expanding budget deficits has been further diminished by the COVID-19 pandemic.

Social policy encompasses the efforts of the government to regulate public conduct with the aim of creating a more improved society. In order to achieve this, the government must successfully navigate the challenging endeavor of striking a balance between the rights and liberties of its population. The right to privacy of an individual may require restriction if there is a threat to the safety of another person. To what degree should the government encroach onto the personal affairs of its citizens? According to a recent survey, 54 percent of respondents expressed the belief that the U.S. government was excessively engaged in addressing matters of morality.

Abortion is a contentious social policy matter that has sparked controversy for almost a century. A certain demographic seeks to safeguard the rights of the fetus. Another individual seeks to safeguard women's bodily autonomy and the privacy rights pertaining to the relationship between a patient and her doctor. The division is evident in public opinion surveys, with 59 percent of respondents supporting the legality of abortion in most situations, while 39 percent oppose it. Similarly, the Affordable Care Act, which expanded government participation in healthcare, has sparked comparable controversy. According to a 2017 survey, the Affordable Care Act (ACA) received support from 56 percent of respondents, which is a 20 percent increase since 2013. On the other hand, 38 percent of respondents voiced dislike of the act. Currently, the ACA is seeing higher levels of popularity than ever before. The popularity of health insurance in the United States can be attributed to several factors, namely the increased number of Americans with health insurance, the prohibition of denying coverage based on pre-existing diseases, and the improved affordability of health insurance for a significant portion of the population.

A significant portion of the general public's initial dissatisfaction with the ACA stemmed from the requirement that individuals must obtain health insurance or face a penalty. This provision was implemented to ensure a sufficiently large group of insured individuals, thereby lowering the overall cost of coverage. However, some individuals perceived this requirement as an encroachment on personal autonomy. After the conclusion of 2018, the penalty for the individual mandate was decreased to zero. The enactment of laws permitting same-sex marriage prompts the inquiry as to whether the government should be responsible for delineating the institution of marriage and overseeing private relationships in order to safeguard individual and marital entitlements. The perception of the general public has undergone a significant and rapid change in the past two decades. In 1996, only 27 percent of Americans supported the legalization of same-sex marriage. However, recent polls indicate that support has risen significantly to 70 percent. Despite this increase, several states had prohibited same-sex marriage until the Supreme Court ruled in Obergefell v. Hodges (2015) that states were required to grant marriage licenses to same-sex couples and recognize same-sex marriages performed in other states. Some churches and businesses argue that the government should not force them to acknowledge or endorse same-sex marriages if it conflicts with their religious beliefs. Undoubtedly, this issue will continue to create a division in public opinion.

Public safety is another domain in which social policy must carefully reconcile rights and liberties. The regulation of gun ownership elicits intense emotions due to its connection to the Second Amendment and the cultural values of the state. Among the respondents surveyed across the country, 50 percent of Americans expressed a preference for prioritizing the reduction of gun violence, while 43 percent favored emphasizing the right to bear arms. Additionally, 53 percent of the participants believe that there should be stricter regulations on gun ownership. It is worth noting that these percentages vary across different states due to differences in political culture. Immigration also generates conflict, as Americans are concerned about the rise in crime and social expenditure resulting from the influx of individuals entering the United States unlawfully. However, 69 percent of the participants expressed support for granting citizenship to undocumented residents already present in the country. Additionally, although marijuana is currently classified as an illegal substance according to the national government's drug policy, 68 percent of the respondents indicated their agreement with the potential legalization of marijuana.

## RELATIONSHIP BETWEEN PUBLIC OPINION AND POLITICAL INSTITUTIONS

Public sentiment towards American institutions is gauged through public approval ratings, rather than through considerations of selecting between positions or individuals. The scrutiny and daily media discussions mostly focus on the congressional and executive arms of government. Survey firms conduct daily approval polls for both of these branches. The frequency of press coverage regarding the Supreme Court is quite low, and approval ratings tend to increase following the announcement of significant court rulings. However, all three branches are vulnerable to fluctuations in public support in response to their activities and national events. Approval ratings tend to be volatile for all three. Next, we will examine each one individually.

The president serves as the most prominent representative of the U.S. government and often attracts strong controversy. Presidents frequently face criticism for the actions taken by their administrations and political parties and are held responsible for economic and foreign policy setbacks. Due to these factors, it is likely that their approval ratings will gradually decrease over time, fluctuating slightly in response to individual occurrences. The average approval rating of presidents upon assuming office is 66 percent, but it declines to 53 percent by the conclusion of their first term. The average initial approval rating for presidents serving a second term is 55.5 percent, but it declines to 47 percent by the conclusion of their tenure. Throughout the most of his term, President Obama's presidency adhered to a consistent pattern. Upon assuming office, his initial public approval rating stood at 67 percent. However, it gradually declined to 54 percent by the third quarter, further dropping to 52 percent following his reelection. As of

October 2015, his approval rating had reached 46 percent. Nevertheless, starting from January 2016, his popularity rating saw an upward trend, and he concluded his term with a 59 percent approval rating. President Trump's approval ratings were notably below average, starting his term with a 45 percent approval rating and ending in January 2021 with a 34 percent approval rating. Furthermore, during his administration, Trump's approval rating never exceeded 49 percent. As of March 2021, President Biden's approval rating stood at 54 percent.

Occurrences throughout a president's tenure can cause a sudden increase in public approval ratings. The public approval rating of George W. Bush had a significant increase, rising from 51 percent on September 10, 2001, to 86 percent by September 15, in response to the 9/11 attacks. After the first Persian Gulf War in 1991, George H. W. Bush, the user's father, experienced a significant increase in his approval ratings, rising from 58 to 89 percent. However, these surges of popularity are typically short-lived, lasting only a few weeks. As a result, presidents make an effort to promptly utilize the political influence they gain during these periods. For instance, the rally effect following the 9/11 attacks facilitated the swift approval of a legislative joint resolution granting the president the authority to deploy military forces. This led to the actualization of the "global war on terror". However, the rally effect was short-lived, and support for the wars in Iraq and Afghanistan declined rapidly after 2003.

Public approval ratings of presidents vary, making it challenging to compare them due to the influence of external factors such as national and global events, which are outside a president's jurisdiction. Some chief executives oversaw economies in decline or times of conflict, while others had the advantage of robust economy and periods of peace. On the other hand, Gallup calculates the average approval rating for each president for their whole tenure in office. The mean approval rating of George W. Bush from 2001 to 2008 was 49.4 percent. Ronald Reagan's approval rating from 1981 to 1988 was 52.8 percent, even though he won all but thirteen electoral votes in his bid for reelection. Bill

Clinton's average approval rating from 1993 to 2000, which encompasses the period when the Monica Lewinsky affair occurred and his subsequent impeachment, stood at 55.1 percent. When comparing other prominent presidents, John F. Kennedy had an average approval rating of 70.1 percent, whereas Richard Nixon had an average of 49 percent. Kennedy's high average can be attributed to the fact that his presidency was cut short due to his assassination, which limited the time for his ratings to decrease. Nixon's atypically low approval ratings are a consequence of extensive media and congressional investigations into his complicity in the Watergate scandal, as well as his decision to resign in anticipation of probable impeachment.

## KEY TERMS

**Approval ratings**: A measure of public support for a political figure or institution, typically expressed as a percentage.

**Civil liberties**: Individual rights protected by law from governmental interference.

**Coalition of the ascendant**: A term referring to the growing demographic groups that support the Democratic Party.

**Coalition of restoration**: A term referring to the shrinking, older demographic groups that support the Republican Party and desire a return to past social norms.

**Electoral College**: The body of electors established by the United States Constitution to elect the president and vice president.

**Exit polls**: Surveys conducted immediately after voters leave the polling stations, used to predict the outcome of an election.

**Fake polls**: Polls released to manipulate public opinion without accurately reflecting reality.

**Gallup Organization**: A Washington, D.C.-based analytics company known for conducting public opinion polls.

**Get-out-the-vote (GOTV)**: Efforts by political parties or organizations to encourage their supporters to vote in elections.

**House effects**: Systematic differences in polling results that favor one political party over another due to the polling methodology used by a particular polling firm.

**Likely voter polls**: Polls that attempt to gauge the opinions of individuals most likely to vote in an upcoming election.

**Margin of error**: A measure of the accuracy of a public opinion poll, indicating the range within which the true opinion of the entire population is likely to fall.

**Nonresponse bias**: A type of bias that occurs in polls when certain groups are less likely to respond, leading to an unrepresentative sample.

**Online processing**: The phenomenon where people form opinions based on information acquired on the fly without clear reasoning.

**Opinion leaders**: Individuals who are well-informed and actively engaged in civic activities, influencing the opinions of others.

**Opinion followers**: The majority of citizens who look to opinion leaders for guidance on political matters.

**Party identification**: The political party with which an individual identifies, often a significant influence on their opinions and voting behavior.

**Polling aggregators**: Methods that combine the results of multiple polls to arrive at a more accurate overall result.

**Public opinion polls**: Surveys conducted to gauge the public's views on various issues, often used to guide political campaigns and policymaking.

**Random digit dialing**: A method used by pollsters to create a random sample by calling telephone numbers randomly generated.

**Random sample**: A subset of a population where each member has an equal chance of being selected, used in polling to ensure representativeness.

**Sampling bias**: A distortion in polling results caused by a sample that is not representative of the entire population.

**Sampling errors**: Errors in polling results due to the nature of sampling, which can never perfectly represent the entire population.

**Two-step flow of information**: A process where opinion leaders first receive information and then pass it on to opinion followers, influencing their views.

**Voter turnout**: The percentage of eligible voters who cast a ballot in an election.

**Weighting**: A statistical process used in polling to adjust the results to better reflect the wider population, compensating for any sampling bias.

# CHAPTER 15

---

# CAMPAIGNS AND ELECTIONS

Campaign managers understand that in order to secure victory in an election, they must accomplish two essential tasks: effectively communicate their candidate's information to the electorate and motivate voters to actively participate by casting their votes. To achieve these objectives, candidates and their campaigns frequently attempt to focus their efforts on individuals who are most inclined to participate in the voting process. Regrettably, these voters exhibit variability from one election to another and occasionally from one year to another. Primary and caucus voters differ from voters who only participate in presidential general elections. Certain years experience a rise in the participation of younger voters in the electoral process. The outcome of elections is inherently uncertain, and political campaigns must be flexible and responsive in order to have their desired impact.
Fundraising

Early funding is crucial for politicians, even if they have meticulously planned and executed their presidential campaign. Financial resources contribute to their success, and the capacity to generate funds distinguishes those who are capable. Indeed, the greater the amount of funds a candidate accumulates, the more they will persist in raising. At the beginning of the 2016 election season, a number of Republican candidates had raised a significant amount of money compared to their opponents. Jeb Bush and Ted Cruz emerged as the leading fundraisers by July 2015, with Cruz claiming $14 million and Bush reporting $11 million in contributions. By contrast, Bobby Jindal and George Pataki, who withdrew from the race at an early stage, each disclosed contributions of less than $1 million during the same timeframe. Bush subsequently disclosed a sum above $100 million in contributions, although the remaining Republican candidates consistently claimed lesser contribution amounts. Media coverage of Bush's fundraising highlighted his influential financial connections, whereas the coverage of other contenders centered on their limited financial resources. Donald Trump, who would later become the Republican nominee and president, had a relatively small amount of money raised during the primary phase. This was due to the fact that he received a significant amount of media attention for his controversial reputation, which did not require him to spend as much on advertising. In addition, he entertained the notion of becoming a candidate who would finance his own campaign totally.

The Democratic field in 2020 was initially filled with numerous candidates, but it gradually narrowed down to a small number of contenders in early March. At that point, most of the candidates withdrew from the race, leaving only Senator Bernie Sanders and former Vice President Joseph Biden as the remaining candidates. The individuals who withdrew from the race include former New York City mayor Michael Bloomberg, Pete Buttigieg, former congresswoman Tulsi Gabbard, Senator Amy Klobuchar, and Senator Elizabeth Warren. The candidates' cash-on-hand balances in March were $11,179,565, $6,011,814, $640,210, $2,281,636, and $4,534,180, respectively. Sanders subsequently withdrew from the race on April 8, having $16,176,082 remaining in his campaign funds, so allowing Biden to easily secure the nomination.

## COMPARING PRIMARY AND GENERAL CAMPAIGNS

While the ultimate objective of candidates in both primary and general elections is to secure victory, both races diverge significantly from each other and necessitate distinct strategic approaches. Voting in primary elections poses greater challenges for the voter. There is an increased number of candidates competing to become the nominee of their respective political party. Party identification is not a reliable indicator as each party has multiple candidates instead of simply one. In the 2016 presidential election, Republican voters in the early primaries were offered a variety of choices, including as Mike Huckabee, Donald Trump, Jeb Bush, Ted Cruz, Marco Rubio, John Kasich, Chris Christie, Carly Fiorina, Ben Carson, and others. (Huckabee, Christie, and Fiorina withdrew from the race at an early stage.) In the year 2020, Democrats were faced with the decision of choosing between Joe Biden, Bernie Sanders, Kamala Harris, Pete Buttegieg, Michael Bloomberg, Cory Booker, Amy Klobuchar, and Elizabeth Warren. In order to determine which candidate aligns most closely with their preferred issue viewpoints, voters can seek out additional information about each contender. Given the constraints of time, voters may be unable to thoroughly investigate every candidate. Furthermore, not all candidates will receive sufficient media coverage or debate opportunities to effectively communicate with the people. The challenges posed by these concerns make it arduous to conduct a campaign in a primary election, thereby prompting campaign managers to customize their strategy accordingly.

Initially, the significance of name awareness cannot be overstated. It is improbable that voters will choose to vote for someone who is not well-known. While certain candidates, such as Hillary Clinton and Jeb Bush in 2016 or Joe Biden and Bernie Sanders in 2020, have either had or have familial ties to individuals who held national office, the majority of candidates are often governors, senators, or municipal officials who are not as widely recognized on a national scale. Barack Obama served as a junior senator representing Illinois, while Bill Clinton held the position of governor of Arkansas before both of them pursued the presidency.

Voters nationwide had limited access to information about the candidates, and both contenders required media exposure to gain recognition. Established candidates with extensive track records are more susceptible to opposition attacks, but they also have more ease in gathering campaign funding due to their higher chances of winning. Emerging candidates encounter the obstacle of substantiating their worth during the limited duration of the primary season, rendering them more prone to defeat. In 2016, both final party nominees possessed substantial familiarity and awareness among the public. Hillary Clinton gained prominence due to her roles as First Lady, a U.S. senator representing New York, and secretary of state. Donald Trump gained widespread recognition due to his prominent status as a renowned real estate magnate, with his Trump towers being present across the globe, as well as his television career as a reality TV personality on shows such as The Apprentice. In 2020, Joe Biden, the Democratic nominee, gained name recognition because to his prior service in the United States. He has been a member of the Senate for a long time and has served two terms as vice president under President Barack Obama.

Furthermore, exposure plays a key role when a candidate is just one among a multitude of others in a lengthy procession. As voters want efficient and valuable information, candidates will strive to attract media attention and gain momentum. Media coverage is particularly crucial for candidates who are relatively new to the political scene. The majority of voters think that a candidate's website and other campaign materials will be biased, presenting only the most favorable information. Contrarily, the media is commonly regarded as more dependable and impartial compared to a candidate's promotional materials. Consequently, voters rely on news networks and journalists to gather information regarding the candidates' backgrounds and stances on many issues. Candidates are cognizant of voters' inclination for expeditious information and news and endeavor to secure interviews or press coverage for themselves. Candidates also gain an advantage from news coverage that is more extensive and cost-effective compared to campaign advertisements.

Campaign commercials in primary elections seldom reference political parties and instead prioritize issue viewpoints or name familiarity. Several of the most effective primary advertisements assist voters in identifying shared issue viewpoints with the candidate. In 2008, Hillary Clinton sponsored a holiday advertisement where she was observed packaging gifts. Each gift was accompanied by a card indicating a specific stance on an issue, such as "withdrawal of troops" or "universal pre-kindergarten." Similarly, Mike Huckabee garnered popularity and established his opinion on issues through a hilarious primary advertisement in 2008. In the "HuckChuck" advertisement, Chuck Norris repeatedly mentioned Huckabee's name while enumerating the candidate's stance on several issues. Norris's statement, "Mike Huckabee desires to abolish the IRS," was among several declarations that consistently mentioned Huckabee's name, so enhancing voters' familiarity with him. Although neither of these contenders secured the nomination, the advertisements garnered millions of views and proved to be effective as primary campaign advertisements.

During the general election, each political party is limited to a single candidate, and their campaign advertisements must aim to achieve distinct objectives among various groups of voters. Given that the majority of people who are affiliated with a political party will vote for their party's candidate, political campaigns must focus on targeting independent and undecided voters. Additionally, they must also make efforts to persuade their own party members to actively participate in the voting process. Certain advertisements may prioritize addressing specific issues and policy perspectives, while also drawing comparisons between the two primary candidates from different political parties. Additional advertisements will serve as a reminder to devoted supporters of the political party about the significance of casting their vote. President Lyndon B. Johnson employed the notorious "Daisy Girl" advertisement, which juxtaposed a little girl counting daisy petals with the detonation of an atomic bomb, in order to elucidate the imperative for people to participate in the electoral process and support his candidacy. Johnson insinuated that if the voters abstained from voting, his Republican opponent Barry Goldwater may initiate a nuclear war. The advertisement was broadcasted once as a paid advertisement on NBC before it was removed. However, the footage was shown on other news stations as news presenters discussed the controversy surrounding it. In the 2020 campaign, Joe Biden utilized the "What Happens Now" advertisement to highlight his experience in crisis management, contrasting it with President Trump's mishandling of the COVID-19 pandemic.

One factor contributing to the success of Johnson's campaign ad is the higher voter turnout in general elections compared to earlier elections. These supplementary voters typically exhibit less ideological inclinations and greater independence, rendering them more challenging to pinpoint yet potentially susceptible to persuasion. Moreover, they are less inclined to engage in extensive research on the candidates, prompting campaigns to frequently resort to crafting negative advertisements that appeal to emotions. Although negative advertisements have the potential to reduce voter participation by fostering cynicism towards politics and the electoral process, they are nevertheless effective in capturing the attention and retention of voters.

## EXTERNAL ORGANIZATIONS

External organizations also contribute to the proliferation of bad advertisements. Occasionally, political action committees and other organizations execute shadow campaigns, which are independent of candidates and without their coordination or guidance, to employ negative advertisements as a means of reaching voters. Prior to the Citizens United ruling, which granted corporations and interest groups the ability to air advertisements in favor of political candidates, covert operations were already in existence. In 2004, the Swift Boat Veterans for Truth organization aired advertisements criticizing John Kerry's military service history, while MoveOn criticized George W. Bush's choice to engage in the conflicts in Afghanistan and Iraq. During the year 2020, an amount over $2.3 billion was contributed by super PACs to endorse political candidates. Furthermore, general campaigns also aim to mobilize people in hotly disputed states to participate in the electoral process. In 2004, recognizing the challenge of persuading Ohio Democrats to vote in favor of the Republican party, George W. Bush's campaign strategically prioritized mobilizing the state's Republican voters to participate in the election. The volunteers canvassed precincts and visited Republican households to generate enthusiasm for Bush and the upcoming election. Volunteers, including individuals affiliated with the Republican party and those who were previously affiliated with the Republican party, made phone calls to remind people of their voting obligations, including the date and location. This approach proved successful and served as a reminder to future political campaigns that a well-coordinated initiative to encourage voter turnout remains an effective method to secure victory in an election.

## TECHNOLOGY

Historically, campaigns have consistently incurred high costs. Furthermore, they have occasionally exhibited a pessimistic and malicious attitude. The 1828 "Coffin Handbill" used by John Quincy Adams during his campaign included a detailed account of the executions that Andrew Jackson, his opponent, had authorized. This information was presented with the names of the individuals executed. In addition to engaging in gossip and verbal attacks, there were also criticisms directed on Jackson's wife, who unintentionally committed bigamy by marrying him without obtaining a valid divorce. Since then, campaigns and politicians have not grown more friendly or cooperative. After television became a common feature in households, political campaign advertising transitioned to broadcasting over the radio. Television enabled candidates to establish a connection with people by means of video, so enabling them to directly appeal to and forge an emotional bond with voters. Although Adlai Stevenson and Dwight D. Eisenhower were pioneers in utilizing television during their 1952 and 1956 campaigns, their advertisements primarily consisted of catchy tunes accompanied by visuals. Stevenson's advertisement titled "Let's Not Forget the Farmer" featured a memorable melody, but its animated visuals lacked seriousness and made no contribution to the intended message. The "Eisenhower Answers America" segments provided Eisenhower with the opportunity to respond to policy inquiries, but his responses were superficial and unhelpful.

John Kennedy's campaign pioneered the use of visual imagery to convey the message that the candidate was the preferred choice for all voters. The advertisement titled "Kennedy" featured a catchy melody "Kennedy for me" and showcased photos of a varied populace navigating life in the United States. The Museum of the Moving Image has amassed presidential campaign advertisements from 1952 to the present day, which includes the aforementioned "Kennedy for Me" commercial. Observe and analyze how candidates have devised advertisements to capture the attention and secure the votes of voters throughout the years.

Gradually, advertisements evolved to become increasingly pessimistic and deceptive. The Bipartisan Campaign Reform Act of 2002, also known as McCain-Feingold, mandated that candidates must endorse their advertisements and add a recorded statement within the ad confirming their approval of the message. Despite the persistently hostile nature of advertisements, particularly those funded by super PACs, candidates are now held accountable for their content.

Candidates often utilize interviews on late night television as a means to disseminate their messaging. Infotainment, sometimes known as soft news, is a contemporary style of news that merges fun and informative elements. Television programs such as The Daily Show and Last Week Tonight use humor and satire to inform viewers about current events both nationally and globally. In 2008, political candidates Huckabee, Obama, and McCain appeared on popular shows like The Daily Show, The Colbert Report, and Late Night with Conan O'Brien to appeal to well-informed voters under the age of 45. The candidates successfully demonstrated their humorous sides and projected an image of relatability to the common American, all while briefly discussing their policy opinions. By autumn 2015, The Late Show with Stephen Colbert has already conducted interviews with the majority of the prospective presidential candidates, such as Hillary Clinton, Bernie Sanders, Jeb Bush, Ted Cruz, and Donald Trump.

The advent of the Internet has provided candidates with a novel venue and a fresh approach to reach out to voters. In the 2000 election, political campaigns transitioned to the internet and established websites as a means of disseminating information. In addition, they commenced utilizing search engine results to specifically target voters with advertisements. In 2004, Democratic candidate Howard Dean utilized the Internet as a means of connecting with prospective contributors. Instead of organizing costly dinners to generate donations, his campaign opted to share a video on his website showcasing the candidate consuming a turkey sandwich. The ploy generated almost $200,000 in campaign contributions and reaffirmed Dean's dedication to being an approachable candidate. Candidates furthermore utilize social media platforms, like as Facebook, Twitter, and YouTube, to engage with their followers and capture the interest of younger voters. Internet websites are increasingly being used in political campaigns, but the rise of social media has significantly amplified the impact of online information and communication. Candidates utilize social media platforms, including as Facebook, Twitter, and YouTube, to engage with their followers and capture the interest of the younger electorate. Significantly, social media has emerged as a highly significant platform for citizens to engage in political discourse, exchanging viewpoints, memes, and barbs with their selected networks of contacts and friends. Facebook and Twitter initiated monitoring measures to detect falsehoods and partiality in that context, resulting in the removal of social media accounts belonging to offenders, including President Trump.

## VOTER DECISION-MAKING

When citizens participate in voting, how do they arrive at their decisions? The electoral landscape is intricate, and the majority of voters lack the time to thoroughly investigate all aspects of the candidates and issues. However, they must do a comprehensive and logical evaluation of the options available for an elected position. In order to achieve this objective, they often resort to expedient measures.

One commonly used method is to vote based on party affiliation. Party-line voting is often regarded as reasonable by political scientists, as voters typically align themselves with political parties based on either their policy preferences or socialization. Likewise, candidates associate themselves with political parties depending on their stances on certain issues. A Democrat who casts their vote for a Democrat candidate is very likely to choose the candidate who aligns most closely with the voter's personal beliefs. Party identity serves as both a voting cue and a rational decision.

Citizens also employ party identification as a means of decision-making through straight-ticket voting, wherein they select all candidates from either the Republican or Democratic Party listed on the ballot. Certain states, such as Texas or Michigan, employ a system where checking a single box at the top of the ballot grants all the votes on the ballot to a single political party. Straight-ticket voting poses challenges in states that feature non-partisan positions on the ballot. In Michigan, the uppermost section of the ballot, which includes the presidential, gubernatorial, senatorial, and representative seats, is organized along party lines. By casting a straight-ticket vote, all candidates from the chosen party will receive a vote. However, the center or bottom section of the ballot contains positions for local officials or judicial seats, which are not affiliated with any political party.

These offices would not receive any votes as straight-ticket votes are exclusively allocated to partisan positions. In 2010, the cast members of the political drama series The West Wing collaborated to produce a promotional video in support of Bridget McCormack, the sister of Mary McCormack. Bridget was a candidate for a non-partisan position on the Michigan Supreme Court. The advertisement served as a reminder to voters who consistently vote for candidates from the same political party to also vote for the court seats. Failure to do so would result in them missing a significant election. McCormack emerged victorious in the election and secured the seat.

Straight-ticket voting offers the benefit of alleviating ballot fatigue. Ballot fatigue refers to the phenomenon where an individual chooses to vote just for the prominent or significant positions on a ballot, such as the president or governor, and then ceases to vote rather than proceeding to the lower places on a lengthy ballot. In 2012, 70 percent of registered voters in Colorado participated in the presidential election, yet only 54 percent voted either in favor or against keeping Nathan B. Coats as a member of the state supreme court. Voters often rely their votes on politicians' physical attributes, such as appearance or facial features. Additionally, they may also consider factors like gender or race, assuming that the elected official will prioritize policy decisions that align with the voters' demography. Candidates are very cognizant of voters' emphasis on these non-political characteristics. In 2008, a significant segment of the voting population desired to choose between Hillary Clinton and Barack Obama due to their representation of new demographic groups, namely the possibility of electing either the first female or the first African American president. John McCain's demographics proved to be a disadvantage for him during that year, as a significant number of individuals held the belief that, at the age of 71, he was too elderly to serve as president. In a similar vein, Hillary Clinton had a similar predicament in 2016 when she became the first female contender from a major political party. Essentially, the perception of attractiveness can enhance the perceived competence of a candidate, hence increasing their chances of winning. The 2020 election encompassed a diverse range of elements. Although the two primary candidates from the major parties were older Caucasian males, similar to the last remaining Democrat, Bernie Sanders, who was even older than McCain in 2008, several contenders of various ages and backgrounds competed for the Democratic candidacy. Elizabeth Warren, Amy Klobuchar, and Kamala Harris, all U.S. senators, conducted rigorous and tough political campaigns. Kamala Harris, in addition, was selected as the vice-presidential candidate. Representative Tulsi Gabbard, a Democrat from Hawaii, also participated in the race. Harris has a racial and cultural background that includes Black and South Asian ancestry. Senator Cory Booker is Black, former HUD Secretary Julián Castro is Latino, while Tulsi Gabbard and entrepreneur Andrew Yang have Asian-American/Pacific Islander heritage.

In addition to party affiliation and demographic factors, voters will also consider topics and the state of the economy when making their selection. Certain voters who prioritize a particular topic may consider a candidate's position on abortion rights to be of utmost importance, while other voters may evaluate the candidates' views on the Second Amendment and gun regulation. While single-issue voting may not demand much work from voters, it is common for many voters to examine a candidate's stance on other subjects before reaching a conclusion. They will utilize the information they discover in multiple ways.

Retrospective voting refers to the act of a voter using a candidate's previous conduct and the past economic conditions as the sole basis for making a decision. This phenomenon might manifest itself in times of economic recession or in the aftermath of political scandals, as voters demand accountability from leaders and are unwilling to grant them another opportunity. Pocketbook voting refers to the practice of voters making their voting decisions based on their individual financial situations and circumstances. Individuals who experience difficulty in securing employment or witness a decline in their investments under the governance of a specific candidate or political party are more likely to vote for an alternative candidate or party rather than the current officeholder. Prospective voting is the act of using a candidate's past behavior as a basis for predicting their future actions. Will the candidate's voting record or actions have a positive impact on the economy and enhance their ability to lead as president amid an economic downturn? The primary difficulty associated with this voting approach is in the necessity for voters to assimilate a substantial amount of information, which may be contradictory or irrelevant, in order to make an informed prediction regarding the future performance of a candidate. It seems that voters tend to rely on both future-oriented and past-oriented voting more frequently than on voting based on their personal financial situation.

Occasionally, a voter may strategically exercise their right to cast a ballot. In such scenarios, an individual may opt to cast their vote for a candidate who is not their first choice, either due to the realization that their preferred candidate has little chance of winning or with the intention of thwarting the victory of another candidate. Such voting occurs when there are multiple candidates vying for a single position or multiple parties competing for a single seat. For instance, in Florida and Oregon, Green Party voters, who typically hold liberal views, may opt to vote for a Democrat if doing so prevents a Republican candidate from winning. In Georgia, although a Libertarian candidate may be favored, voters would still prefer the Republican candidate to win over the Democrat and will vote accordingly.

## INCUMBENCY

Another factor that influences voters' decision-making is the incumbency of a candidate. Essentially, this is a form of voting based on past performance, but it demands minimal effort from the voter. The incumbency advantage refers to the phenomenon where incumbents in congressional and local elections are reelected up to 90 percent of the time. What factors contribute to this advantage and frequently dissuade capable competitors from participating? Firstly, incumbents possess the advantage of being widely recognized by their name and having established voting histories. The media is more inclined to interview them due to their extensive name recognition from multiple election campaigns and their involvement in passing legislation that impacts the state or district. Previous electoral victories by incumbents enhance the likelihood of receiving financial contributions from political action committees and interest groups, as most interest organizations refrain from supporting candidates with a high probability of losing.

Incumbents possess franking privileges, granting them a restricted quantity of complimentary mail for communication with the constituents in their district. Although these mailings are prohibited in the days immediately preceding an election (sixty days for a senator and ninety days for a House member), congressional representatives can establish a mutually beneficial connection with voters through them. Additionally, incumbents have established campaign organizations, whereas challengers must create new organizations from scratch. Finally, the current officeholders own a greater amount of funds in their campaign reserves compared to the majority of their opponents.

Another advantage that incumbents have is the practice of gerrymandering, which involves strategically drafting district lines in order to ensure a specific electoral result. Every decade, in accordance with the United States. The allocation of House of Representatives representatives to each state is established based on the state's population as recorded in the census. If a state experiences an increase or decrease in the number of members in the House, it is required to redraw districts in order to achieve equal representation by ensuring that each district has an equivalent number of inhabitants. States have the option to redraw these districts on different occasions and for various purposes. If a district is redrawn with the intention of including a majority of members from either the Democratic or Republican Party inside its boundaries, candidates from those parties will gain an advantage.

Gerrymandering greatly benefits local legislative candidates and House of Representatives members, who consistently achieve a reelection rate of 90 percent. Senators and presidents are not affected by gerrymandering as they do not participate in district-based elections. Presidents and senators secure victories in states, therefore deriving advantages only from their substantial campaign funds and widespread familiarity. One factor contributing to the reelection rate of senators in 2020 was that they were successful in retaining their seats just 84 percent of the time, but the United States as a whole had a higher reelection rate. The house rate was 95 percent.

## PRESIDENTIAL ELECTIONS

The ones that usually attract the most attention are the *general elections* held every four years. On the ballot are the president, every member of the House of Representatives, one-third of the Senate, various state and local offices, and any petition initiatives that may make the ballot in some states.

What are the requirements to run for president? Which are the steps to follow? There are three critical steps in the election process:

The first step usually takes place behind the scenes. The *invisible primary* is when candidates test the waters to see if they can obtain support and promises of big money without launching a viable campaign.

The second step is about *getting the nomination*. *Party primaries* are held, statewide elections among members of the same party, or in some states, *party caucuses*, which are meetings where party members may debate the merits of the various candidates, and delegates can then decide for whom they wish to stand. The earlier state contests attract many candidates and media attention, so naturally, everyone wants to be among them. However, New Hampshire and Iowa have made it their business to remain first in line. *Frontloading* is a process by which states try to move their primaries or caucuses to earlier dates, which may not be suitable for democracy. Only the most fervent party activists are paying attention to politics that early in the season. During the primary season, the goal is to be the front runner and hold on to that position through the final contest. The *front runner* is the leader of the pack, as seen in the polls.

Candidates attempt to grab and keep the *momentum* by winning debates and maintaining an advantage in the early contests. If, for some reason, one does not perform as well as one has set up the media to expect, one may look like a loser, which can diminish the momentum during the campaign.

The third step is about rallying the party in the *national nominating conventions*, which are party conventions held near the end of summer or early in the autumn before the election, offering a chance to bring the party together behind a political candidacy. Conventions are party mending, strengthening, and rallying events that the media does not have serious interest in covering. The upshot is that most voters will not be paying close attention until the summer ends in the election year.

## THE GENERAL ELECTION AND THE ELECTORAL COLLEGE

The general election campaigns open on Labor Day, even though it may feel like they have been going on forever by then. The campaigns keep their eyes on the ultimate prize--more valuable even than the popular vote! When it comes to presidential elections, the final prize is the *Electoral College*, a body of electors from each state who votes for the president. When a citizen votes for a presidential candidate, one is doing it for a delegate (or an elector) to the Electoral College. He will ultimately go on to vote for one's candidate on behalf of the state.

The Electoral College's inner workings may appear mysterious to the average citizen, established in the United States Constitution in 1787 as a compromise between electing a president by a vote in Congress or a popular vote in an election. State distribution indicates electoral votes. Each state has a certain number of electors equal to their total number of Congress members, including two senators. Except for two, Maine and Nebraska, all states cast all their votes to their state's plurality winner. Any state can change its method of how to allocate its votes. The critical point is that different allocation methods may produce different winners and losers.

The Electoral College has a significant impact on candidates' campaign strategies. Some states have much higher elector payoffs than others, and some states are not really in contention.

There are 538 total electoral votes, and a candidate has to get at least 270 to win. So he or she has to win enough states to get to 270. This changes how candidates pursue their campaigns, because all of them are smart enough to realize that a state such as Texas likely will vote Republican, while California will vote Democrat. The election then tends to come down to "swing states"— states that can go either way depending on the year. Candidates thus concentrate their efforts on those states, while not completely neglecting the others. On the other hand, the states with only three electoral votes don't get as much attention.

The political coloring book with which candidates concern themselves is red, blue, and purple. While these colors do not have any significance in and of themselves, they are a media convention that has become a tradition. Those states that are not reliably Democratic blue or Republican red, even though they may trend one way or the other in a given election, are called swing states.

These "purple" political entities have become the battlegrounds in which elections are ultimately contested. There are also swing voters who do not reliably vote for either party and must be vigorously courted by aspiring officeholders' campaigns because they often display a resistance toward traditional candidates. Independents become independents because one is repelled by the current political system--by the self-dealing and arrogance of politicians and political parties.

Winning campaigns are usually notable for having competent teams behind them. These days, campaigns are professional organizations. Generally, the campaign with the most money, expertise, and best data-gathering operation will be able to out-strategize and out-perform those that may be less adept. Also, increasingly necessary to gain access to the winner's circle is a solid and memorable message. Most swing voters will want to know what a candidate stands for before casting ballots for them. Thus, citizens expect candidates to clearly explain why they are running for office and towards which goals and objectives. They may also search for *wedge issues*, political disputes that they can use as levers to divide an opponent's voting coalition.

Furthermore, because paid advertising is incredibly costly for any campaign, one of the campaign's first goals is to maximize free coverage by staging events and making appearances that the media will cover. Still, for candidates, a good commercial that goes viral and is seen multiple times on cable news and the internet without paying for it is a great thing. *Negative advertising*, or criticizing the opponent, even without mentioning the advertising candidate's name, runs the risk of turning people off and restraining them from coming out to vote. Still, if the issue over which a candidate goes negative connects with the voters, it may prove to be an effective strategy. *Issue advocacy ads* help a candidate by promoting his or her issues or criticizing the opponent's stances.

One absolute certainty is that advertising requires money, and money is a resource to which candidates devote a great deal of their time chasing. Campaign finance law limits how much hard money an individual can donate (currently $2,900 per election).[129] *Hard money* is those funds donated directly to a candidate, *while soft money* is that they give to parties and other groups that can spend it on a candidate's behalf. Wealthy individuals spend *dark money* without having to identify themselves. *Citizens United v. Federal Election Commission* (2010) was a Supreme Court decision that tilted the financial playing field of elections toward corporations, outside groups, and wealthy donors by allowing them to spend without limit and without identifying themselves.[130]

The court's 5-4 majority opinion held that limiting "independent political spending" violated the right to free speech. In doing so, it overturned election spending restrictions that dated back more than a century. The court ruled that there was no threat of corruption if the spending was not coordinated with a candidate's campaign. The upshot of all this is that elections are big business, and all of the citizens are stakeholders in them and in their results, which will significantly affect our lives.

## LEGISLATION GOVERNING THE FINANCING OF POLITICAL CAMPAIGNS

In the 2020 presidential election cycle, candidates from various political parties collectively amassed a staggering sum of 5.7 billion dollars

---

[129] The Federal Election Commission clearly states the contribution limits, *see* Contribution limits, https://www.fec.gov/help-candidates-and-committees/candidate-taking-receipts/contribution-limits/, Federal Election Commission, accessed 19 March 2021.

[130] Dark money is usually election-related spending where the source is disclosed or secret. Citizens United contributed to a major jump in this type of spending, which often comes from nonprofits that are not required to reveal their donors. See Tim Lau and Brennan Center for Justice for more details.

to fund their campaigns. Candidates running for Congress collectively raised a staggering $8.7 billion in campaign funds. The aggregate funds amassed by political action committees (PACs), entities established to generate and allocate financial resources to shape political outcomes and support candidates' electoral campaigns, amounted to almost $2.7 billion. How does the government oversee the substantial sums of money that are currently involved in the electoral process?

The origins of campaign finance monitoring may be traced back to a federal statute enacted in 1867, which explicitly forbade government officials from soliciting donations from Naval Yard personnel. In 1896, the Republican Party allocated approximately $16 million in total, encompassing the campaign expenses of William McKinley, which amounted to $6-7 million. This caused significant concern, leading to the attention of various influential politicians, such as Theodore Roosevelt. Upon assuming the presidency in 1901, Roosevelt urged Congress to investigate political corruption and the exertion of influence in government and elections. Soon after, Congress passed the Tillman Act (1907), which imposed a ban on corporate donations to candidates participating in federal elections. Subsequent legislative legislations were enacted to restrict the amount of money that individuals may donate to candidates, regulate how candidates might utilize campaign contributions, and determine the extent of information that would be made available to the public.

Although these rules were designed to promote transparency in campaign financing, the government lacked the authority to effectively curb the influx of large sums of money into elections, and no efforts were made to implement the laws. In 1971, Congress attempted to address the issue by enacting the Federal Election Campaign Act (FECA), which established guidelines for candidates to disclose all financial donations and expenses associated with their campaigns. The FECA established regulations for the manner in which organizations and companies could make contributions to federal campaigns, hence enabling the formation of political action committees. The statute was amended in 1974 to establish the Federal Election Commission

(FEC), an independent body responsible for enforcing election laws. Although several provisions of the FECA were deemed illegal by the courts in Buckley v. Valeo (1976), such as restrictions on personal expenditures by candidates who do not rely on federal funds, the FEC commenced the enforcement of campaign finance legislation in 1976. Despite the implementation of new legislation and the establishment of the Federal Election Commission (FEC), financial resources continued to be directed towards electoral campaigns.

Exploiting legal loopholes, political parties and political action committees made substantial donations to candidates, necessitating the implementation of new measures. Senators John McCain (R-AZ) and Russ Feingold (former D-WI) together introduced the Bipartisan Campaign Reform Act of 2002 (BCRA), popularly known as the McCain–Feingold Act. McCain–Feingold legislation imposes limitations on the financial contributions made to political parties, which had been utilized as a means for corporations and political action committees (PACs) to wield their power. The legislation imposed restrictions on the overall amount of donations that could be made to political parties, banned any collaboration between politicians and political action committees (PACs) during campaigns, and mandated that candidates must provide personal endorsements in their political advertisements. Additionally, it imposed restrictions on the dissemination of advertisements by unions and businesses, namely during the thirty-day period preceding a primary election and the sixty-day period preceding a general election.

Shortly after the McCain-Feingold Act was passed, the Federal Election Commission's implementation of the statute led to legal actions questioning its validity. In McConnell v. Federal Election Commission (2003), the Supreme Court affirmed the act's limitations on the utilization of campaign contributions by candidates and parties. However, further legal disputes resulted in the elimination of restrictions on individual expenditures and the lifting of the prohibition on advertisements conducted by special interest organizations in the period preceding an election. The Supreme Court's decision in 2010 in the case of Citizens United v. Federal Election Commission resulted in the elimination of restrictions on corporate expenditure. The majority of justices contended that the BCRA infringed upon a corporation's freedom of speech. The court verdict also authorized businesses to contribute unrestricted funds to super PACs, also known as Independent Expenditure-Only Committees. These organizations are prohibited from making direct contributions to a candidate or engaging in campaign strategizing with a candidate. They have the freedom to raise and spend unlimited amounts of money to either support or criticize a candidate, which includes activities such as running commercials and organizing events. The Senate Leadership Fund, a conservative super PAC, allocated $293.7 million towards endorsing conservative candidates in 2020, whilst the Senate Majority PAC dedicated $230.4 million to help liberal candidates. In the 2020 election, super PACs alone spent a total of $2.13 billion. In 2012, the super PAC "Restore Our Future" generated $153 million in funds and allocated $142 million towards endorsing conservative politicians, such as Mitt Romney. "Priorities USA Action" amassed $79 million in funds and allocated $65 million towards endorsing progressive politicians, notably including Barack Obama. In the 2012 election, super PACs alone spent a total of $609 million, while in the 2014 congressional elections, their expenditure amounted to $345 million.

The courts have maintained some restrictions on campaign contributions, which are still in effect. The maximum allowable contribution per candidate every election is $2,900. In Nebraska, a teacher is allowed to donate $2,900 to a candidate's campaign for the Democratic presidential nomination. If that candidate wins the nomination, the teacher can then contribute an additional $2,900 to their general election campaign. Individuals have the option to contribute $5,000 to political action committees and $36,500 to a national party committee. Political Action Committees (PACs) are allowed to donate $5,000 to any candidate they support in an election and can donate up to $15,000 to a national party. PACs that are established with the purpose of providing financial support to a single candidate are subject to a maximum contribution limit of $2,900 per candidate. The quantities are modified biennially, in accordance with inflation. The purpose of these limits is to establish a fairer competitive environment for the candidates, ensuring that they must gather their campaign funds from a diverse range of contributors.

## KEY TERMS

**Ballot fatigue**: The phenomenon where voters cast votes for the top positions on a ballot but skip voting for lower positions.

**Campaign finance legislation**: Laws and regulations that govern the funding of political campaigns to ensure transparency and fairness.

**Caucuses**: Meetings of party members where they debate the merits of various candidates and select delegates to support them.

**Electoral College**: A body of electors from each state who vote for the president based on the popular vote in their respective states.

**External organizations**: Political action committees (PACs) and other groups that run independent campaigns to support or oppose candidates.

**Franking privileges**: The right of incumbents to send mail to constituents at no cost, except during certain periods before an election.

**Frontloading**: The process by which states try to move their primaries or caucuses to earlier dates to gain more influence.

**General election**: The election held every four years in which voters choose the president, members of the House of Representatives, one-third of the Senate, and various state and local officials.

**Gerrymandering**: The practice of drawing electoral district boundaries to favor a particular party or candidate.

**Incumbency advantage**: The benefits that current officeholders have, such as name recognition and established campaign organizations, which help them get re-elected.

**Invisible primary**: The period before a campaign officially begins when candidates test their support and seek commitments from key donors and influencers.

**Media coverage**: The reporting and broadcasting of campaign events and advertisements, which play a crucial role in shaping public perception of candidates.

**Negative advertising**: Campaign ads that criticize an opponent, often appealing to voters' emotions rather than providing substantive information.

**Nomination**: The process by which a political party selects its candidate for the general election.

**Party identification**: The loyalty of voters to a particular political party, which influences their voting behavior.

**Political action committees (PACs)**: Organizations that raise and spend money to influence elections and support candidates.

**Primary elections**: Statewide elections where party members vote for their preferred candidate to represent their party in the general election.

**Retrospective voting**: Voting based on a candidate's past performance or the current economic conditions.

**Swing states**: States that can vote either Democratic or Republican in a given election and are heavily targeted by campaigns.

**Super PACs**: Independent expenditure-only committees that can raise and spend unlimited amounts of money to support or oppose candidates, but cannot coordinate directly with candidates.

**Swing voters**: Voters who do not consistently vote for the same party and can be persuaded to vote for different candidates in different elections.

**Voter turnout**: The percentage of eligible voters who actually cast a ballot in an election.

# CHAPTER 16

# BUREAUCRACY

## WHAT IS BUREAUCRACY AND WHY DO WE NEED IT?

B ureaucracy comes from the French *bureaucratie* – from *bureau* (office) and *cratie* (power) – and it originally indicated the group of officials who, divided into various hierarchical levels, carry out the functions of the public administration in the state. In this broad sense, bureaucracy is a hierarchical structure that operates following precise rules. At the same time, bureaucracy has been widely considered as being the most efficient form of organization achieved so far - at least at the level of the ideal model - since it is a functional structure for the management of large quantities of work. Hence, this term does not only define political management, but any set of officials of a body, who in some way conduct the management of this organization (Albrow 1970; 16-30).[131]

Drawing from these features, there have been several definitions of bureaucracy in the literature, of which the most famous is Max Weber's definition of bureaucracy as: "an organization where tasks are divided among technical specialists who devote their full working capacity to the organization and whose activities are coordinated by rational rules,

---

[131] Albrow M. (1970), *Bureaucracy*, Macmillan International Higher Education, New York.

hierarchy and written documents".[132] According to Weber, bureaucracy was an improvement compared to previous societal forms of political management and it was necessary to resolve many political issues in current societies. Whereas in ancient democracies, such as the Athenian one, small dimensions of the republic and a conception of political involvement based on liberty as self-government required the whole citizenry to take part in the political management of the community, current societies are too complex and large to grant equal direct political participation to each citizen. For this reason, current political systems have shifted towards representative forms of government, which means that citizens elect ruling elites which are afterwards in charge of the political decisions of the country (Manin 1997; 67-80).[133]

Representative systems yet encompass certain problematic features from a democratic point of view, since elections are simultaneously aristocratic and democratic. On the one hand, elections are aristocratic because they do not produce similarity between rulers and ruled, rather the opposite. Elections tend to create aristocracies, since they select candidates that prove to have the politically relevant qualities and that are deemed superior by the dominant values in the culture. Yet, on the other hand, elections are also democratic: even if there is inequality regarding who can be selected, citizens possess an equal power in deciding who is worth assuming a certain position (Manin 1997; 156-160).

This dual character is reflected by bureaucracy, since this mechanism can be good at some things - making decisions quickly and consistently and maximizing expertise - but at the same time it can also be easily corrupted because of the lack of transparency and democratic accountability. For this reason, bureaucracy has been a central topic of study in political science over the last centuries. That is, political literature has

---

[132] Weber, M. (1978). Bureaucracy. In Economy and society: An outline of interpretive sociology. Trans. and ed. G. Roth and C. Wittich. Berkeley: University of California Press.
[133] Manin B. (1997), *The Principles of Representative Government*, Cambridge University Press, Cambridge.

tried to explain why certain public policy decisions are preferred over others and how relevant officials in the government use these policies to protect or promote their own agency's special interests against other bodies. To understand this debate better, it is first essential to consider how bureaucratic theory has developed over time and how it has been connected to the development of modern society.

## THE FRAMEWORK AND HISTORY

Bureaucracy is a result of both an economic and political development of our societies. On the one side, the development and enlargement of capitalist industries required economic companies not only to employ more employees, but also more technical and managerial personnel within the industry to deal with the increased managerial requirements of these businesses. On the other side, the expansion of the State into new areas of welfare provision and economic regulation, and the emergence of a mass political party required the expansion of a bureaucratic administration. In this regard, bureaucratization has become a universal feature of modern society and because of its indispensability, any modern organization must rely on some form of bureaucratic management to carry out its tasks. In Weber's words (1968; 223)[134]: "the choice is only between bureaucracy and dilettantism in the field of administration".

Bureaucratization was thus the management response to the development of the territorial state and the capitalist economy, whose administrative needs could not be met by traditional means employed by previous societies. In this regard, the wave of democratization that has occurred in western societies over the last centuries has played a significant part in fostering bureaucracy's importance. Democracy has levelled traditional status differences by requiring a system operating on the basis of impartiality between citizens and by offering opportunities

---

[134] Weber M. (1968), *Economy and Society. An Outline of Interpretative Sociology*, Bedminister Press, New York.

for bureaucratic careers that are linked to education and merit rather than family status only.

However, democracy did not foster bureaucratic development by itself, since this latter has always been intertwined with another process typical of modern societies, namely the process of rationalization. This latter can be defined as the historical drive towards a world in which "one can, in principle, master all things by calculation" (Weber 1946 [1919]; 139).[135] As for bureaucracy, rationalization processes can be found in many different spheres of society. In the economy, modern capitalism depends on a calculable process of production structured on division of labor, centralization of production control and other processes that enhance the calculability of the production process. For what concerns the legislative and administrative sphere, precise rules, an autonomous judiciary and a professional bureaucracy enhance the predictability in the sociopolitical environment, thus making it easy to govern a large mass society.

This process of rationalization has become so intertwined with modern society that it has influenced the people's values and identity. It is in this regard that Weber maintained that modern organizations require a "person of vocation", namely a rational personality type connected to the protestant ethic (Weber 1946; 140-141). Hence, according to Weber, the interplay between rationalization and bureaucracy structured modern rational western civilization in three main regards.[136]

First, rational action presupposes *knowledge* of the ideational and material circumstances structuring the action. To act rationally is to act conscious of the consequences of the action and it thus requires a means-ends relationships in order to maximize the outcome of the action with the least expenditure of resources. Weber called this process 'intellectualization', whereby modern knowledge replaces old metaphysics based on superstitions and irrational thoughts. Second, rational processes must be *impersonal and objective*. For example, workers in industrial capitalism

[135] Weber M. (1919), "Science as a Vocation", in Gerth. H.H., and Wright Mills C. (1946), *From Max Weber: Essays in Sociology*, Oxford: Oxford University Press.
[136] Brubaker R. (1992), *The Limits of Rationality*, London: Routledge.

are reduced to sheer numbers and non-economic considerations are not relevant to their judgment. In the same way, rules obey formal codes and apply equally to all the citizenry. Third, *control* is essential, since technological and scientific development have offered societies the chance to impose their mastery not only over nature, but also over human beings' social life. It is in this regard then that a rational and disciplinary ethos has increasingly penetrated into every aspect of social life.

Finally, bureaucracy and rationalization are also connected because the latter is essential in giving bureaucracy a different source of legitimacy than traditional powers. That is, while traditional societies relied on societal custom and habit to legitimize their power, modern societies achieved this legitimation simply by adhering to precisely defined rules, such as following the conduct of office, governing the criteria for appointment and the scope of authority (Albrow 1970; 84.91). In a nutshell, bureaucracy imposed itself as an indispensable system of administration rooted in the requirements of the modern world, since it allowed governments to coordinate action over a large area, to ensure continuity of operation, to acquire a monopoly of expertise and to guarantee an internal social cohesion and morale.

However, the development of bureaucracy did not lead to positive consequences only, since it also paved the way to political debates concerning its efficiency and negative consequences. One of the first debates arose regarding the patronage system, namely the political system where the appointment or hiring of a person to a government post is decided on the basis of partisan loyalty. By means of this system, elected officials had the opportunity to use their power to reward the people who helped them win and maintain office. Originally, proponents of patronage sustained that it promoted direct accountability of those who were selected and it also diminished elitism in politics by allowing commoners to occupy important roles.[137]

---

[137] Pollock, J.K. (1937), "The cost of the patronage system.", *The Annals of the American Academy of Political and Social Science*, 189 (1), 29-34.

Political patronage has a long history in the United States, since it was already included in the Article 2 of the constitution. In this article, it is specified that the President has powers of appointment to choose a large number of U.S. officials, such as ambassadors, agency heads, military office and other high-ranking members of government. This power is yet not absolute, since the Senate has confirmation powers to check this selection. Nonetheless, this practice has often been a powerful political tool for the President. For this reason, appointments became so widespread that they formed a 'spoils system', namely a political organization where the political party which won the elections gives high-ranking civil service jobs to its supporters, both as a reward for working toward victory and a way to make sure that they continue working for the party after the victory.[138]

This process is different from a merit system in which offices are assigned independently of political affiliation and according to impartial procedures meant to award candidates on the basis of some measure of merit. This difference created problems at the end of the 19th century, when 'spoils system' became too widespread, especially at local level, thus giving political leaders the opportunity to dominate local government and politics by building a community of supporters whose main aim was to maintain power from one election to another. Hence, patronage encompasses also several deficiencies that may erode public confidence in this system, since it can favor corruption and it can create a system where those appointed are unlikely to speak freely and to criticize their bosses on whom their job depends.[139]

For this reason, at the end of the 19th century, the Pendleton Act of 1883 shifted the appointment process to a merit-based system, in which recruitment was made by means of competitive exams meant to assess competence rather than partisan affiliation. In this way, neutral

[138] Folke, O., Hirano S., and Snyder Jr J.M. (2011), "Patronage and elections in US states.", *American Political Science Review*, 105 (3), 567-585.

[139] Friedrich C.J. (1937), "The rise and decline of the spoils tradition.", *The Annals of the American Academy of Political and Social Science*, 189 (1), 10-16.

competence became the primary selection method and rulers used it to deliver the message that in an ideal bureaucratic structure power is hierarchical and rule based. That is, a well-functioning bureaucratic system must appoint individuals according to their expertise and it must promote bureaucrats on the basis of merit, not personal affiliations. In this way, a neutral bureaucratic organization can make decisions better and more quickly than a patronage system and even than a democracy based on a self-government ideal.

The percentage of civil service employees recruited according to a neutral competence principle has steadily increased over the years in any society, and in the United State it reached more than 90% after both the Civil Service Reform Act signed by President Jimmy Carter in 1978 and the amendments enacted by the Supreme Court over the years to limit the externalities of partisan patronage (Ingraham & Ban 1984).[140] Nowadays, political patronage is less prevalent than in the past, since presidents now appoint less than 1% of all federal positions. Yet, this does not mean that patronage has lost all its relevance, since strategic appointments are still an important political means used by presidents to reward their supporters and to create a working relationship with members of congress.

In sum, the historical development of bureaucracy describes that this form of organization has become an essential feature for the management of complex modern societies. However, at the same time, bureaucracy transfers political power from the citizenry to technical officers, so the former may question the latter's power and they could request increased accountability and transparency in return for the transfer of power. That is, citizens want to have some form of control over the elites ruling government and other institutions and corporations. Above all, citizens want to know how governments are using the people's money, especially concerning taxpayer funds.

---

[140] Ingraham, P. W. and Ban C. (1984), *Legislating Bureaucratic Change: Civil Service Reform Act of 1978*, SUNY Press, New York.

One way of posing such control is to make bureaucrats accountable by requiring them to follow rules designed to treat people fairly, to refrain from politics on the job, and to fill out paperwork. However, these requests may also lead to unforeseen externalities, such as the Red Tape issue, which defines an excessive regulation or conformity to formal rules that is considered redundant and hinders action or other decision-making processes. This issue draws its name from the case in the 16th century when Henry VIII besieged Pope Clement VII with a significant amount of petitions for the annulment of his marriage to Catherine of Aragon. The pile of documents was rolled and stacked in original condition, each one sealed and bound with the obligatory red tape, as was the custom. Hence, the name red tape issue to describe an excessive amount of procedures to follow.[141]

The problem is thus that in order to respond to the people's request for accountability, civic service employees may be asked to fill out unnecessary paperwork, to obtain unnecessary licenses, to have multiple people or committees approve a decision and finally, to follow various minor rules that unavoidably slow down the whole bureaucratic process. In short, "red tape" indicates the governmental problem for which any official routine or procedure marked by excessive complexity results in delay or inaction. Therefore, governments must find a way to balance their need to get things done and to satisfy the people's need for transparency and accountability. To resolve this problem, the US government divided the federal bureaucracy in three branches: legislative, executive and judiciary.

## BUREAUCRACY IN THE UNITED STATES

The legislative branch drafts proposed laws, confirms or rejects presidential nominations for heads of federal agencies, federal judges and the Supreme Court, it has the authority to declare war and finally, it also

---

[141] Bozeman, B. (1993), "A theory of government "Red tape", *Journal of public administration research and theory*, 3.3, 273-304.

disposes of substantial investigative powers. American citizens have the right to vote for Senators and Representatives through free, confidential ballots. This branch includes a *Congress* composed of two parts: The Senate and the House of Representatives. In order to pass legislation and send it to the President for the signature, both these bodies must pass the same bill by majority vote (Little & Ogle 2006; 25-31).[142]

The Senate includes two elected senators per state for a total of 100 Senators, with the Vice-President serving as President of the Senate. These latter are in charge for a period of six years and their terms are staggered so that about 1/3 of the Senate is up for reelection every two years, even though there is no limit to the number of terms an individual can serve. Overall, the Senate is meant to confirm President's appointments that require consent, to provide advice on treaties' ratification, to impeach cases for federal officials and it has also to approve appointments to the Vice Presidency and any treaty that involves foreign trade.[143]

The House of Representatives has several powers, such as initiating revenue bills, impeaching federal officials, and electing the President in the case of an Electoral College tie. This institution includes 435 elected Representatives, which are divided among the 50 states in proportion to their total population. There are additional 6 non-voting delegates who represent the District of Columbia, Puerto Rico and the territories. The presiding officer of the chamber is the speaker of the House and it is elected by other representatives. These elected officials serve a two-year term, and there is no limit to the number of terms an individual can serve.

The legislative branch encompasses also special agencies and offices that provide support services to Congress, the list of which includes agencies such as the Architect of the Capitol, the Congressional Budget

---

[142] Little, T. H., Ogle D. B. (2006), *The legislative branch of state government: people, process, and politics*, ABC-CLIO, California.
[143] The White House Government, "The Legislative Branch", retrieved at: https://www.white-house.gov/about-the-white-house/our-government/the-legislative-branch/

Office, the Congressional Research Service, the Copyright Office, the Government Accountability Office, the Government Publishing Office, the House Office of Inspector General, the House Office of the Clerk, the Joint Congressional Committee on Inaugural Ceremonies, the Library of Congress, the Medicaid and CHIP Payment and Access Commission, the Medicare Payment Advisory Commission, the Office of Compliance, the Open World Leadership Center, the Stennis Center for Public Service, the U.S. Botanic Garden, the U.S. Capitol Police and the U.S. Capitol Visitor Center.

Second, the executive branch carries out and enforces laws. Executive power is vested in the President of the United States, namely the individual in charge of leading the country. He or she is the head of state, leader of the federal government, and Commander in Chief of the United States armed forces. The president serves a four-year term and can be elected no more than two times. During his or her mandate, the president is responsible for implementing the laws written by Congress, while it is responsibility of the Cabinet and of independent federal agencies to take care of the day-to-day enforcement and administration of federal laws. These bureaucracies do so by providing regulations and restrictions on businesses and individuals, like limitations on allowable air pollution from factories, or the requirements that cars have airbags, or making sure that people do not have unfettered access to certain classes of drugs or overstay their visas.[144]

The president is supported by the Vice-president and when the former is unable to serve, the latter becomes president. The vice president can be elected and can serve an unlimited number of four-year terms as vice president, even under a different president. Vice-President is part of The Cabinet together with other advisors such as the heads of executive departments and other high ranking government officials. These advisors

[144] The White House Government, "The Executive Branch", retrieved at: https://www.white-house.gov/about-the-white-house/our-government/the-executive-branch/.

are nominated by the President and must be approved by a simple majority of the Senate.

Much of the work in the executive branch is thus done by executive departments, independent agencies and other boards, commissions, and committees. The most important executive department is 'The Executive Office of the Presidency' which was born in the New Deal expansion of federal power and that is aimed at coordinating the bureaucracy. The Executive Office of the Presidency (EOP) is home to agencies that the president appoints to help him manage the large range of issues that the White House has to deal with on a daily basis. This office – composed by different bodies such as the office of the President, the National Security Council, the Office of the United States Trade Representatives, etc. - is in charge of communicating the president's message and deals with the federal budget, security, and other high priorities.[145]

The office of the president cooperates with the Executive Departments, namely the 15 main agencies of the federal government that cover essential government functions or policy areas where clientele groups have been effective at lobbying for representation at the executive level, such as the U.S. department of Defense, Commerce, Justice, Labor and so on. The heads of these 15 agencies – also called "secretaries", except for the head of the Justice Department, who is called the "attorney general" are also members of the president's cabinet. These 15 main agencies are divided in Executive Sub-agencies and Bureaus, namely smaller sub-agencies aimed at supporting specialized work within their parent executive department agencies.

Finally, there are also independent agencies that are not represented in the cabinet and are not part of the Executive Office of the president, but which are structured similarly to other executive bodies with a presidential appointee at the top (some of whom can be fired by the president, and some of whom cannot). These bodies deal with government

---

[145] Branches of the U.S. Government, USA Government, retrieved at: https://www.usa.gov/branches-of-government.

operations and issues concerning the economy and regulatory oversight. In case there are areas that do not fall under these agencies (historic preservations, endangered species, Nuclear waste, etc.), Congress or the President can establish Boards, Commissions and Committees to manage these specific tasks. Even though they are not officially part of the executive branch, these bodies are also quasi-official agencies, namely organizations that are required by federal statute to release certain information about their programs and activities in the Federal Register, the daily journal of government activities.[146]

Overall then, the executive branch consists of several agencies as the president's cabinet, the departments under the responsibility of the cabinet members and all the agencies, boards, and commissions that put the laws of Congress into action. Moreover, these bodies also include everyone serving in the U.S. military and public corporations like the U.S. Post Office. Overall then, the Federal bureaucracy performs different central functions like diplomacy, defense, and internal affairs. Yet, these branches also perform 'minor' tasks such as responding to clientele groups of veterans, farmers, teachers, or other groups who feel that they have particular concerns.

Third, the Judicial Branch interprets the meaning of laws, applies laws to individual cases, and decides if laws violate the Constitution. It is composed of the Supreme Court and other federal courts. The former is the highest court in the United States, whose nine Justices – a Chief Justice and eight Associate Justices - are nominated by the president and must be approved by the Senate. To decide a case. there must be a minimum or quorum of six Justices, while if there is an even number of Justices and a case results in a tie, the lower court's decision stands. These Justices' service is not fixed term, since they serve until their death, retirement, or removal in exceptional circumstances.[147]

---

[146] Cohen, J. E. (1988), *The politics of the US cabinet: Representation in the executive branch, 1789-1984.* University of Pittsburgh Press, Pennsylvania.

[147] The White House. "The Judiciary Branch", retrieved at: https://www.whitehouse.gov/about-the-white-house/our-government/the-judicial-branch/

Together with the Supreme Court, the Constitution gives Congress the authority to establish other federal courts to handle cases that involve federal laws including tax and bankruptcy, lawsuits involving U.S. and state governments or the Constitution, and more. Other federal judicial agencies and programs support the courts and research judicial policy. The appointments for these federal judgeships follow the same basic process as the one for the appointment of Supreme Court Justices.

First, the President nominates a person to fill a vacant judgeship, then the Senate Judiciary Committee holds a hearing on the nominee and votes on whether to forward the nomination to the full Senate. If the nomination moves forward, the Senate can debate the nomination. Debate must end before the Senate can vote on whether to confirm the nominee. A Senator will request unanimous consent to end the debate, but any Senator can refuse. Without unanimous consent, the Senate must pass a cloture motion to end the debate. It takes a simple majority of votes - 51 if all 100 Senators vote - to pass cloture and end debate about a federal judicial nominee. Once the debate ends, the Senate votes on confirmation. The nominee for Supreme Court or any other federal judgeship needs a simple majority of votes - 51 if all 100 Senators vote - to be confirmed.

Therefore, these three sides of government are bureaucracies that perform essential tasks for the management of the United States, since they provide administration, rule-making which is filling in all the technical details in the laws Congress passes so that they can be enforced, and bureaucratic discretion when the bureaucracy exercises legislative power delegated to it by congressional law through judgment.

## BUREAUCRACY MODELS

Bureaucracies are intricate organizations created to achieve specific objectives. The intricate nature of bureaucracies, along with their composition of human individuals, can present difficulties in comprehending their functioning. Nevertheless, sociologists have constructed several models to comprehend the process. Each model emphasizes distinct characteristics that elucidate the organizational behavior of governing bodies and their associated functions.

The Weberian Model refers to a theoretical framework developed by sociologist Max Weber.

The conventional paradigm of bureaucracy is sometimes referred to as the ideal Weberian model, which was formulated by Max Weber, a pioneering German sociologist. Weber posited that the progressive intricacy of existence will concomitantly augment the expectations of individuals for governmental provisions. Thus, the Weberian concept of bureaucracy is characterized by agencies that are politically neutral, structured in a hierarchical structure, and governed by formal rules. In addition, highly skilled bureaucrats would possess superior problem-solving abilities through the use of logical reasoning. These efforts would eradicate deeply rooted favoritism, prevent flawed decision-making by those in positions of authority, establish a framework for handling and executing routine tasks that involve minimal or no judgment, establish organization and effectiveness, foster a clear comprehension of the services rendered, diminish arbitrary actions, guarantee responsibility, and restrict the exercise of personal judgment.

The Acquisitive Model refers to a theoretical framework that focuses on the acquisition and accumulation of resources or possessions. Weber believed that the bureaucracy, as shown by his ideal type, was not only essential but also a beneficial advancement for humanity. Subsequent sociologists have not consistently held a positive view of bureaucracies and have established alternative frameworks to elucidate the mechanisms and rationales behind their functioning. An example of such a model is referred to as the acquisitive model of bureaucracy. The acquisitive model posits that bureaucracies inherently exhibit a competitive nature and a strong desire for power. This indicates that bureaucrats, particularly those in top positions, acknowledge the scarcity of resources allocated to support bureaucracies. Consequently, they will strive to elevate the prestige of their own bureaucracy at the expense of others.

This endeavor may manifest as simply highlighting to Congress the significance of their bureaucratic duty, but it also entails the bureaucracy striving to optimize its budget by fully utilizing all its allocated resources annually. This tactic increases the challenge for lawmakers to reduce the budget of the bureaucracy in the future, a technique that achieves its goal at the cost of frugality. Thus, the bureaucracy will gradually expand beyond its essential needs, resulting in bureaucratic inefficiency and a misallocation of resources among other bureaucracies.

The Monopolistic Model refers to a market structure in which there is a single dominant firm that has exclusive control over the production and distribution of a certain product or service. Other theories have determined that the level of competition among bureaucracies for limited resources is not the most illuminating factor in understanding how a bureaucracy operates. Instead, it is the lack of competition. The model that resulted from this finding is the monopolistic model. Advocates of the monopolistic model acknowledge the parallels between a bureaucratic organization such as the Internal Revenue Service (IRS) and a private monopoly like a regional power company or internet service provider that operates without any competition. These firms often face criticism for their inefficiency, subpar service, and lack of responsiveness towards clients. Take, for instance, the Bureau of Consular Affairs (BCA), which is the government organization responsible for granting passports to individuals. There is no alternative institution that a U.S. citizen can lawfully approach to formally apply for and obtain a passport, a procedure that typically requires a duration of ten to twelve weeks, unless one is willing to pay an increased charge for expedited processing, which will reduce the timeframe to four to six weeks. Therefore, there is no justification for the BCA to enhance its efficiency and responsiveness or expedite passport issuance.

There are a few uncommon bureaucratic exceptions that usually vie for presidential favor, particularly entities like the Central Intelligence Agency, the National Security Agency, and the intelligence agencies inside the Department of Defense. In addition to these factors, bureaucracies lack incentives to improve efficiency or responsiveness, and they are rarely held accountable for persistent inefficiency or ineffectiveness.

Consequently, they have minimal incentive to implement cost-saving or performance measurement systems. Although several economists contend that privatizing specific tasks could effectively address the government's problems by reducing widespread incompetence, bureaucrats are not easily persuaded.

## KEY TERMS

**Acquisitive Model**: A theoretical framework that sees bureaucracies as competitive and power-seeking, with bureaucrats striving to maximize their agency's prestige and budget.

**Bureaucracy**: A hierarchical structure that operates according to precise rules and is considered the most efficient form of organization for managing large quantities of work.

**Civil Service Reform Act**: A law signed by President Jimmy Carter in 1978 that reformed the hiring and employment practices in the federal government to promote merit-based recruitment.

**Executive Branch**: The branch of the United States government responsible for implementing and enforcing laws, led by the President.

**Judicial Branch**: The branch of the United States government responsible for interpreting laws, applying them to individual cases, and deciding if laws violate the Constitution.

**Legislative Branch**: The branch of the United States government responsible for drafting proposed laws, confirming presidential nominations, and declaring war, consisting of Congress (the Senate and the House of Representatives).

**Max Weber**: A pioneering German sociologist who developed a well-known definition of bureaucracy and emphasized its efficiency and necessity in modern societies.

**Merit System**: A system of hiring and promoting individuals based on their competence and qualifications rather than partisan affiliation.

**Monopolistic Model**: A theoretical framework that sees bureaucracies as similar to private monopolies, often criticized for inefficiency, subpar service, and lack of responsiveness due to the absence of competition.

**Patronage System**: A political system where appointments to government positions are made based on partisan loyalty, often leading to the 'spoils system.'

**Pendleton Act**: A law passed in 1883 that shifted the U.S. government's appointment process from a patronage system to a merit-based system.

**Rationalization**: The historical drive towards mastering all things by calculation, influencing values and identity in modern society.

**Red Tape**: Excessive regulation or adherence to formal rules considered redundant, hindering action or decision-making processes.

**Representative Government**: A system where citizens elect ruling elites to make political decisions on their behalf, as opposed to direct political participation by the whole citizenry.

**Spoils System**: A practice where a political party that wins an election gives civil service jobs to its supporters as a reward for their work and to ensure continued support.

**Weberian Model**: Max Weber's ideal type of bureaucracy characterized by hierarchical structure, formal rules, political neutrality, and skilled bureaucrats using logical reasoning to solve problems.

# CHAPTER 17

## POLITICAL PARTIES AND INTEREST GROUPS

B oth political parties and interest groups are social bodies bound together by shared interests. Political parties are modern forms of factions in the sense that they seek goals particular to their interests. Interest groups have a shared vision to use the political system to attain their goals. Parties can develop higher degrees of cohesion in fragmented political systems. Interest groups use lobbying as a tool. Lobbying can be both direct and indirect; it is trying to persuade government officials to do something.

In countries with more than two parties, partisanship likely bows to practicalities and compromise. In the United States, it is challenging for third parties to get any relevant traction at the national level. There may be structural reasons that justify the maintenance of the two-party system in the United States. The Democrats and the Republicans dominate the national political spectrum today, which will likely remain so for the following years.

## PARTIES AND INTEREST GROUPS

Both political parties and interest groups are social bodies bound together by shared interests. They do their best to take advantage of the political system to accomplish their political goals. These are the factions James Madison feared would be so destructive of democracy. The way they go about working the system to get political goals realized is very different.

Political parties are modern forms of factions in the sense that they seek goals particular to their interests. *Political parties* are groups bound by common interests which seek to use the political system to attain their goals from inside the system by controlling government. Different factors may affect and influence parties and interest groups' internal processes, such as choosing a favorite candidate and getting him elected. This form of *electioneering* is nominating and electing candidates to office. Once they are in office, they are *governing public officials* and run the political show.

Interest groups have a shared vision to use the political system to accomplish their goals. *Interest groups*, including corporations, are societies bound by common interests which endeavor to use the political system to achieve their policy goals by persuading inside people in power that will give them what they want. This form of action is known as lobbying. The act of persuading officials is a type of lobbying. It is typical for party representatives in government and interest group lobbyists outside the government to develop close working relationships where their interests overlap. These actions magnify their power.

## THE ROLE OF PARTIES IN A DEMOCRACY[148,149]

What is involved with the duties of a political party? A political party must represent the interests of its members by gaining control of the

---

[148] For information on the role of political parties in socialist countries, see Corwin 11-24. Generally, in Cuba, as in China, only members of the Communist Party are allowed to vote or hold public office, and the party's most relevant members make all government decisions. Some exceptions to this rule may apply in China since the Asian country has a multiparty system, in which the Communist Party has authority over the rest.

[149] Under certain conditions, The Chinese political system allows for the participation of some non-CCP members (independents) and members of minor parties in the National People's Congress (NPC). The CCP is the only party that effectively holds power at the national level.

government. Parties have vital advantages and tools to strengthen and facilitate democracy in some crucial ways. Parties act as democracy-strengthening agents by providing a bridge and connection between voters and their elected officials.

Political parties also practice partisan politics. *Partisanship* is about identifying one's interests with a party's platform. Elected officials can be held accountable to the people who vote for them through re-election. *Accountability* is about ensuring our elected officials do what they say they are going to do. When a political party is helping to create accountability, they provide cohesion. Parties can develop higher degrees of cohesion in fragmented political systems. Parties also provide a voice to those in power, and they provide the opposition voice to those who are not in government.

## POLITICAL PARTIES CREATE THE NORMALITY

Political parties create the normality that people countenance since they politically shape the social and cultural environment. The *responsible party model* is when political parties conform to paragons about how parties should ideally operate. One of these tools is the party platform. A *party platform* is a distinct set of policies based on a party's ideology, whose candidates align. People expect them to follow the party's platform and promises. If elected, citizens expect candidates to enact the values and policies of the party.

Voters make their choices based on the public policies political parties promote through their platforms; they are willing to vote against the party's candidates if they fail to keep their campaign promises successfully. Voters will likely reject party officials at the polls if party officials poorly carry out their partisan platforms' commitments. In the United States, the responsible party model is nothing but a yardstick against which actual parties can be measured.

United States parties can create unique party platforms different from each other in the political system. With several levels and branches, the national system offers many places where people and groups can engage the government. Candidates, in general, promise to support their party's platform if elected. People choose the political party they want to support through a process called partisan sorting. *Partisan sorting* identifies with the party because it most closely stands for their views and values and not for regional or other non-ideological reasons. Partisan sorting has historically been enforced by voters rather than by tight political party regulations. Increasingly, party members are not only partisan (that is, they identify with the political team); they are hyperpartisan.

*Hyper-partisanship* is when people are loyal to the party at all costs. Hyper-partisanship is an ideology that suggests that someone would choose their team over the other every time, even if it may require that they change their minds on policy priorities or values to do so. When voters are unwilling to vote against their party, even when it lets them down because the priority is to deny their opponents a win, they send a message to their party that it is acceptable not to keep promises.

To follow the dictates of the political party leaders to which they belong, House members and senators in the United States Congress may sometimes ignore the voters in their home states and the groups that represent them. For example, a member of the United States Congress from a state with a sizable elderly population may be inclined to vote in favor of legislation that will likely increase the benefits for retired people. However, their political party leaders, who disapprove of government spending on social programs, may ask for a vote against the legislation. The opposite can also occur, especially in the case of a legislator soon facing re-election. With two-year terms of office, it is more likely to see House members buck their party in favor of their constituents. (Corwin, 21)

## PARTY ORGANIZATION AND DECISION-MAKING

In liberal democratic countries, political parties no longer choose leaders in smoke-filled rooms behind the scenes. There is a formal and transparent process. Historically, *party machines* were organizations in which party leaders or "bosses" made the decisions and kept their voters' loyalty by providing them with services and support. Reforms included bringing party decisions, like whom to nominate, out of the proverbial "smoke-filled rooms." The way we are choosing political candidates today is in the smoke-free air of democratic transparency.

Political parties choose candidates through primaries and caucuses. *Primary elections*, often abbreviated to *primaries*, are processes by which voters can indicate their political preference for their party's candidate, or a general candidate, in an upcoming general election, local election, or by-election. *Primaries* are usually party-held preliminary elections.

A *caucus* is a meeting of political supporters or members (usually active) of a specific political party or movement. The definition of this term varies between countries and political cultures. *Caucuses* are the party gatherings where partisans debate candidate choices openly. While party officials still have a great deal of clout and resources, they are no longer "the boss."

Generally, political parties in the United States do not like nominating methods that allow non-party members to participate in selecting party nominees. In 2000, the United States Supreme Court heard a case brought by the California Democratic Party, the California Republican Party, and the California Libertarian Party. At the time, the parties argued that they had the right to determine who associated with the party and who participated in choosing the party nominee. The Supreme Court ultimately agreed to limit the states' choices for nomination methods to closed and open primaries.

## A FOUR-PART PARTY STRUCTURE

The party structure rests in, more or less, four essential elements that make the party structure. The people in the electorate who identify with the party are people who vote party lines. These citizens are known as the *party followers* (1). On the other hand, *party activists* (2) are the party base, the most ideologically extreme of the party's voters. These activists are the ones that are the core group of people within the political party. *Party leaders* (3) are those who act as the official representatives of the political party.

The *party organization* is the official group, whose career party officials are part of it, that runs the party. This party organization is the functioning of the party within the state. Those who win an election are known as the *party-in-government members* (4) because they represent the people. *Party identification* is when people think of themselves as partisans (team members) and generally vote for the party. Identity politics are crucial to understanding national politics since political representation is, for some experts, rooted in the representatives' racial, ethnic, socioeconomic, gender, and sexual identity.

## WHY DOES THE UNITED STATES HAVE A TWO-PARTY POLITICAL SYSTEM?

In countries with more than two parties, partisanship likely bows to practicalities and compromise. If not, a party typically gets left out in the cold. In the United States, it is challenging for third parties to get any traction at the national level. There are structural reasons for the two-party system in the United States. The primary structural reason is that the United States does not have a proportional representation system, often found in parliamentary governments. The United States follows a *single member, first past the post district* model. These congressional districts in the United States have only one person elected—the person who gets the most votes.

The United States has made legal barriers to third parties to access federal funds. This situation implies that candidates are no longer dependent on the parties for their infrastructure. Third parties are vulnerable to the ability of social media to be manipulated and weaponized against them.

Third parties are cutting into fundraising against the major two parties. The parties are struggling to keep financial control in the age of the Internet. There is now much more opportunity for those not blessed by a major party's nomination to stage a campaign. Unlimited corporate and interest group funds are available to parties. A third-party candidate must get a certain number of signatures on a petition to get on the ballot in most states. Usually, when a third party begins to get traction, one of the parties will co-opt the winning issues.

## THE PARTIES TODAY

The Democrats and the Republicans dominate the United States political spectrum today. Democrats seek an activist government that believed it could and should solve economic and social problems at the national level. Republicans seek a hands-off, anti-regulatory business party. By the 1960s, Democrats had a solid hold on the United States Congress. *Richard Nixon's "southern strategy"* took advantage of race as a wedge issue to break conservative southern Democrats away from the Democrats and give the Republicans a majority.

Republicans seek a government that attends to its inherent responsibilities of maintaining a stable monetary and fiscal climate, encouraging a free and competitive economy, and enforcing law and order. Republicans seek a balance between the branches of government and every level. The Republican Party perceives that communism is the principal significant disturber of peace in the world today. Thus, they are reluctant to have relations with countries run by communist leaders and parties.[150]

The "new" Republican coalition began with the rise of evangelical Christian politics. Generally, traditional southerners were far more hierarchical, authoritarian, and evangelical-Christian than the average economic conservative Republican. The relationship between these two Republican groups ultimately led to considerable political friction because of broken promises and misunderstandings. For a time,

---

[150] For an in-depth analysis of the values of the two leading parties of the United States, see Donaldson, Robert. *Modern America: a Documentary History of the Nation Since 1945: A Documentary History of the Nation Since 1945*, 2014. London: Routledge. Internet resource.

economic conservatives paid lip service to social conservatives' concerns to keep the peace.

As one understands them today, national political parties did not exist in the United States during the republic's early years. At various points in the past 170 years in the United States history, national elites and voters have sought to create and foster alternatives to the existing party system. Political parties formed as alternatives to the Republican and Democratic parties are known as third parties or minor parties. Third parties, often born of frustration with the current political system, attract supporters from one or both of the existing and leading parties during an election but fail to attract enough votes to win. No third-party candidate has ever won the presidency, and historians still discuss why.

The Republican Party and the Democratic Party still have their economic and social left-right divisions. Trump's coalition's conservative social dimension is an interesting one, as critics argue that social conservatives seem to have set aside the traditional values that so motivated them in years past.

In the United States, two political movements formed fifteen years following John Kennedy's election: the American New Left and the American New Right. The New Left supports the call for social, economic, and political justice based on the equality of class, gender, and race rather than by the traditional leftist-Marxist dogma that socialism would replace the decadent capitalist system. On the other hand, the New Right focuses on downsizing the federal government, supporting state's rights, resisting communism, and reducing government regulations. Even if experts often describe both tendencies as radical movements, they are less orthodox than the traditional Left and the traditional Right.

## INTEREST GROUPS' BASICS

Madison's definition of factions can apply to both interest groups and political parties. Political parties and interest groups both work together and compete for social influence, although in different ways. Even though its writers did not mention the term interest group in the United States Constitution, the text's framers were aware that individuals would eventually band together in an attempt to use the governmental structure in their favor. One should especially consider that, while interest group activity often transcends political party lines, one can perceive many interests as more supportive of one party than the other. Thus, interest groups and political parties are related and may even closely work together as long as they support similar causes. For example, The American Conservative Union, Citizens United, the National Rifle Association, and National Right to Life will likely have relationships with Republican lawmakers than with Democratic ones.[151]

Interest groups do not need to be moderate—in fact, it is quite the opposite. The more stalwart and uncompromising interest groups stand on their positions, the better situated they are to draw a membership who shares their particular views. Individual citizens can join interest groups that promote and support the causes they favor.

Interest groups help provide representation to the people. The United States Constitution bases political representation almost entirely on geography. Interest groups give people a chance to get other interests they care about represented in government policy pursuing. Interest groups also help with political participation. *Political efficacy* is when people's sense of their ability to have a higher degree of control of their lives. Interest groups give people political participation opportunities that they would not typically have. Interest groups amplify the power of one. What one voice may not achieve, a chorus of multitudes may do much more quickly.

The role the interest groups provide in educating the public is essential. Interest groups usually provide information on their cause to policymakers by testifying in front of congressional committees, working with

---

[151] Corwin, Edward. "The Basic Doctrine of American Constitutional Law." *Michigan Law Review*, vol. 12, no. 4, 1914, pp. 247–276. *JSTOR*, www.jstor.org/stable/1276027. Accessed 8 Mar. 2021.

bureaucrats, or communicating directly with their members. Interest groups provide agenda building. By publicizing the values and interests they care about to the public and policymakers, interest groups can get onto their radar screens. This focus provides program alternatives and program monitoring.

## UNDERSTANDING INTEREST GROUPS

Interest groups can benefit society. Interest groups provide collective goods. *Collective goods* are benefits that, if the group is successful in obtaining them, can be enjoyed by everyone, whether they were members of the group and contributed to the purpose or not. There may be a problem with people who do not contribute to the interest group and only profit from it. *The free-rider problem is* a quandary with getting people to join an interest group if they enjoy the benefit? Does a member get *material benefits* provided of actual monetary worth, like insurance discounts or professional paybacks? Are there *solidary benefits* that appeal to one's desire to associate with other people who care about the same things one does? Are there *expressive benefits* which are the opportunity to do work for something that matters deeply to one? Does the interest group provide *selective incentives* which benefit offered to induce people to join up?

We can understand interest groups' politics best if we think about the kinds of interests that bind their members together into different groups. *Economic interest groups* are those which seek to influence policy for the pocketbook issues of their members. On the other hand, *equal opportunity interest groups* pretend to influence the policymaking process by politically targeting citizens who feel unrepresented. These are different from public interest groups which aspire to change policy according to values that they consider are good for every citizen. *Government interest groups* are groups hired by governments to lobby other governments.

*Interest Group Politics*

What does one mean by "interest group politics"—are lobbyists politicians? Interest groups and their lobbyists are political actors in that they can bring considerable power to bear on elected officials. Power is relative amongst interest groups. Power can come from strength in numbers and resources.

Interest groups use lobbying as a tool. Lobbying can be direct and indirect. *Lobbying* is trying to persuade government officials to do something. *Lobbyists* are professionals who promote agendas and persuade public officials. *Direct lobbying* impacts public officials directly, while *indirect lobbying* focuses on the public to get the public to put pressure on public officials.

Professional lobbyists come from the ranks of professional politicians. There is a *revolving door* between lobbyists and politicians. The revolving door theory explains how people move from the public to the private sector and then sometimes back to the public sector. With direct lobbying of Congress, the Congress member's lobbyists focus on the committees and subcommittees that deal with the policies they mind. Interest groups research and investigate policy options and bring their findings to Congress members who cannot become experts on every topic they pass a law on.

Interest groups give money. *Political action committees (PACs)* can raise money but are limited in their contributions to candidates. One practical way for interest groups to increase their power is to form coalitions with other groups conveniently. Interest groups are as interested in influencing the people who implement the laws as they are interested in determining who makes them. The result is the public being shut out of the policymaking process, known as the Iron Triangle. Often, lobbyists, bureaucrats, and Congress members end up working together closely on laws affecting a particular sector that they finally come to identify with each other's interests. *Iron triangles* are the close policymaking relationships between legislators, regulators, and state-regulated groups.

Interest groups provide direct and indirect lobbying. Direct lobbying of the courts happens at the state level. State judges are frequently elected and willing to take campaign contributions. Lobbyists also operate in the Supreme Court and carry out their political mission by writing and submitting amicus curiae briefs on behalf of groups with interest in a particular case. Challenging a law in court is one way of lobbying the court to change the law. Indirect lobbying occurs when groups find it more beneficial to stay concealed behind an ostensible social movement. In these cases, they attempt to persuade the public to put pressure on our representatives.

People outside the political culture can lobby as well. When citizens become lobbyists, they are known as grassroots. Groups that orchestrate *grassroots lobbying* are usually those that arise from spontaneous popular movements and revolts. Fake grassroots movements are known as *Astro-turf lobbying*. This lobbying type occurs through an orchestrated effort by an established interest group dressed up to look like a genuine popular movement. Astroturf lobbying is made more convenient by the Supreme Court rulings that say that spending money by individuals, groups, or corporations is a form of *protected free speech*.

## KEY TERMS

**Accountability**: Ensuring elected officials are responsible to the people who vote for them, often through mechanisms like re-election.

**Astroturf Lobbying**: Orchestrated efforts by established interest groups designed to appear as spontaneous grassroots movements.

**Caucus**: A meeting of political supporters or members of a specific party or movement to debate and choose candidates openly.

**Closed Primary**: A type of primary election in which only registered party members can vote to select their party's candidates.

**Collective Goods**: Benefits that, if obtained by an interest group, can be enjoyed by everyone, regardless of whether they contributed to the effort.

**Direct Lobbying**: Efforts by lobbyists to directly influence public officials and policymakers.

**Free-Rider Problem**: The issue of individuals benefiting from collective goods without contributing to the effort to obtain them.

**Grassroots Lobbying**: Lobbying efforts that arise from spontaneous popular movements and involve ordinary citizens as lobbyists.

**Hyper-Partisanship**: Extreme loyalty to a political party, often leading to a refusal to compromise or vote against party lines.

**Iron Triangle**: Close policymaking relationships between legislators, regulators, and interest groups focused on specific sectors.

**Lobbying**: The act of attempting to influence government officials to enact or oppose legislation, policies, or decisions.

**Open Primary**: A type of primary election where all voters, regardless of party affiliation, can participate in selecting a party's candidate.

**Partisan Sorting**: The process by which individuals identify with a political party that aligns most closely with their views and values.

**Partisanship**: Loyalty to a political party and its platform.

**Political Action Committee (PAC)**: Organizations that raise and spend money to influence elections and legislation.

**Primary Election**: A preliminary election used by political parties to nominate candidates for a general election.

**Public Interest Groups**: Organizations that seek to change policy according to values they consider beneficial for the public.

**Revolving Door**: The movement of individuals between roles as legislators and regulators and positions in the industries affected by the legislation and regulation.

**Selective Incentives**: Benefits offered by interest groups to induce people to join and support their efforts.

**Solidary Benefits**: Social advantages gained by associating with others who share similar interests and goals.

**Third Parties**: Political parties formed as alternatives to the two major parties, often focusing on specific issues or representing a broader dissatisfaction with the existing system.

# CHAPTER 18

# MEDIA AND POLITICAL COMMUNICATION

People make decisions throughout their lives according to their perceptions and biases, eventually shaped by the information they receive from the media. News agencies influence our actions, judgments, and beliefs. Depending on how critical citizens are, media corporations will alter their perception of the world more or less. In countries like the United States, the government controls the media by the use of licensing. Reporting is not only about accurately reporting facts but also about increasing advertiser revenues and audience shares. Media outlets are looking to make a profit. Real reporting means digging out nuggets of truth and stitching them together into a coherent story that accurately informs the public of what is happening in their world. Ideally, in the entertainment and media industry, stories, pieces, and narratives are both fact-based and fact-checked. Respectable journalists do not write or spread fake news. Journalists can lose sight of what is necessary and still ethically acceptable for the sake of media sales and revenues.

# INTRODUCTION TO MEDIA AND POLITICAL COMMUNICATION

How politicians and governments communicate with people occurs in all types of forms, such as the internet, books, television, and advertisements in mass media. The media can influence the governmental implementation of public policies and the development of public opinion. The media uses established communication channels for transmitting news, as well as influencing human behavior. The powerful complex of media technology not only carries information to us, but it also collects information about us.

The way media companies monitor and collect data about us creates a narrative and empowers companies. A significant component of power-building is control of the information or how one assembles data into narratives that influence public opinion. The rise of both cable and satellite television audiences translates into more options for media dissemination.

The phenomenal increase in channels through which information can flow for the informed citizen has made understanding the relationships among power, narratives, and political communication all the more central. The media are all-encompassing, enormously powerful and invasive, and yet, at the same time, more porous and open to our influence than ever before. The past decades have witnessed dramatic changes in the media environment, which have deepened during the social media revolution.

By intending to democratize political participation, social media has changed the way politicians, journalists, and public figures interact with the citizens. In real-time, social media users can respond to each other and influence public opinion. Citizens deliberate about policy-making in social media networks such as Facebook, Twitter, Instagram, Reddit, and more. Social media have these days the potential to both shape political campaigns and influence power relations in political parties as they allow candidates to campaign with a higher degree of independence than before.

## MEDIA SOURCING

The origin of media and the stories reported is a relevant aspect to verify. The roots of our thoughts and beliefs can be very blurry. Some media channels create their own stories through scientific reporting methods, while other sources merely report other news stories. A *media aggregator* is a channel that only picks and chooses from the reporting of others. Media aggregators do not always verify facts. They disseminate stories, even if the narrative is false.

Competent media reporting rests on reporting up to standards. *Reporting* in the media is the process by which professional journalists track down facts, check them, and ask hard questions, not settling for easy answers and pushing until they have found the truth. When looking for truth, the truth is not relative it is verifiable with empirical (real-world) evidence. More and more news sites rely on using others' work, including the wire services like the Associated Press. Without the reporting of skilled, assiduous, and persistent journalists, our system would be in serious trouble.

Even though traditional forms of international diplomacy persist, one can see that modern hybrid wars also take place in the media. In this context, global public opinion is the prize. Governments, business organizations, religious-related entities, terrorist groups, and large-scale international NGOs pursue their political objectives by using the media. Throughout the world, public opinion is essential to the welfare of every government. Publicists do their best to create powerful narratives that are convincing enough for people all around the globe.

## HOW WE GET AND CONSUME OUR NEWS

A hallmark of authoritarian political systems is the state's effort to control the narrative by managing the press[152]. When the government controls the story, then truth can be relative to the media producer. He who con-

---

[152] On media biases and political repression, see Davenport, Christian. *Media Bias, Perspective, and State Repression: The Black Panther Party.* Cambridge University Press, 2010.

trols the narrative-setting process also regulates what people think and feel about something. Our media channels that seek out truth include word of mouth, print media, broadcast media, or electronic media sources.

Print media is in decline and it is struggling to figure out its role in the electronic world. The use of magazines and newspapers has evolved to appease today's audiences and advertisers. TV news, especially local news, still draws older generations, and its audience is dwindling. The internet is rapidly becoming the go-to place for people, predominantly the youth, to seek information.[153]

In today's busy world, we get in touch with the media from numerous sources and places. *Media convergence* is the process by which most of us get our news from many different sources. You may receive information from a multiplicity of news sources every day—paper, the internet, and television. People are becoming acclimatized to the media narrative in their life. A *mediated citizen*[154] is a citizen whose media dictate his lines of communication and thought. People live within a media bubble; however, it is possible to pop that bubble.

When people are comfortable in their information bubble, they are less likely to make changes. An *information bubble* is a person's media comfort zone, in which they listen to the news, curate social media, and meet new people, all of which reinforce the ideas they already have. Popping the bubble should be a fundamental goal of an educated person. We are vulnerable to manipulation tactics. Public opinion-influencing tactics leave us especially vulnerable to be controlled by those who guide the information we get. We live our lives according to the information we receive from the media. News agencies influence our actions, decisions, and beliefs.

---

[153] Newspaper revenues declined considerably between the years 2008 and 2018. Advertising revenue fell from $37.8 billion in 2008 to $14.3 billion in 2018, which evidences a 62% decline. For more information on this, see Grieco, Elizabeth. "Fast Facts about the Newspaper Industry's Financial Struggles as McClatchy Files for Bankruptcy." *Pew Research Center*, 14 Feb. 2020.

[154] On mass media depictions of citizens and the influence of those depictions, see Shumow, Moses. *Mediated Communities: Civic Voices, Empowerment and Media Literacy in the Digital Era.* Peter Lang, 2015.

Depending on how critical we are, the media will more or less be able to alter our perception of the world. They have the adequate tools to do so.

## MEDIA OWNERSHIP AND GOVERNMENT REGULATIONS

In the United States, the government does not own the media and news sources. Who owns media agencies if the government does not own them? And how does the government regulate the media? The government controls the media by the use of licensing. The government sells licenses to radio and TV stations and is now questioning the role social media plays in national security-related issues. Because of that, policymakers carefully examine which threats the media represent and boost. News agencies are big businesses all around the world.

Only in the United States, six corporations own most of the major media outlets. What difference does that fact make? How important is media ownership for us? How having little to no diversity in media ownership can affect us? Those who control the media are known as gatekeepers. *Gatekeepers* are the people in charge of what information gets to us, and most importantly, how it does. Today, most news comes from—or at least through—massive, corporate-owned sources. One can these days see a *commercial bias* in the media toward what will increase advertiser revenues and audience shares. When taking news stories and information from the media in a context that could be considered reliable, one should adequately contextualize and understand the media bias nature and the outlets' ideological and political views.

Having money, however, does not necessarily help when building effective political communication. Innovation and creativity play a crucial role in political communication, as in other forms of cultural integration, and are not only a thing of the wealthy. Money certainly gives an advantage over the rest, but there are other factors that one should consider. Small and medium-sized news outlets can adjust to their budget and still create engaging and convincing narratives.

There is a continuous effort to get large audiences and keep them engaged. The media does that while also making way for increased advertising, which results in a reduced emphasis on political news, particularly for local television. Journalists lighten and dramatize the content of the information we get through the media. News is turned into *infotainment* or *soft news* to keep audiences tuned in and engaged.

Similarly, on the internet, infotainment is used to generate more news leads and story reads. *Clickbait* is the sensational headlines that tease you into clicking a link to find some intriguing-sounding information. By appealing to emotions and feelings, journalists aim to obtain more clicks from you. Today's media's corporate ownership means that the media outlets frequently face conflicts of interest in deciding what news to cover and how to cover it.

When doing their best to avoid getting "scooped" by another station or newspaper, reporters and editors alike sometimes jump the gun. Today, anyone can start a blog, a website, a podcast, or a YouTube Channel and start publishing his/her independent views. Social media networking has given voice to many new actors that influence public opinion.

If small media outlets and new-coming influencers look like they will be profitable, enterprising corporations likely have an incentive to scoop them up. Today, some outlets look like alternative media but have the funding of giants behind them. They are not independent at all. By appearing to be alternative or independent can attract new potential audiences that mistrust larger media outlets.

Media in the United States of America functions like a private enterprise system in which large businesses seek profit. The media in this country is almost entirely privately-owned, but they do not operate without some degree of public control. With fewer limitations on how many stations an owner can possess, the potential for media monopoly has become enormous over the years.[155]

---

[155] On media monopoly and the hilling effects of corporate ownership and mass advertising on the nation's news, see Bagdikian, Ben. *The Media Monopoly.* Beacon Press, 2000.. Since 1983, the number of corporations controlling most of America's daily newspapers, magazines, radio and television stations, book publishers, and movie companies has dwindled from fifty to ten to six.

The internet is known as a place in which the media can freely operate. However, that is only true as long as there is internet freedom in that country. Should the internet be regulated? Is it time to consider internet connectivity a basic human right? And are we prepared if it turns against us? Supporters of net neutrality believe that the internet should be an open-access forum for innovation. In the aftermath of Russian hacking and social media manipulation during the 2016 election, the internet has been up for scrutiny in Congress.

It is important to note that U.S. Congress members are mostly not among the generations that are internet savvy. It comes as no surprise that they often don't seem to know what they are searching for. Even though there has been significant-tech adoption since 2012 among older generations, Millennials still stand out for their technology use. On the other hand, Gen Z's are tech native.

## WHAT DO JOURNALISTS DO?

Both reporters and journalists gather information to later present it as news stories, feature articles, or documentaries. Journalists usually work on the staff of news organizations, but they work freelance as well. Freelance journalism means that they write stories for whoever pays them. General reporters cover all kinds of news stories, while other journalists specialize in specific areas such as politics, business, or fashion.

Journalists play a relevant, far-reaching, and essential role in our political system because they chase the news and deliver information to the rest of society. Valid-reporting means seeking answers. Reporting means digging out nuggets of truth and stitching them together into a coherent story that truly informs the public of what is happening in their world. Self-claiming that one is a journalist is not enough to be an authentic journalist. Citizens have to keep a keen eye on whether they contribute valuable, high-quality, factual, and not-strongly biased information to the public debate.

Journalism falls into four principal journalistic roles. The first role is to be a *gatekeeper* of truth. Editors and high-authority reporters who decide about what should be covered and what should not are the gate-keepers of truth for society. The second role is to be a disseminator. A *disseminator* is a reporter who mainly focuses on getting out facts rather than opinions. The third role of a journalist is to be a *researcher/analyst.* This type of journalist is a person who digs for information and interprets both its transcendence and significance by contextualizing it. The fourth type of reporter is a *public mobilizer.* This journalist usually has an agenda, and it is part of their job to make citizens aware of what is going on around them and encourage them to take action.

Journalists do not only communicate about what is going on in the world but also influence public opinion. In his seminal study of *Public Opinion,* Walter Lippmann observed that political action mostly derived from voting rights and mass media communications rather than from the collectively arrived at the will of rational, enlightened men. Citizens politically decide, more or less, through the exercise of the vote and the influence of public opinion. Lippmann recognized in 1922 that public opinion was a constructed and manufactured thing that could be shaped and manipulated by those with the resources and interests in doing so[156]. Publicists, press agents, and journalists are part of a social class situated between political organizations and media institutions. Their job is often to influence the public opinion-building process according to the needs of their clients.[157]

## ISSUES, CHALLENGES, AND CONTROVERSIES PROFESSIONAL JOURNALISM FACES

Professional journalists are often in a position that does not allow them to earn money from their work. It is too easy to make money off their

---

[156] On the role of news in the process of manufacturing public opinion, see Lipmann.

[157] For more information about how the press agents influence public opinion, see McNair, Brian. *An Introduction to Political Communication.* Routledge, Taylor & Francis Group, 2018. Political programs, policy agendas, electoral messages, pressure group campaigns, and acts of domestic and global terrorism have the potential for communicative effectiveness.

work without paying them for it. News aggregators pose a threat to journalism because high-quality reporting costs both time and money. If a news source only retells another agency's story, the original story writer loses revenue for their work.

Another problem with professional journalism is that people have equated journalism with print journalism. Nowadays, people do not buy or subscribe to print outlets as they used to in the past. People object to paying for content online. There is a slow appreciation of electronic media. Major outlets are doing their best to maintain old business models based on subscription and print ad revenue while still successfully venturing into the digital world. As citizens distrust the media in general, it becomes more difficult for the public to trust the media. The public distrusts the media, which lacks credibility these days.

Respectable journalists do not write fake news. Fake news is out there, but credible journalists do their best to confront it. What is distinctive about good journalism is the reporters' commitment to accuracy, objectivity, and detail in telling their stories. Journalists have to properly research and verify their facts because they act as communicators who work in service of the truth, even if it is troublesome.

Low-quality journalism may allow disinformation and misinformation to originate in or leak into the news industry, which is likely to mislead public opinion. Strong ethical journalism and professional standards are required as antidotes to both disinformation and misinformation. As long as we do not control the avalanche of disinformation, the public may come to disbelieve all content, including journalism. Citizens are likely to take as credible whatever content their close friends and preferred influencers share in social networks. Disinformation campaigns do not necessarily aspire to convince the public to believe that its content is veracious but rather impact the agenda-setting. Fake news can shape what people think is relevant and what is not.

One should consider that when people use the phrase "fake news," for the most part, what they are trying to do is to control the narrative. Fake news accusations are used as a way of delegitimizing a journalist's work. Because of its popularity, the term has recently been weaponized to leverage attacks against the media. Citizens may use the term "fake news" to satisfy their need for structure in the world. Cognitively speaking, people need to satisfy their need to see the world around them as an orderly, coherent, and structured place rather than solely to express their political, cultural, or personal ideology. One can already see the negative impacts of this situation on public beliefs about health, science, and intercultural affairs.

News organizations in the United States recognize fake news as a sociopolitical problem while acknowledging the challenge in defining it because of its many uses and connotations depending on the context. In general, specialists consider fake news as a social media phenomenon thriving on political polarization driven by mostly ideological and partisan, but sometimes also cultural and financial motivations. It has become common throughout the world to blame for the rise of fake news to the current political environment, to technological platforms Google, Twitter and Facebook, and some particular audiences as well.

## MEDIA SHAPES THE POLITICAL NARRATIVE

The media has historically played an integral role in influencing social trends. The information era, a new history term used to capture the way the world has recently developed to rely on information for most of the actions that people take, remains significantly different from all the other periods in the history of humankind.

More than ever, information and narratives now have significant powers to change and influence the way people think and act. Most importantly, the reasoning they help portray on various relevant topics in society. The media is essential to push for specific narratives and messages in the modern world.

The contemporary media industry has emerged as the most advanced system of communication that humanity has ever experienced. Unlike in the past, when information and narratives could take long periods to reach citizens, the situation is radically different in our times since information travels the world in seconds. Researchers have studied the role of the contemporary media in political driving narratives quite extensively. The media drives our social, economic, and political trends. Communication outlets influence the reasoning that people hold as truths.

The primary purpose of the mass media outlets is to tell convincing yet engaging stories. Ideally, in the media industry, stories and narratives are not only fact-based but also fact-checked. And who exactly are the storytellers? At the pinnacle of political reporting are the Washington press corporations. Some of them have been politicians or at least members of the political world. As politicians move from the political to the private sector, the list of government officials regularly changes. This *revolving door-like process* consists of moving from the political sector to the public or the private ones. Some journalists are ethically stellar, but others' loyalty may lie more toward their political allies than their audiences.

## MEDIA AND POLITICIANS WILL TRY TO CREATE A NARRATIVE LINE AND SPIN THE FACTS THAT FIT THE NARRATIVE

When a politician *spins* a story, they are likely to purposely select pieces of information that fit their political narrative and intentionally interpret data to make things look different by distorting facts and ignoring relevant factors. In political journalism, spins are attempts to control communication to deliver one's preferred message and persuade audiences. The term is commonly used to refer to the sophisticated art of promoting one's agenda by selling and spreading specific messages in favor of one's interests and views. Political spins often imply a certain degree of deception. A person who offers to give their opinion or commentary to mass media outlets on a particular subject area (most typically *political analysis*) is a pundit. A *pundit* is a person who can sometimes fall into the "analyst" category of journalists and sometimes into the bloviator category. The journalist can spin a story through different methods.

Journalists can spin a tale by creating an agenda for their news source and creating an important story that people focus on. *Agenda setting* is what a journalist, editor, or producer decides is important, becomes news and ends up on the political agenda.[158] This agenda-setting can frame issues so that one or two topics become relevant in the national discussion for the day. *Framing* the political debate and public opinion is about telling people what matters the most and what to pay attention to when reading the news. There should be a reliance on skilled and professional communicators who stick to engaging, easy, and already existing narratives to shape and influence political debates.

Journalists can lose sight of what is necessary for the sake of media sales and revenues. A *feeding frenzy* is a process by which a scandal turns average journalists into sharks-like beings waiting for the next tidbit of news to drop. This situation can cause trouble when people focus on scandal and clickbait instead of seeking the truth. During election cycles, it is a common problem to only focus on the person winning a race. This *horse race-type of journalism* in election reporting focuses on who is ahead, who is losing support, and who is a surprisingly long shot, but not on the substance of what the election is really about. Much of the time, the end result is the *soundbite* generated, which is a short and snappy memorable line that commentators may repeat over and over. Often, they do so by taking facts out of context.

## MEDIA AND THE FIRST AMENDMENT

The U.S. Constitution was drafted clandestinely. Journalists were excluded from observing the writing process, and the framers did not engage with the press to discuss their disputes and decisions. Upon completion, the Constitution was then made available to the public,

---

[158]   See Zaller, John. *The Nature and Origins of Mass Opinion.* Cambridge University Press, 2011 for more information on the tactics to influence public opinion throughout history.

leading to its widespread publication in nearly all newspapers. Newspaper editors additionally disseminated discussion and opinion regarding the newly introduced constitution and its suggested structure of governance. The initial backing for the Constitution was robust, while those against it, known as Anti-Federalists, contended that their apprehensions were inadequately addressed by the media. The final publication of The Federalist Papers, as well as the lesser-known Anti-Federalist Papers, bolstered the contention that the press was indispensable to American democracy. Furthermore, it was evident that the press possessed the capacity to influence public opinion, and hence, public policy. The inclusion of the First Amendment in the Bill of Rights demonstrated the framers' conviction that safeguarding a free and robust press was of utmost significance. The message stated that "Congress shall make no law respecting an establishment of religion, or prohibiting the free exercise thereof; or abridging the freedom of speech, or of the press; or the right of the people peaceably to assemble, and to petition the government for a redress of grievances." This amendment forms the foundation for the political liberties of the United States, and the freedom of the press plays a significant part in maintaining a robust democracy. Without it, the press would lack the freedom to inform citizens about governmental misconduct and dishonesty.

The New York Weekly Journal, founded by John Peter Zenger in 1733, aimed to eradicate corruption within the colonial government, making it one of New York's earliest newspapers. Following the arrest and allegation of seditious libel against Zenger by provincial governor William Cosby in 1735, his legal team effectively fought his case resulting in a verdict of not guilty. This outcome reinforced the significance of a free press in the colonies.

The media functions as a source of information and communication, enabling citizens to stay informed and functioning as a platform for citizens to publicly declare their intentions to gather and protest against their government's activities. However, it is imperative for the government to ensure that the media operates with integrity and refrains from using their authority. Similar to other rights protected by the First Amendment, freedom of the press is not without limitations. The media are subject to restrictions on their freedom to publish and broadcast.

## DEFAMATION, LIBEL AND SLANDER

The media lack the authority to engage in slander, which involves making false statements with the intention of damaging a person or entity, or to commit libel, which involves publishing false material with the intention of harming a person or entity. These actions amount to character defamation, which can result in a negative impact on one's reputation and financial earnings. In circumstances of libel and slander, the media do not possess the right to exercise free speech as the information they disseminate is acknowledged to be false. However, newspapers and magazines consistently publish articles on a weekly basis that have a negative impact and are detrimental. How can people engage in such actions without facing legal consequences?

Libel and slander only arise when incorrect information is presented as fact. Editors and columnists enjoy protection from numerous libel and slander provisions when expressing their ideas, as they do not assert that their words are factual. Furthermore, the responsibility lies with the person or organization that has been subjected to defamation to initiate legal action against the media entity. The legal standards applied by the courts vary based on whether the claimant is a private individual or a public figure.

In order to hold a public figure accountable for defamation, it is necessary to demonstrate that the publisher or broadcaster behaved with a clear and conscious disregard for the truth or that the author had a deliberate intention to harm. This examination dates back to the landmark case of New York Times v. Sullivan (1964), wherein a police commissioner in Alabama filed a lawsuit regarding the dissemination of false information in a newspaper advertisement. Due to the commissioner's status as a public figure, the United States. The Supreme Court utilized a rigorous examination of malice to ascertain whether the adver-tisement constituted libel; the court concluded that it did not.

An individual in a private capacity must either present one of the aforementioned justifications or contend that the author was remiss in failing to verify the accuracy of the information prior to its publication. Due to this rationale, newspapers and magazines are less inclined to devi-ate from objective information while reporting on private individuals, but they may be more inclined to exaggerate the truth when writing about politicians, celebrities, or public figures. However, even distorting the truth might incur significant expenses for a publisher. In 2010, Star magazine released a headline titled "Addiction Nightmare: Katie Drug Shocker," which insinuated that actress Katie Holmes was involved in drug use. The article in the magazine mostly discusses the addictive nature of Scientology sessions rather than narcotics. However, the connotation and the headline conveyed a different message. Due to the unpredict-able behavior caused by drug addiction, directors may be less willing to hire Holmes if she were addicted to drugs. Therefore, Holmes may assert that she had suffered a deprivation of both opportunity and money as a result of the headline. Although the publisher first refused to rectify the story, Holmes initiated a $50 million lawsuit, and Star's parent company, American Media, Inc., ultimately reached a settlement. Star issued a for-mal apology and made a charitable contribution on behalf of Holmes.

## SENSITIVE INFORMATION

The media possess a restricted entitlement to publish material that the government designates as classified. If a newspaper or media outlet acquires classified material, or if a journalist becomes aware of classi-fied information, the government may demand that certain content be censored or deleted from the piece. Government personnel and former employees frequently provide media with confidential documents to raise public awareness about an issue. If a journalist contacts the White House or Pentagon to obtain quotes regarding a secret subject, the president has the authority to issue an order to halt the publishing of the newspaper in order to protect national security. Subsequently, the courts are requested to adjudicate on matters of censorship and determine what content can be published.

The demarcation between the public's entitlement to information and the imperative of safeguarding national security is frequently ambiguous. In 1971, the Supreme Court presided over the Pentagon Papers case, where the U.S. government filed a lawsuit against the New York Times and the Washington Post in an attempt to prevent the disclosure of classified information from a study on the Vietnam War. The Supreme Court has determined that although the government has the authority to impose prior restrictions on the media, which allows the government to block the release of material, this power is very restricted. The court granted the newspapers the authority to publish a significant portion of the study. However, the disclosure of military movements and the identities of covert agents are among the few justifications for which the government can lawfully prevent publishing or reporting.

During the second Persian Gulf War, FOX News correspondent Geraldo Rivera successfully persuaded the military to allow him to be embedded with a U.S. military unit. An army unit stationed in Iraq will offer real-time coverage of its daily operations. While accompanying the 101st Airborne Division on a trip, Rivera had his camera operator film him sketching a map in the sand. The map indicated the location of his battalion and used Baghdad as a point of reference. Rivera subsequently deliberated on the next destination for the unit. Rivera was promptly expelled from the unit and accompanied out of Iraq. The military invoked its prerogative to uphold confidentiality regarding troop movements, asserting that Rivera's journalism had divulged troop positions and jeopardized the unit's security. Rivera's subsequent communications and news coverage were subjected to censorship until he was physically separated from the military unit.

Regulations pertaining to media and the Federal Communications Commission (FCC) The freedoms exercised by newspapers are supervised by the U.S. judiciary, whereas television and radio broadcasters are subject to scrutiny by both the judiciary and a governmental regulatory authority. The Radio Act of 1927 marked Congress' initial endeavor to govern broadcast content. The legislation was enacted to regulate the burgeoning proliferation of radio stations and the excessive utilization of frequencies. However, legislators were concerned that televised media could contain explicit or prejudiced content. The Radio Act included provisions that granted the government authority to regulate the content of broadcasts sent through public airwaves and to ensure that stations prioritized the public's welfare.

The Communications Act of 1934 superseded the Radio Act and established a more authoritative body, the Federal Communications Commission (FCC), consisting of seven members, to regulate both radio and telephone communication. The Federal Communications Commission (FCC), now consisting of a mere five members, mandates that radio stations must submit applications for licenses. These licenses are only given if stations adhere to regulations regarding advertising restrictions, the provision of a platform for public discourse, and the promotion of local and minority communities. Television's introduction led to the FCC being granted the same power to license and oversee television stations. The FCC currently enforces ownership restrictions to prevent monopolies and filters content that is considered undesirable. The jurisdiction of print media is not within its purview, mostly due to the fact that print media is acquired through purchase rather than broadcast.

In order to retain a license, stations must satisfy a set of criteria. The equal-time rule mandates that registered candidates seeking public office must be provided with equitable opportunities for airtime and commercials on non-cable television and radio stations, commencing forty-five days before a primary election and sixty days before a general election. If WBNS in Columbus, Ohio, decides to sell Senator Marco Rubio thirty seconds of airtime for a presidential campaign commercial, the station is obligated to sell all other candidates in that race thirty seconds of airtime at the same price. The amount must not exceed the fee charged by the station to preferred commercial advertisers for running advertisements of the same category and duration. If Fox5 in Atlanta decides to provide Bernie Sanders with a five-minute infomercial, they are obligated to provide the same opportunity to all other candidates in the race for an equal amount of free airtime. Failure to do so may result in a complaint being filed with the FCC. Donald Trump made an appearance on Saturday Night Live in 2015 while he was campaigning for the Republican presidential nomination. Subsequent Republican contenders submitted requests for equal television time, which NBC granted by allocating twelve minutes and five seconds to each candidate. This airtime was scheduled for Friday and Saturday nights, as well as a later episode of Saturday Night Live.

The FCC grants an exemption to the equal-time rule in cases when the coverage is exclusively focused on news. If a newscaster is reporting on a political event and manages to obtain a brief interview with a candidate, the principle of equal time does not come into play. Similarly, if a news program produces a concise documentary on the issue of immigration reform and opts to incorporate footage from only a select few candidates, the rule does not become applicable. However, the regulation may encompass programs that are not categorized as news. Therefore, certain stations will refrain from broadcasting a movie or television program if it features a candidate. Arnold Schwarzenegger and Gary Coleman, who are both actors, ran as candidates in California's governor recall election in 2003. Television stations refrained from broadcasting Coleman's sitcom Different Strokes or Schwarzenegger's movies due to the application of the equal time clause. Given the presence of 135 candidates on the official ballot, it would have been challenging for stations to provide thirty-minute and two-hour time slots to each candidate. Even the airing of the president's State of the Union speech can activate the equal-time restrictions. Following the State of the Union, opposing parties in Congress utilize the opportunity to officially counter the president's initiatives.

The equal-time norm, although rooted in the principle of fairness, may not extend to encompass supporters of a candidate or a cause beyond the candidates themselves. Therefore, there is a possibility of a loophole where broadcasters can provide free airtime exclusively to supporters of a single candidate. During the 2012 Wisconsin gubernatorial recall election, there were allegations that Scott Walker's supporters were provided with complimentary air time to solicit donations and recruit volunteers, whereas Tom Barrett's supporters did not receive the same opportunity. As per a source familiar with the issue, the FCC chose not to get involved when a complaint was lodged, stating that the equal-time requirement only pertained to the official candidates and that the case fell under the now-defunct fairness concept. The fairness policy was implemented in 1949 and mandated that licensed stations present controversial topics in an equitable manner by offering listeners information from all viewpoints on these topics. If a candidate, cause, or supporter was provided with an opportunity to communicate with the viewers or listeners, the opposing side would also be granted a chance to offer their perspective. The fairness concept was terminated in the 1980s following a series of court disputes, leading to its repeal by the FCC in 1987. Stations and detractors contended that the doctrine restricted discussion of contentious subjects and gave the government editorial authority.

The Federal Communications Commission (FCC) enforces regulations on television, radio, and other broadcasters to restrict indecent content and ensure that the public airwaves remain free from obscene material. Although the Supreme Court has refrained from providing a specific definition for obscenity, it is determined by the application of a set of criteria established in the Miller v. California (1973) case. According to the Miller test, obscenity refers to material that attracts individuals with abnormal or deviant interests, violates local or state regulations, and lacks any significant value. The Supreme Court ruled that the presence of children in the audience outweighed the right of broadcasters to broadcast indecent and profane material. Nevertheless, broadcasters are permitted to transmit indecent programs or use vulgar language between the hours of 10 p.m. between 12 midnight and 6 in the morning.

The Supreme Court has confirmed that the FCC possesses the power to regulate content. Despite the radio station providing a warning about potentially harmful content, the Federal Communications Commission (FCC) still decided to prohibit a sketch performed by George Carlin. The station filed an appeal against the decision and was unsuccessful. Penalties can vary from tens of thousands to millions of dollars, and a significant number of them are imposed for making sexual jokes on radio talk shows and displaying nudity on television. Janet Jackson's wardrobe malfunction during the Super Bowl's half-time show in 2004 resulted in a financial loss of $550,000 for the CBS network.

Although certain FCC infractions, such as Jackson's incident at the Super Bowl, are observed firsthand by commission members, the primary source of information for the FCC regarding violations of equal time and indecency regulations is the filing of complaints by individuals and customers. Radio programming accounts for approximately 2 percent of complaints to the FCC, while television programming accounts for 10 percent. In contrast, telephone complaints make up 71 percent of the total, and Internet complaints make up 15 percent. However, the criteria for determining a violation may not always be apparent to persons seeking to file a complaint, nor is it evident what actions may result in a punishment or the revocation of a license. In October 2014, parent advocacy groups and consumers lodged complaints and urged the FCC to impose penalties on ABC for airing a sexually provocative opening scene in the drama series Scandal right after It's the Great Pumpkin, Charlie Brown, without any advertisements or the credits of the cartoon to serve as a transitional buffer between the two vastly distinct types of programming. ABC was not fined by the FCC.

The radio and television industries saw substantial transformations as a result of the implementation of the Telecommunications Act of 1996. The restriction on the maximum number of radio stations (forty) and television stations (twelve) that a single firm could possess was eliminated. Furthermore, it enabled networks to acquire a substantial quantity of cable stations. Essentially, it diminished competition and enhanced the quantity of conglomerates. According to Common Cause and other critics, the act not only increased cable costs but also facilitated firms in disregarding their commitments to the public interest. The legislation also transformed the role of the FCC from that of a regulator to that of a monitor. The Commission is responsible for regulating the acquisition of stations to prevent media monopolies and resolving consumer grievances against radio, television, and telephone businesses.

A significant alteration in government regulation of the press, aimed at ensuring equitable coverage, pertains to net neutrality. The Obama administration implemented net neutrality regulations in 2015. These regulations mandated that internet service providers provide equitable access to their services for all users and prohibited discriminatory pricing of internet access fees. In the early stages of the Trump Administration, the Federal Communications Commission (FCC) decided to abandon the principle of net neutrality. Subsequently, the Trump administration legally contested California's state statute that established net neutrality. The Biden administration dismissed the lawsuit within a fortnight of assuming office in 2021. In March 2020, a consortium of technology firms urged the FCC to take additional action and officially restore net neutrality.

# KEY TERMS

**Agenda-setting:** The process by which journalists and media producers determine which issues are most important and deserving of public attention.

**Aggregators:** Media channels that compile and disseminate stories from other news sources without independent verification of the facts.

**Clickbait:** Sensational headlines designed to attract clicks and increase web traffic, often at the expense of accurate or meaningful content.

**Equal-time rule:** An FCC regulation requiring broadcast stations to provide equal airtime opportunities to all registered political candidates during election campaigns.

**Fake news:** False or misleading information presented as news, often intended to deceive or mislead the audience.

**Framing:** The way media outlets shape and present news stories to influence public perception and interpretation of the events.

**Gatekeepers:** Editors and high-authority journalists who decide which news stories are covered and how they are presented to the public.

**Infotainment:** A blend of information and entertainment in news reporting, designed to engage audiences while delivering news content.

**Mediated citizen:** An individual whose thoughts and opinions are heavily influenced by media consumption and the narratives presented within their media bubble.

**Net neutrality:** The principle that internet service providers should treat all data on the internet equally and not discriminate or charge differently based on user, content, or website.

**Public mobilizer**: A type of journalist who aims to inform the public about issues and encourage them to take action.

**Spin**: The practice of presenting information in a biased or manipulative way to favor a particular political agenda or viewpoint.

**Telecommunications Act of 1996**: A law that significantly deregulated the telecommunications industry, allowing for greater media consolidation and the rise of media conglomerates.

**Yellow journalism**: Journalism that is based on sensationalism and crude exaggeration, often sacrificing truth for the sake of attracting readers.

# CHAPTER 19

# DOMESTIC POLICY

A policy is a prescribed course of action for those who work for the government. It creates a set of operational principles through which to accomplish desired goals.

Setting domestic policy creates standard operational procedures by which a government operates. Policies are put in place to guide the bureaucratic agencies that work under the Executive Branch.

When governments create laws and policies, either domestic or foreign, it is called policymaking. Policymaking is the process by which the Congress creates public policies. A public policy is a government plan of action to solve a problem that people share collectively or that they cannot solve on their own. These public policies are meant to create solutions to problems for the greater good of society. We can understand public policy as a purposeful course of action intended by officials to solve problems of society.

## MAKING PUBLIC POLICY

The power to make public policy in the United States begins with Congress. Policies are usually created by legislators in the form of new proposals or bills, which are passed by both the House and Senate and signed into law by the president. The role of influencing and creating public policy also resides in limited form within the Executive Branch.

A president may also create policy through multiple pathways: by placing an issue on the public agenda, including in their budget proposal, vetoing a law passed by Congress, or issuing an executive order that establishes a new policy or augments an existing one. Executive orders are directed only to government bureaucracies at the federal, state, or local levels. These agencies can wield enormous control over policy through how they enforce such orders.

The court system also can make public policy. When a court rules on what the government can, should or should not do, it is clearly taking an active policy making role. The courts, especially the Supreme Court, can create public policy by hearing cases that change policy adoption, allow for policy to be formulated, or create standards by which we interpret public law.

## TYPES OF DOMESTIC PUBLIC POLICY

Scholars have come up with a typology of domestic problems that require different kinds of policies to solve them. These categories help determine the types of social and economic policies that the nation adopts.

The method by which a policy is implemented may vary according to the type of economic and political policy. Some policies are considered redistributive in nature. These redistributive policies use resources from affluent segments of society to provide benefits for those less likely to participate in the political sector. Redistributive policies are less likely to occur in more capitalistic market systems.

Domestic policies that are equally taxing on all of the population are called distributive in nature. A distributive policy is one whose costs are borne by the entire population. An example would be a flat-based tax system that is the same across all income brackets.

Some domestic policies, however, do not deal with the allocation of goods and resources in society. A domestic policy that does not distribute resources but exerts control within society through behaviors it requires is called a regulatory policy. Regulatory policies control behavior rather than distributing resources.

## SOCIAL POLICY

Many domestic policies are designed as social policies. Social policies are primarily distributive and redistributive policies that improve Americans' quality of life. If a social policy is distributive or redistributive for social welfare needs, it is a social welfare policy, a government program designed to provide for those who cannot, or sometimes will not, provide for themselves. Those programs that care for those who cannot care for themselves are the most redistributive in nature. Often there are rules and requirements, usually based on income potential.

Social policies that filter who is eligible or not for the redistribution of wealth often utilize means-tested programs. Means-tested programs require that beneficiaries prove they lack the necessary income or resources to provide for themselves, according to the government's definitions of eligibility. This is usually based on income-earning potential. In the United States, these types of programs often carry a social stigma and are contentious during elections.

Certain types of means-tested social programs are designed to help families in need. One example is the Temporary Assistance to Needy Families (TANF) program that replaced AFDC. This program provides block grants to state governments, giving states greater control over how they spend their money. The TANF program caps the amount that the federal government will pay for welfare and requires work in exchange for time-limited benefits. Other requirements may include recipients finding jobs within two years, then removing them from welfare rolls after a total of five years or less, depending on the state.

Another domestic policy program for helping people who make less than a federally legislated income level is the Supplemental Nutrition Assistance Program (SNAP). SNAP is the largest United States food assistance program for low-income families, providing vouchers to purchase food. This program helps those without enough resources for food and sustenance.

In modern times, many Americans are unaware that the policy we have referred to for years as "welfare" is mostly gone.

One of the best-known social policies is Social Security Insurance. Social insurance policies are longer-term distributive programs that provide benefits to a specific segment of the population. Social Security is a program born in the Great Depression to provide retirement funding for the elderly. It works through an economic input, or buy-in, when workers pay into the federally backed program. People contribute to Social Security during their working lives in order to receive benefits after they retire. Current workers pay the Social Security of retirees, with any leftover money going into the Social Security trust fund. Most people, at least those who are older, see Social Security as something they have earned and to which they are entitled, not as a government handout.

Still, there are problems with Social Security. With longer life spans, most people end up getting much more back from Social Security and Medicare than they may have contributed. Many workers who have paid into the system see Social Security as an entitlement. Entitlement programs require benefits to be paid to people who are entitled to receive them. They are not needs-based nor do they follow a means-tested approval system. Even though there is talk of the Social Security system going insolvent, it could be made sustainable. Some potential remedies, however, are politically unpalatable and vigorously opposed by interest groups, including the American Association of Retired People (AARP).

Domestic policies to ensure the health care of people are increasing. The Patient Protection and Affordable Care Act established and made access to health insurance more available and affordable for most Americans. The United States stands out among industrialized nations as the only one that doesn't have a universal health-care system guaranteeing minimum basic care to all. Historically, health-care in America pre-2010 utilized Medicare (covering old people) and Medicaid (covering the poorest people) for health care coverage of those without insurance. The consequences were that many unin-sured people fell through the cracks.

Medicare was a social insurance program designed to help the elderly pay their medical costs. This program has been modified since the incep-tion, however, it is still focused on elderly care. Medicare has become an extraordinarily expensive program. Medicaid is a means-tested welfare pro-gram designed to assist the poor -- especially children -- with their medical costs. This program undergoes adjustments when domestic policies allow for increased coverage and care for different segments of society.

## ECONOMIC POLICY

Government creates economic policies to keep the economy stable, growing, and functioning smoothly. Economic policies include all the different strategies that government officials, elected and appointed, employ to solve economic problems, to protect economic rights, and to provide procedural guarantees to keep the financial markets running smoothly. The government can control and regulate the marketplace or allow it to go mostly unregulated, with each approach depending on the political policy and party in power.

The consequences of a largely unregulated market vary. More regula-tion of the commerce of food and energy can increase the cost of goods and services for consumers. Traditionally, policymakers have felt that the government should pursue a hands-off economic policy. This allows for consumers to decide how much they are willing to pay for goods and ser-vices. Since the Great Depression, the goal of economic policymakers has been to even out the dramatic cycles of inflation and recession without undermining the vitality and productivity of a market-driven economy. America has gone through various series of recessions, depressions, and economic growth, often influenced by the domestic policies set by the government.

Economic policies are complicated, so for the sake of brevity we will provide a short and simple description. The government uses fiscal policy to grow or shrink the economy through taxation. Fiscal policy is the government's power to tax and spend with the aim of stabilizing the economy. This is done to create both surpluses and deficits in national spending. A surplus is money saved after spending on the government's domestic policy. A deficit is money owed after spending beyond what is actually available.

There are many tools available to create a healthy fiscal policy. One power of the government is known as monetary policy. Monetary policy is the power to control the money supply by manipulating interest rates. When interest rates are low, people can borrow money at a lower cost, spurring more business activity. The monetary policy of the United States is run by the Federal Reserve System (the Fed). The Federal Reserve System is a group of 12 banks run by a board of governors whose chair is appointed by the president. It sets interest rates for the nation and is autonomous of the Executive Branch or Congress.

The government has the power to take from every citizen and business a share of their revenue for the purpose of ensuring the national interest. Taxation is the power to charge people a percentage of their income for the domestic and foreign policy needs of the government. Tax policy is the way in which the government requires that individuals and businesses contribute to collective costs. Taxation levels may be different for people depending on their income levels. A progressive income tax is a tax on people with more money at a higher rate than the rate applied to people with less money. This is different from a regressive tax.,. A regressive tax may take a higher percentage of a poorer person's gross resources, like sales taxes or value-added taxes (VATs) or some proposals for a flat income tax. There are other types of taxes as well, including capital gains taxes, a controversial tax that may be levied on the return from capital investments.

## ENVIRONMENTAL POLICY

President Richard Nixon in 1970 signed a National Environmental Policy Act that a year later became the Environmental Protection Agency, or EPA. During the 1970s, laws were passed regarding clean air and clean water, as well as protections for endangered species. With these, sources of air and water pollutants came under federal regulation. Environmental policy attempts to balance the protection and conservation of natural resources with economic growth and jobs. Industries are required to follow federal and state rules designed to protect the natural environment. The rigor with which these regulations are enforced often depends on the political party in power at any particular time. For example, President Ronald Reagan in 1982 cut EPA funding by 30 percent.

The Department of the Interior was established in 1849 to manage natural resources, and oversees energy development on federal lands as well as offshore leases. A division, the Bureau of Land Management, was formed in 1946 to manage the federal lands that total almost 250 million acres.

## ENERGY POLICY

U.S energy policy is sometimes connected to environmental policy, especially when energy production and consumption involves the exploitation of natural resources and creates pollutants. Legislation, regulations, international treaties, subsidies and taxation are all modes of policy implementation. Coal, oil, natural gas, hydroelectric and nuclear power, and more recently renewables including wind and solar power have powered America through the years and been subjects of energy policies. Fossil fuels still account for most United States energy consumption. Federal tax policies and subsidies can be used as incentives for the development of specific energy sources.

There is concern in the United States and worldwide over greenhouse gas emissions that are related to climate change. China and the United

States are the biggest carbon polluters, and many nations and industries are taking steps to reduce such emissions and move toward energy efficiencies and renewable sources, though there has been no firm global agreement on such policies as yet.

## HEALTH POLICY

America's massive and complex health-care industry accounts for about 17 percent of all spending, mostly on medical services to diagnose and treat illnesses and injuries, both physical and mental. Health policy has therefore become a contentious issue between political parties and is often adjusted, depending on who is in power. The United States system is a third-party payer arrangement in which health insurance companies reimburse medical providers a portion of the cost of services to patients. Almost half of Americans participate in private health insurance plans through their employers. Medicare (15 percent), for people over 65, and Medicaid (16 percent), for low-income people, are public programs touched on earlier under social policies. While the Affordable Care Act, also known as Obamacare, has helped expand coverage since its passage in 2010, there are still about 30 million (13 percent) of Americans who are uninsured, mostly because of the high costs of healthcare. Soaring costs have also driven employers to reduce the reimbursements paid to medical providers and to increase the burden of insurance premium payments on their employees.

## TRANSPORTATION POLICY

The Department of Transportation (DOT) plans and coordinates federal transportation projects to enhance national economic competitiveness, facilitating the movement of people and goods and also setting safety regulations for all major modes of transport, including air, water, and land – both roads and railways. National Transport Policy also attempts to reduce negative impacts on the environment. The Federal Aviation

Administration, Highway Administration, Railroad Administration, Transit Administration and other agencies are related to the DOT.

Many federal infrastructure programs and policies have failed to modernize in recent decades, according to DOT research, leading to five major challenges, which involve crumbling infrastructure, congestion, climate change, injuries and fatalities as well as unequal economic opportunity.

Transportation is the biggest source of United States greenhouse gas emissions, with more than 100 million people living amid pollution that exceeds health-based air quality standards. Traffic congestion costs the economy more than $165 billion in wasted productivity and fuel each year. Additionally, many infrastructure assets including highways, public transit and rail systems have come to the end of their useful lives and require repair or replacement. New modes of transport will also be necessary to handle the demands of both the economy and the environment in the future.

## KEY TERMS

**Affordable Care Act (ACA)**: A health reform law enacted in 2010 that aims to make health insurance more affordable and accessible for Americans.

**Bureau of Land Management (BLM)**: A division of the Department of the Interior formed in 1946 to manage federal lands.

**Distributive Policy**: A type of domestic policy that allocates resources equally among the population, such as a flat-based tax system.

**Entitlement Programs**: Government programs that provide benefits to individuals who meet certain eligibility criteria, such as Social Security.

**Environmental Policy**: Government actions and regulations aimed at protecting the natural environment and conserving resources.

**Executive Order**: A directive issued by the president that manages operations of the federal government and has the force of law.

**Fiscal Policy**: Government policies on taxation and spending aimed at stabilizing the economy.

**Means-Tested Programs**: Social programs that require beneficiaries to prove they lack the necessary income or resources to provide for themselves.

**Monetary Policy**: The regulation of the money supply and interest rates by the Federal Reserve System to control inflation and stabilize the economy.

**Social Welfare Policy**: Government programs designed to provide assistance to individuals and families in need, often through redistributive policies.

# CHAPTER 20

# FOREIGN POLICY

## FOREIGN POLICY

Foreign policy determines how the United States reacts and responds to governments and non-governmental groups beyond its borders. Foreign policy is the official policy designed to solve problems that occur between the United States and actors from abroad. It is important to have successful policies for national self-preservation. Without a strong and effective foreign policy, America's security as a rich and peaceful country could come under threat. However, the United States has little control over the other actors involved. its foreign policy is generally carried out for the good of American citizens or in the interest of national security.

## TWO FUNDAMENTAL PERSPECTIVES ON OUR RELATIONSHIP WITH THE WORLD

Relationships with other nations can be seen through two distinct perspectives: isolationism and interventionism. Isolationism is a foreign policy view holding that Americans should put themselves and their problems first and not interfere in global concerns. The United States pursued an isolationist policy after World War I, but this experiment was seen largely as a failure. The second fundamental perspective is interventionism, which holds that to keep the republic safe, the United States must be actively engaged in shaping the global environment and willing to intervene in order to create desired outcomes.

## FOREIGN POLICY AND EXTERNAL ACTORS

Many organizations are external actors within the current foreign policy environment. Intergovernmental organizations are bodies that have countries as members, including the United Nations, NATO, OPEC, and the EU. These international bodies work together to create agreements among nations regarding international policies. American foreign policy relies on the concept of American Exceptionalism, which teaches that the United States is unique, marked by a distinct set of ideas, including equality, self-rule, and limited government. The aim of foreign policy is to create a commonly held theory of democratic peace teaching that democratic nations are less likely to engage in wars with one another.

The president is the chief negotiator for the United States, and any treaty negotiated must then be ratified by the Senate. The president has ample resources available to fulfill the obligations of the office. The National Security Council (NSC) is the president's inner circle that advises on matters of foreign policy and is coordinated by the national security adviser. Foreign policy is negotiated through the Department of State, which is charged with managing foreign affairs. The secretary of state is part of the president's cabinet and fulfills a variety of foreign policy roles, including maintaining diplomatic and consular posts around the world, sending delegates and missions (groups of government officials) to a variety of international organization meetings, and negotiating treaties and executive agreements with other countries. The Department of Defense (DOD) manages the United States military and its equipment in order to protect the nation. It is headed by the secretary of defense, and under that office are the Joint Chiefs of Staff, service chiefs of the Army, Navy, Marine Corps, Air Force, Space Force, and the National Guard Bureau.

While the chief of the Coast Guard is not an official member of the Joint Chiefs, a Coast Guard admiral routinely meets with the group.

The Defense Department is the government's biggest agency and accounts for a large portion of the national budget, along with health spending and Social Security. It employs almost 3 million service members and civilians in more than 160 countries and is headquartered in the iconic Pentagon building in Arlington, Virginia, just outside Washington DC.

## TRADE POLICY

United States trade policy objectives in recent decades have included reducing protections both at home and abroad, opening foreign markets for American exports, and increasing global economic integration. While there has much success in integrating the world's economies, the United States has seen its share of the gross world product (GWP) plummet since the post-war period, and its position as the world's biggest economy challenged first by Japan in the 1990s and now by China, which is expected to overtake it in the future. America's international trade deficit now routinely exceeds $600 billion annually, as the United States buys far more foreign goods and services than it sells.

The Department of Commerce is charged by the president with helping the economy expand through working to ensure fair trade and providing the data necessary to support commerce. It also helps negotiate bilateral trade agreements, enforces laws and issues sanctions that attempt to ensure a level playing field for United States businesses.

Even more directly concerned with trade policy is the office of the United States Trade Representative (USTR), which is responsible for developing and recommending trade policy to the president. It also conducts trade negotiations for the executive branch and participates in the World Trade Organization (WTO).

Tariffs are customs duties levied on imported and exported goods and services. They are typically used to protect domestic industries or as leverage in trade negotiations and disputes. While Congress originally had the power to levy tariffs granted by the Constitution, the president has the power to negotiate international agreements, so Congress has partially delegated to the executive the latitude to negotiate trade agreements and set tariff policy. The United States has been a member of the WTO since 1995, and as such makes tariff policies within the regulatory context of the global trading system.

Tariffs are actually a type of tax paid on goods sourced from other countries and usually paid to United States customs authorities by importing companies. While tariffs may offer some protection to domestic industries by raising prices of competing imported goods, they are ultimately paid by United States consumers to whom cost increases are passed by importers.

## STRATEGY AND FOREIGN POLICY

Foreign policy refers to a government's strategy and approach in dealing with other countries and international relations. It can be understood from multiple perspectives, such as "the objectives that government officials of a country aim to achieve in foreign affairs, the principles that underlie those goals, and the methods or tools employed to pursue them." This definition emphasizes the fundamental subjects in U.S. foreign policy, including the objectives of the nation overseas and the methods employed by the United States to accomplish them. It is important to note that we differentiate between foreign policy, which is directed towards external matters, and domestic policy, which establishes plans within the United States. However, these two types of policies can often become closely interconnected. For instance, when discussing educational strategies aimed at boosting the enrollment and graduation rates of Hispanic Americans in American colleges and universities, one could refer to Latino politics as a matter pertaining to the country's internal affairs. Nevertheless, the primary discussions before the 2016 election revealed that Latino politics can swiftly transform into a foreign policy concern when examining issues like immigration from and international trade with nations in Central America and South America. The objectives of U.S. foreign policy are the specific goals and aims that the United States seeks to achieve in its interactions with other countries. The goals of a nation's foreign policy are subject to debate and revision, but there are four main objectives that largely guide the actions of the U.S. government in this realm: (1) safeguarding the United States and its citizens, (2) ensuring access to crucial resources and markets, (3) maintaining a global balance of power, and (4) defending human rights and democracy.

The primary objective is to safeguard the United States and the well-being of its inhabitants, both within the country's borders and on their journeys overseas. Linked to this security objective is the intention of safeguarding the United States friends or nations with whom it shares a friendly and mutually helpful relationship. Within the global arena, various types of threats and perils might arise, encompassing military threats emanating from foreign governments or terrorist organizations, as well as economic concerns arising from trade boycotts and the imposition of steep tariffs. An economic sanction is the act of one or more countries halting commerce or other financial interactions with another country as a means of expressing their disapproval of the other country's actions.

An economic boycott is a situation when the United States stops engaging in trade with another country unless that country modifies a policy that the United States finds objectionable. Imposing trade restrictions results in the prohibition of selling U.S. products in the targeted country and the prohibition of selling the targeted country's products in the United States. As of late, the United States and other nations have enforced an economic blockade on Iran due to its increasing advancement of the nuclear energy program. The recent Iran nuclear deal is a bilateral agreement in which Iran commits to ceasing nuclear development, while the United States and six other nations agree to withdraw economic sanctions, so restoring trading relations with Iran. Trade barriers can also encompass tariffs, which are charges imposed on the transportation of commodities between different countries. Protectionist trade policies impose higher taxes, making it challenging for imported goods, which are now more costly, to effectively compete with domestic goods in terms of pricing. Free trade agreements aim to decrease these trading obstacles.

One of the primary objectives of U.S. foreign policy is to secure continued access to crucial resources and markets worldwide. Resources encompass both natural resources, such as oil, and economic resources, which involve the injection of foreign capital investment into U.S. domestic infrastructure projects, such as buildings, bridges, and military systems. Undoubtedly, having access to the worldwide economy also entails having access to commodities that American consumers may desire, such as Swiss chocolate and Australian wine. The primary objective of U.S. foreign policy is to promote the interests of American businesses by facilitating the sale of domestic products in the global market and fostering economic growth worldwide, particularly in emerging nations.

One other primary objective is to maintain a global equilibrium of power. A balance of power refers to a situation where no single nation or region possesses significantly greater military might than the other countries in the world. Attaining a state of complete power equilibrium is likely unattainable, but achieving overall stability, predictability in governmental operations, robust institutions, and the lack of violence both internally and externally may be feasible. Throughout a significant portion of United States history, policymakers perceived global stability primarily from a European perspective. If the European continent maintained a state of stability, then the entire world was also stable. In the post-World War II era known as the Cold War, stability was maintained by the presence of two dominant superpowers, the United States and the Soviet Union. The constant threat of nuclear destruction, which both countries possessed the capability for, instilled genuine terror and contributed to this stability. Until around 1989-1990, sophisticated industrial democracies formed alliances with either of the two superpowers.

In the present era following the Cold War, numerous regions in Europe have achieved greater political freedom compared to the period when they were under the influence of the Soviet bloc. Additionally, the threat of nuclear war has significantly diminished as the United States and the Soviet Union no longer have missiles aimed at each other after forty consecutive years. Nevertheless, despite the predominantly stabilizing influence of the European Union (EU), which currently encompasses twenty-eight member nations, numerous conflicts have taken place in Eastern Europe and the former Soviet Union. In addition, the European Union is confronted with several obstacles, such as the referendum in the United Kingdom about its exit from the EU, the persistent dispute on how to address Greece's national debt, and the European crisis triggered by the influx of numerous refugees from the Middle East.

The primary objective of U.S. foreign policy is to safeguard human rights and promote democracy. The benefit of stability resulting from other objectives of U.S. foreign policy is the attainment of peace and calm. Although the United States prioritizes its own strategic interests when formulating foreign policy, it also strives to promote global peace through various means, including foreign aid and active involvement in international organizations like the United Nations, NATO, and the Organization of American States.

The United Nations (UN) is often regarded as the preeminent international institution in the contemporary world. The primary institutional entities of the United Nations (UN) consist of the General Assembly and the Security Council. The General Assembly comprises all member nations and grants membership to new nations while also approving the UN budget through a two-thirds majority vote. The Security Council comprises fifteen nations, with five being permanent members (including the United States) and ten being non-permanent members that rotate every five years for a two-year tenure. All members of the organization are obligated to follow the decisions made by the Security Council, which has authority over matters concerning global peace and security. The International Court of Justice in The Hague (Netherlands) and the UN Secretariat, which comprises the Secretary-General of the UN together with the directors and employees of the UN staff, are two other significant entities within the UN.

A persistent dilemma for the United States in its efforts to combat terrorism is the extent to which it should collaborate with the United Nations to implement global anti-terrorism measures in a cooperative manner, as opposed to pursuing an independent approach of unilateralism. The U.S. government's ability to make this decision indicates the optional nature of a country like the United States recognizing global control in foreign policy. If the United States genuinely acknowledged the authority of the United Nations in determining how it conducts its counterterrorism operations, it would seek approval from the UN Security Council.

The United States is connected to another international organization called the North Atlantic Treaty Organization (NATO), which aims to strongly advocate for Western allies and promote peace. NATO was established in the aftermath of World War II, coinciding with the emergence of the Cold War between the Eastern and Western blocs. Although NATO has a more militant approach compared to the United Nations, its primary objective is to safeguard the interests of Europe and the Western countries. Additionally, NATO ensures the provision of support and defense from its partner nations. Although the military coalition is formidable, it has not pursued territorial expansion or the conquest of other nations. Instead, the primary objectives of Europe are to achieve peace and stability. NATO originally comprised solely of Western European nations and the United States. Nevertheless, with the conclusion of the Cold War, other Eastern countries, like Turkey, have joined the NATO alliance.

In addition to its involvement in the UN and NATO, the United States allocates substantial amounts of money annually in international aid to enhance the living standards of individuals in developing nations. The United States may also consider granting debt forgiveness to these countries. Developing countries, by definition, lack modernization in terms of infrastructure and social services, which consequently leads to instability. Assisting them in modernizing and establishing stable regimes is aimed at providing them with advantages and supporting global stability. Another perspective on U.S. assistance suggests that it may have ulterior motives, such as seeking to gain influence in developing nations, establish a strategic position in the region, acquire access to valuable resources, or cultivate a sense of reliance on the United States.

The United States achieves its four primary foreign policy objectives through several foreign policy types, which are specific areas of foreign policy in which the United States is involved. The categories include commerce, diplomacy, sanctions, military/defense, intelligence, foreign aid, and global environmental policy. Trade policy refers to the strategic approach adopted by the United States to facilitate the smooth exchange of trade and the movement of commodities and services with other nations. Protectionism refers to the practice of a country restricting or imposing high tariffs on the sale of products and services from other countries within its borders. On the opposite side of the spectrum is a free trade policy, where a country permits unrestricted movement of products and services between itself and other nations. The United States has alternated between being inclined towards free trade and becoming protectionist. One of its most significant actions in favor of free trade was the introduction of the North American Free Trade Agreement (NAFTA) in 1991. This agreement eliminated trade restrictions and additional expenses imposed on the movement of commodities between the United States, Mexico, and Canada.

Critics perceive a free trade strategy as problematic and instead endorse protectionist measures that safeguard U.S. enterprises and their goods from less expensive foreign imports. An illustration of protectionist policies in action may be seen in the steel business, when American corporations faced challenges from Chinese manufacturing in the global steel market. The balance of trade refers to the correlation between the import and export of goods in a country. The United States engages in extensive international trade, however, it consistently experiences a trade deficit, wherein the value of imported goods and services exceeds the value of exported goods and services. The present trade imbalance of the United States stands at $37.4 billion, indicating that the whole worth of imports into the country surpasses the total worth of exports to other nations. Four Some individuals have proposed protectionist trade measures as a response to this trade gap.

For several individuals, foreign policy is equivalent to diplomacy. Diplomacy refers to the process of creating and sustaining a formal relationship between nations, which regulates their interactions on various subjects such as tourism, commerce taxation, and aircraft landing permissions. Although diplomatic ties may not always be harmonious, their existence indicates a positive state of affairs between the countries. Diplomatic ties are established and made official by the exchange of ambassadors. Ambassadors are diplomats who reside in and operate from an embassy in a foreign country, serving as official representatives of their own government. The act of recalling ambassadors serves as a formal indication of the termination of the bilateral relationship between nations, just as the appointment of ambassadors formalizes it. The U.S. government typically use diplomacy as its initial approach in attempting to resolve conflicts with foreign nations.

## KEY TERMS

**Ambassadors**: Diplomats who reside in and operate from an embassy in a foreign country, serving as official representatives of their own government.

**American Exceptionalism**: The belief that the United States is unique, marked by a distinct set of ideas including equality, self-rule, and limited government.

**Balance of Power**: A situation where no single nation or region possesses significantly greater military might than other countries in the world.

**Diplomacy**: The process of creating and maintaining formal relationships between nations, regulating interactions on various subjects such as tourism, commerce, and taxation.

**Economic Sanction**: The act of one or more countries halting commerce or other financial interactions with another country to express disapproval of the other country's actions.

**Foreign Policy**: A government's strategy and approach in dealing with other countries and international relations.

**Intergovernmental Organizations**: Bodies that have countries as members, working together to create agreements regarding international policies, such as the United Nations and NATO.

**Interventionism**: A foreign policy perspective holding that the United States must be actively engaged in shaping the global environment and willing to intervene to create desired outcomes.

**Isolationism**: A foreign policy view holding that Americans should prioritize their own problems and not interfere in global concerns.

**Tariffs**: Customs duties levied on imported and exported goods and services, used to protect domestic industries or as leverage in trade negotiations.

# APPENDIX A

## SELECTED SUPREME COURT CASES

## SELECTED SUPREME COURT CASES

A. *L. A. Schechter Poultry Corp. v. United States,* **295 U.S. 495 (1935).** This case represented a challenge to the constitutionality of a law called the National Industrial Recovery Act. This law was a major part of President Franklin D. Roosevelt's attempt to rebuild the nation's economy during the Great Depression. Major industries in the United States, however, objected to the way the law empowered the president to regulate aspects of American industry, such as labor conditions and even pay. In the unanimous decision, the court determined that the act was unconstitutional because it shifted the power to regulate commerce from the legislative branch to the executive branch.

*Arizona v. United States,* **567 U.S. 387 (2012).** This case involved federal attempts to prevent an Arizona state immigration law (S.B. 1070) from being enforced. The United States brought suit, arguing that immigration law is exclusively in the federal domain. Agreeing with the federal government, a federal district court enjoined specific provisions in the law. Arizona appealed to the Supreme Court to overturn the decision.

In a 5–3 decision, the court found that specific provisions in the law did conflict with federal law, while others were constitutional.

***Brown v. Board of Education of Topeka*, 347 U.S. 483 (1954).** This case represented a challenge to the principle of "separate but equal" established by *Plessy v. Ferguson* in 1896. The case was brought by students who were denied admittance to certain public schools based exclusively on race. The unanimous decision in *Brown v. Board* determined that the existence of racially segregated public schools violated the equal protection clause of the Fourteenth Amendment. The court decided that schools segregated by race perpetrated harm by giving legal sanction to the idea that African Americans were inherently inferior. The ruling effectively overturned *Plessy v. Ferguson* and removed the legal supports for segregated schools nationwide.

***Buckley v. Valeo*, 424 U.S. 1 (1976).** This case concerned the power of the then recently created Federal Election Commission to regulate the financing of political campaigns. These restrictions limited the amount of contributions that could be made to candidates and required political contributions to be disclosed, among other things. In 1975, Senator James Buckley filed suit, arguing that these limits amounted to a violation of First Amendment protections on free speech and free association. In a series of decisions in this complex case, the court determined that these restrictions did not violate the First Amendment.

***Burwell v. Hobby Lobby Stores, Inc.*, 573 U.S. 682 (2014).** This case involved a challenge to the mandate in the Patient Protection and Affordable Care Act that required that all employment-based group health care plans provide coverage for certain types of contraceptives. The law, however, allowed exemptions for religious employers such as churches that held a religious-based opposition to contraception. The plaintiffs in the case argued that Hobby Lobby, a large family-owned chain of arts and crafts stores, was run based on Christian principles and therefore should be exempt as well because of the Religious

Freedom Restoration Act of 1993 (RFRA). The 5–4 decision in *Burwell v. Hobby Lobby* agreed with the plaintiffs and declared that RFRA permits for- profit companies like Hobby Lobby to deny coverage for contraception in their health plans when that coverage violates a religious belief.

***Bush v. Gore*, 531 U.S. 98 (2000).** Following voting in the November 2000 presidential election, observers recognized that the outcome of the very close national election hinged on the outcome of the election in Florida. Because the Florida election was so close, manual recounts were called for by the state's supreme court. Then-governor George W. Bush, who was ahead in the initial count, appealed to the U.S. Supreme Court to halt the manual recount and to declare that the method of manual recount being used violated his rights to equal protection and due process. The court issued a two-part *per curiam* opinion on the case. (In a *per curiam* opinion, the court makes it clear that the decision in the case is not intended to set a legal precedent.) In the first part, the court ruled in a 7–2 decision that the manual recount did violate the plaintiff's right to equal protection. In the second part, decided by a smaller 5–4 margin, the court ruled that there was not sufficient time to adjust the recount procedure and conduct a full recount. The effect of this ruling gave the Florida electoral votes, and thus the presidency, to George W. Bush.

***Citizens United v. Federal Election Commission*, 558 U.S. 310 (2010).** In 2007, the nonprofit corporation Citizens United was prevented by the Federal Election Commission (FEC) from showing a movie about then-presidential candidate Hillary Clinton. The FEC noted that showing the movie violated the Bipartisan Campaign Reform Act (BCRA). BCRA prohibited campaign communications one month before a primary election and two months before a general election, required donors to be disclosed, and prohibited corporations from using their general funds for campaign communications. The plaintiffs argued that these restrictions constituted a violation of the First Amendment. The 5–4 decision in *Citizens United v. FEC* agreed with the plaintiffs and concluded that the restrictions imposed by BCRA and enforced by the FEC violated the corporation's First Amendment right to free expression.

**Dobbs v. Jackson Women's Health Organization, 597 U.S. ___ (2022)** Supreme Court case that reversed *Roe v. Wade* and *Planned Parenthood of Southeastern Pennsylvania v. Casey*, the decisions that originally asserted the fundamental right to an abortion prior to the viability of the fetus. *Dobbs v. Jackson* states that the Constitution does not confer a right to abortion; and, the authority to regulate abortion is "returned to the people and their elected representatives."

**Dred Scott v. Sandford, 60 U.S. 393 (1856).** This case concerned the constitutionality of the Missouri Compromise, which declared that certain states would be entirely free of slavery. Dred Scott, an enslaved person, was brought by his owner into free territories. When the owner brought him back to Missouri, a slave state, Dred Scott sued claiming that his time living in free territory made him free. After failing in his attempts in Missouri, Scott appealed to the Supreme Court. In a 7–2 decision, the court declared that the relevant parts of the Missouri Compromise were unconstitutional, and that Scott remained enslaved as a result.

**Gideon v. Wainwright, 372 U.S. 335 (1963).** In 1961, Clarence E. Gideon was arrested and accused of breaking into a poolroom and stealing money from a cigarette machine. Not being able to afford a lawyer, and being denied a public defender by the judge, Gideon defended himself and was subsequently found guilty. Gideon appealed to the Supreme Court declaring that the denial by the trial judge constituted a violation of his constitutional right to representation. The unanimous decision by the court in *Gideon v. Wainwright* agreed that the Sixth Amendment required that those facing felony criminal charges be supplied with legal representation.

*King v. Burwell,* 576 U.S. 473 (2015). When Congress wrote and passed the Patient Protection and Affordable Care Act in 2010, lawmakers intended for states to create exchanges through which residents in those states could purchase health care insurance plans. For those residents who could not afford the premiums, the law also allowed for tax credits to help reduce the cost. If states didn't create an exchange, the federal government created the exchange for the state. While the intention of the lawmakers was for the tax credits to apply to the federally created exchanges as well, the language of the law was somewhat unclear on this point. Residents in Virginia brought suit against the law arguing that the law should be interpreted in a way that withholds tax credits from those participating in the federally created exchange. In the 6–3 decision, the court disagreed, stating that viewing the law in its entirety made it clear that the intent of the law was to provide the tax credits to those participating in either exchange.

**L. A. Schechter Poultry Corp. v. United States, 295 U.S. 495 (1935).** This case represented a challenge to the constitutionality of a law called the National Industrial Recovery Act. This law was a major part of President Franklin D. Roosevelt's attempt to rebuild the nation's economy during the Great Depression. Major industries in the United States, however, objected to the way the law empowered the president to regulate aspects of American industry, such as labor conditions and even pay. In the unanimous decision, the court determined that the act was unconstitutional because it shifted the power to regulate commerce from the legislative branch to the executive branch.

*Lawrence v. Texas,* 539 U.S. 558 (2003). This case concerned two men in Houston who in 1998 were prosecuted and convicted under a Texas law that forbade certain types of intimate sexual relations between two persons of the same sex. The men appealed to the Supreme Court arguing that their Fourteenth Amendment rights to equal protection and privacy were violated when they were prosecuted for consensual sexual intimacy in their own home. In the 6–3 decision in *Lawrence v. Texas*, the court concluded that while so-called anti-sodomy statutes like the law in Texas did not violate one's right to equal protection, they did violate the due process clause of the Fourteenth Amendment. The court stated that the government had no right to infringe on the liberty of persons engaging in such private and personal acts.

*Marbury v. Madison*, **5 U.S. 137 (1803).** This case involved the nomination of justices of the peace in Washington, DC, by President John Adams at the end of his term. Despite the Senate confirming the nominations, some of the commissions were not delivered before Adams left office. The new president, Thomas Jefferson, decided not to deliver the commissions. William Marbury, one of the offended justices, sued, saying that the Judiciary Act of 1789 empowered the court to force Secretary of State James Madison to deliver the commissions. In the unanimous decision in *Marbury v. Madison*, the court declared that while Marbury's rights were violated when Madison refused to deliver the commission, the court did not have the power to force the secretary to do so despite what the Judiciary Act says. In declaring that the law conflicted with the U.S. Constitution, the case established the principle of judicial review wherein the Supreme Court has the power to declare laws passed by Congress and signed by the president to be unconstitutional.

*McDonald v. Chicago*, **561 U.S. 742 (2010).** This case developed as a consequence of the decision in *District of Columbia v. Heller*, 554 U.S. 570 (2008), which dismissed a Washington, DC, handgun ban as a violation of the Second Amendment. In *McDonald v. Chicago*, the plaintiffs argued that the Fourteenth Amendment had the effect of applying the Second Amendment to the states, not just to the federal government. In a 5–4 decision, the court agreed with the plaintiffs and concluded that rights like the right to keep and bear arms are important enough for maintaining liberty that the Fourteenth Amendment rightly applies them to the states.

*Miranda v. Arizona,* **384 U.S. 436 (1966).** When Ernesto Miranda was arrested, interrogated, and confessed to kidnapping in 1963, the arresting officers neglected to inform him of his Fifth Amendment right not to self-incriminate. After being found guilty at trial, Miranda appealed to the Supreme Court, insisting that the officers violated his Fifth Amendment rights. The 5–4 decision in *Miranda v. Arizona* found that the right to not incriminate oneself relies heavily on the suspect's right to be informed of these rights at the time of arrest. The opinion indicated that suspects must be told that they have the right to an attorney and the right to remain silent in order to ensure that any statements they provide are issued voluntarily.

***National Federation of Independent Business v. Sebelius,*** **567 U.S. 519 (2012).** This case represented a challenge to the constitutionality of the Patient Protection and Affordable Care Act. The suing states argued that the Medicare expansion and the individual mandate that required citizens to purchase health insurance or pay a fine were both unconstitutional. The 5–4 decision found that the Medicare expansion was permissible, but that the federal government could not withhold all Medicare funding for states that refused to accept the expansion. More importantly, it found that Congress had the power to apply the mandate to purchase health insurance under its enumerated power to tax.

***New York Times Co. v. Sullivan,*** **376 U.S. 254 (1964).** This case began when the *New York Times* published a full-page advertisement claiming that the arrest of Martin Luther King, Jr. in Alabama was part of a concerted effort to ruin him. Insulted, an Alabama official filed a libel suit against the newspaper. Under Alabama law, which did not require that persons claiming libel have to show harm, the official won a judgment. The *New York Times* appealed to the Supreme Court, arguing that the ruling violated its First Amendment right to free speech. In a unanimous decision, the court declared that the First Amendment protects even false statements by the press, as long as those statements are not made with actual malice.

***Obergefell v. Hodges,*** **576 U.S. 644 (2015).** This case concerned groups of same-sex couples who brought suits against a number of states and relevant agencies that refused to recognize same-sex marriages created in states where such marriages were legal. In the 5–4 decision, the court found that not only did the Fourteenth Amendment provision for equal protection under the law require that states recognize same-sex marriages formed in other states, but that no state could deny marriage licenses to same-sex couples if they also issued them to other types of couples.

***Plessy v. Ferguson,*** **163 U.S. 537 (1896).** When Homer Plessy, a man of mixed racial heritage, sat in a Whites-only railroad car in an attempt to challenge a Louisiana law that required railroad cars be segregated, he was arrested and convicted. Appealing his conviction to the Supreme Court, he argued that the segregation law was a violation of the principle of equal protection under the law in the Fourteenth Amendment. In a 7–1 decision, the court disagreed, indicating that the law was not a violation of the equal protection principle because the different train cars were separate but equal. Plessy v. Ferguson's "separate but equal" remained a guiding principle of segregation until *Brown v. Board of Education* (1954).

***Roe v. Wade,*** **410 U.S. 113 (1973).** This case involved a pregnant woman from Texas who desired to terminate her pregnancy. At the time, Texas only allowed abortions in cases where the woman's life was in danger. Using the pseudonym "Jane Roe," the woman appealed to the Supreme Court, arguing that the Constitution provides women the right to terminate an abortion. The 7–2 decision in *Roe v. Wade* sided with the plaintiff and declared that the right to privacy upheld in the decision in *Griswold v. Connecticut* (1965) included a woman's right to an abortion. In balancing the rights of the woman with the interests of the states to protect human life, the court created a trimester framework. In the first trimester, a pregnant woman could seek an abortion without restriction. In the second and third trimesters, however, the court asserted that states had an interest in regulating abortions, provided that those regulations were based on health needs.

***Schechter Poultry Corp. v. United States.*** See ***A. L. A. Schechter Poultry Corp. v. United States***.

***Shelby County v. Holder*, 570 U.S. 529 (2013).** After decades in which African Americans encountered obstacles to voting, particularly in southern states, Congress passed the Voting Rights Act of 1965. Among other things, the law prohibited certain congressional districts from changing election laws without federal authorization. In 2010, Shelby County in Alabama brought a suit against the U.S. attorney general, claiming that both section five of the act, which required districts to seek preapproval, and section four, which determined which districts had to seek preapproval, were unconstitutional. In a 5–4 decision, the court found that both sections violated the Tenth Amendment.

***United States v. Windsor*, 570 U.S. 744 (2013).** When Thea Clara Spyer died in 2009, she left her estate to her wife, Edith Windsor, with whom she had been legally married in Canada years before. Because of a 1996 U.S. law called the Defense of Marriage Act (DOMA), this marriage was not recognized by the federal government. As a result, Windsor was compelled to pay an enormous tax on the inheritance, which she would not have had to pay had the federal government recognized the marriage. Appealing to the Supreme Court, Windsor argued that DOMA was unconstitutional because it deprives same-sex couples of their Fifth Amendment right to equal protection. In the 5–4 decision, the court agreed with Windsor, stating that DOMA was intended to treat certain married couples differently in blatant violation of their Fifth Amendment rights.

# AUTHOR BIOGRAPHY

D r. Rodgir Cohen is a university lecturer, educator, and community figure who brings a wealth of experience and insight into his teachings in political science. Rodgir lectures on politics and public policy in Southern California.

Having served in the armed forces during a significant time of conflict, he has firsthand experience of the harsh realities of war, which he leverages to enrich his teachings and activism. His transition from military life to academia and community service speaks volumes of his dedication and resilience. A family man at heart, he cherishes quality time with his loved ones. His interest in boating also offers him a peaceful retreat from his active professional life, allowing him moments of tranquility amidst nature.

# INDEX